Digital Reading and Writing in Composition Studies

As digital reading has become more productive and active, the lines between reading and writing become more blurred. This book offers both an exploration of collaborative reading and pedagogical strategies for teaching reading and writing that reflect the realities of digital literacies.

This edited scholarly collection offers strategies for teaching reading and writing that highlight the possibilities, opportunities, and complexities of digital literacies. Part 1 explores reading and writing that happen digitally and offers frameworks for thinking about this process. Part 2 focuses on strategies for the classroom by applying reading theories, design principles, and rhetorical concepts to instruction. Part 3 introduces various disciplinary implications for this blended approach to writing instruction. What is emerging is new theories and practices of reading in both print and digital spaces—theories that account for how diverse student readers encounter and engage digital texts. This collection contributes to this work by offering strategies for sustaining reading and cultivating writing in this landscape of changing digital literacies.

The book is essential for the professional development of beginning teachers, who will appreciate the historical and bibliographic overview as well as classroom strategies, and for busy veteran teachers, who will gain updated knowledge and a renewed commitment to teaching an array of literacy skills. It will be ideal for graduate seminars in composition theory and pedagogy (both undergraduate and graduate) and teacher education courses, and will be key reading for scholars in rhetoric and composition interested in composition history, assessment, communication studies, and literature pedagogy.

Mary R. Lamb, professor and chair of the department of English at Clayton State University, was formerly director of first-year writing at Clayton State. Publications include the edited collection *Contested(ed) Writing: Re-conceptualizing Literacy Competitions* (Cambridge Scholars 2013); "Teaching Nonfiction through Rhetorical Reading" (*English Journal* 2010); "The 'Talking Life' of Books: Constructing Women Readers in Oprah's Book Club," in *Reading Women: Literary Figures and Cultural Icons from the Victorian Age to the Present* (2005); and "'The Rhetoric of Gender' as Advanced Writing," in *Coming of Age: The Advanced Writing Curriculum,* ed. (Boynton/Cook, 2000).

Jennifer M. Parrott is an associate professor at Clayton State University, where she teaches courses in first-year writing and literature. Topics for her recent publications include 3D printing and pedagogy in the library and collaboration in the academy. Her publication on using Facebook in the literature classroom appeared in *Technology in the Literature Class: Assignments and Materials,* 2016. She earned a PhD in English from Southern Illinois University Carbondale and has completed postdoctoral fellowships focusing on digital pedagogy and digital humanities at Georgia Tech and Bucknell University.

Routledge Research in Writing Studies

Writing Center Talk Over Time
A Mixed-Method Study
Jo Mackiewicz

Writing Support for International Graduate Students
Enhancing Transition and Success
Shyam Sharma

Rhetorical Strategies for Professional Development
Investment Mentoring in Classrooms and Workplaces
Elizabeth J. Keller

Digital Reading and Writing in Composition Studies
Edited by Mary R. Lamb and Jennifer M. Parrott

Digital Reading and Writing in Composition Studies

Edited by Mary R. Lamb
and Jennifer M. Parrott

Routledge
Taylor & Francis Group
New York London

First published 2019
by Routledge
52 Vanderbilt Avenue, New York, NY 10017

and by Routledge
2 Park Square, Milton Park, Abingdon, Oxon OX14 4RN

First issued in paperback 2020

Routledge is an imprint of the Taylor & Francis Group, an informa business

© 2019 Taylor & Francis

Library of Congress Cataloging-in-Publication Data
Names: Lamb, Mary R., editor. | Parrott, Jennifer, editor.
Title: Digital reading and writing in composition studies / edited by
    Mary R. Lamb and Jennifer Parrott.
Description: London ; New York : Routledge, 2019. | Series: Routledge
    research in writing studies.
Identifiers: LCCN 2019001192 (print) | LCCN 2019009628 (ebook) |
    ISBN 9781351052931 (pdf) | ISBN 9781351052917 (mobi) | ISBN
    9781351052924 (epub) | ISBN 9781351052948 (master) | ISBN
    9781138484108 (hardback)
Subjects: LCSH: English language—Rhetoric—Computer-assisted
    instruction. | English language—Rhetoric—Study and teaching. | English
    language—Composition and exercises—Computer-assisted instruction. |
    English language—Composition and exercises—Study and teaching.
Classification: LCC PE1404 (ebook) | LCC PE1404 .D48 2019 (print) |
    DDC 808/.0420285—dc23
LC record available at https://lccn.loc.gov/2019001192

ISBN 13: 978-0-367-66029-1 (pbk)
ISBN 13: 978-1-138-48410-8 (hbk)

Typeset in Sabon
by Apex CoVantage, LLC

Contents

PART 2
Teaching Writing and Reading in Digital Spaces 85

PART 3
Implications and Institutional Contexts 189

Acknowledgments

I would like to thank Mary for giving me the opportunity to work on this project and learn from the process and the product. Kathy, thank you for your attention to detail, good humor, and of course your hard work. Matt, thank you for giving me the extra hours to work on this project. Finally, to my students, I am grateful for and inspired by your hard work and ability to handle whatever the world throws at you.

Jennifer M. Parrott
Decatur, GA

I would like to thank Kathy Daley, graduate research assistant extraordinaire, for all her editorial assistance. Kathy's remarkable attention to detail and style made this project possible. I'd also like to thank my family, especially Kim, for her support and extra work with the home and family work. I am also grateful to my students whose reading, writing, and discussions inspire me.

Mary R. Lamb
Avondale Estates, GA

Contributors

G. Travis Adams is an associate professor of English and director of the writing center at the University of Nebraska Omaha. His teaching and research interests include composition theory/pedagogy, writing center theory/pedagogy, composition, and reading theory/pedagogy. Publications include "The Line That Should Not Be Drawn: Writing Centers as Reading Centered" published in *Pedagogy* (16.1) and the forthcoming mixed-method study "Missions and Toolkits: A Data-Driven Study of Reading in Writing Centers."

Jeanne Law Bohannon is an assistant professor of English at Kennesaw State University. She teaches undergraduate and graduate courses in mixed methods research and digital rhetorics. Her research interests include performing linguistic recoveries of underrepresented populations, conducting empirical studies in information literacies, and evaluating democratic-engagement learning in college writing. She has published in the *Bellaterra Journal*, *Peitho*, the *Purdue Information Literacy Handbook*, and the WAC Clearinghouse *Research Exchange Index*. She is also a blogger with Andrea Lunsford's *Multimodal Mondays* series.

Suzanne Cope is a visiting assistant professor at St. John's University in New York City. Her academic interests include innovative writing pedagogy, the rhetoric of social commentary, and the digital humanities. Publications include "Teaching Creative Nonfiction: The Transformative Nature of the Workshop Method" in *New Directions in Teaching and Learning*; "On Teaching 'Salvation' by Langston Hughes" in *Assay: A Journal of Nonfiction Studies*; and the upcoming "Outside the Box: Incorporating High-Stakes Creative Writing Assignments into Non-Major Literature Classes, A Case Study" in *Writing & Pedagogy*.

Jacob W. Craig is an associate professor at the College of Charleston in Charleston, South Carolina, where he teaches courses in composition theory and digital rhetoric. His research focuses on the relationships between practices, technologies, and locations of writing. His work has appeared, among other venues, in *Composition Forum* and *Literacy in Composition Studies* as well as in the edited collections *The Tablet Book* and *Deep Reading*.

Molly E. Daniel is an assistant professor of rhetoric and composition at the University of North Georgia. She has presented papers at the College English Association, Conference on College Composition and Communication, Computers and Writing, and the International Writing Center Association.

Matthew Davis is an assistant professor in composition and new literacies at the University of Massachusetts Boston. He has published in *enculturation*, *South Atlantic Review*, *Computers and Composition*, *The WAC Journal*, and in several edited collections.

Catherine Gabor is an associate professor and director of composition at the University of San Francisco in the Department of Rhetoric and Language. Her teaching interests include service learning and the intersection of digital, oral, and written rhetoric; her research focuses on these topics as well as the scholarship of administration. Selected publications are "Magic, Agency and Power: Mapping Embodied Leadership Roles" in *WPA: Writing Program Administration* and "Writing Partners: Service Learning as a Route to Authority for Basic Writers" in *Journal of Basic Writing*.

Lynée Lewis Gaillet, distinguished professor and chair of the English department at Georgia State University in Atlanta, Georgia, is author of numerous articles and book chapters. Her book projects include: editor of *Scottish Rhetoric and It Influence* (1998); co-editor of *Stories of Mentoring* (2008), *The Present State of Scholarship in the History of Rhetoric* (2010), *Publishing in Community: Case Studies for Contingent Faculty Collaborations* (2015), *On Archival Research* (2016), and *Writing Center and Writing Program Collaborations* (2017). She coauthored *Scholarly Publication in a Changing Academic Landscape* (2014) and *Primary Research and Writing: People, Places, and Spaces* (2015).

Alice Horning is professor emerita of Writing and Rhetoric at Oakland University, where she held a joint appointment in Linguistics. Her research over her entire career has focused on the intersection of reading and writing, concentrating lately on the increasing evidence of students' reading difficulties and how to address them in writing courses and across the disciplines. Her work has appeared in the major professional journals and in books published by Parlor Press and Hampton Press. Her most recent books include Reading, Writing, and Digitizing: Understanding Literacy in the Electronic Age published in 2012 by Cambridge Scholars Publishing and Reconnecting Reading and Writing co-edited with Beth Kraemer, published in 2013 by the WAC Clearinghouse and Parlor Press, What is College Reading?

co-edited with Cynthia Haller and Deborah-Lee Gollnitz, published by the WAC Clearinghouse, and Literacy Then and Now, published by Peter Lang. Her current project is entitled Literacy Heroines: Women and the Written Word, under contract to Peter Lang. She is the editor of the Composition and Rhetoric book series for Peter Lang.

Mary R. Lamb, professor and chair of the English department at Clayton State University, was formerly director of first-year writing at Clayton State. Publications include the edited collection, *Contested(ed) Writing: Re-conceptualizing Literacy Competitions* (Cambridge Scholars 2013); "Teaching Nonfiction through Rhetorical Reading" (*English Journal* 2010); "The 'Talking Life' of Books: Constructing Women Readers in Oprah's Book Club," in *Reading Women: Literary Figures and Cultural Icons from the Victorian Age to the Present* (2005); and "'The Rhetoric of Gender' as Advanced Writing," in *Coming of Age: The Advanced Writing Curriculum, ed.* (Boynton/Cook, 2000).

Amanda Licastro is the assistant professor of digital rhetoric at Stevenson University in Maryland and a member of the editorial collective of the *Journal of Interactive Technology and Pedagogy.* Her research explores the intersection of technology and writing, including book history, dystopian literature, and digital humanities. Publications include articles in *Kairos, Digital Pedagogy in the Humanities, Hybrid Pedagogy,* and *Communication Design Quarterly.* Amanda's current grant-funded project on Virtual Reality has been featured in the *Baltimore Sun* and *Baltimore Magazine.*

Jason McIntosh is an assistant professor of English and the director of composition at New Mexico Highlands University. His teaching and research interests include place-based writing and education, computers and writing, writing program administration, and the National Writing Project.

Janine Morris is an assistant professor in the writing and communication department at Nova Southeastern University in Fort Lauderdale, Florida. Her research interests include digital and multimodal writing, reading, and literacy studies, and composition theory and pedagogy. Her scholarship has appeared in the *College English Association (CEA) Critic; Pedagogy: Critical Approaches to Teaching Literature, Language, Composition, and Culture; Computers and Composition; Composition Studies;* and *Community Literacy Journal.*

Julie A. Myatt is an associate professor of English at Middle Tennessee State University, where she co-directs the General Education English program. Her research interests include writing program administration and feminist rhetorical practices. Her most recent project finds her studying suffragists' productive uses of past failures when seeking ratification of the Nineteenth Amendment. Her scholarship appears in

Bad Ideas about Writing; Composing Feminist Interventions: Activism, Engagement, Praxis; and *Teaching the New Writing: Technology, Change, and Assessment in the 21st-Century Classroom.*

Ed Nagelhout is a professor of professional writing at the University of Nevada, Las Vegas. His research interests include writing program administration, teaching in digital environments, digital composing, and writing in the disciplines. Recent publications include "Blogging Advanced Composition" with Denise Tillery and Elisa Cogbill-Seiders for the collection *Twenty Writing Assignments in Context: An Instructor's Resource for the Composition Classroom* and "Student-Centered Assessment Design in a Professional Writing Minor" with Denise Tillery for the journal *Programmatic Perspectives.*

Jennifer M. Parrott is an associate professor at Clayton State University, where she teaches courses in first-year writing and literature. Topics for her recent publications include 3D printing and pedagogy in the library and collaboration in the academy. Her publication on using Facebook in the literature classroom appeared in *Technology in the Literature Class: Assignments and Materials,* 2016. She earned a PhD in English from Southern Illinois University Carbondale and has completed post-doctoral fellowships focusing on digital pedagogy and digital humanities at Georgia Tech and Bucknell University.

Donna Qualley is a professor of English at Western Washington University in Bellingham, Washington, where she was the WPA of the first-year writing program for many years. Currently, she invents and teaches courses in writing studies, literacy studies, qualitative research methods, and young adult literature. She has written articles and chapters on reading and reading pedagogy over the last twenty-five years, including guest-editing a special issue of *Reader: Essays in Reader-Oriented Theory, Criticism and Pedagogy* on disciplinary ways of teaching reading in English studies. Her recent chapter "Building a Conceptual Topography of the Transfer Terrain" (*Critical Transitions: Writing and the Question of Transfer*) was published in 2017.

Philip Rusche is an associate professor at the University of Nevada, Las Vegas, where he teaches Old and Middle English literature. He researches what manuscripts were available in early medieval England and how these texts were studied and translated. Selected publications include "The Glosses to the Lindisfarne Gospel and the Benedictine Reform: Was Aldred Trained in the Southumbrian Glossing Tradition?" in *The Old English Glosses to the Lindisfarne Gospels: Language, Author and Context,* (2016) and "The Translation of Plant Names in the Old English Herbarium and the Durham Glossary," in *Rethinking and Recontextualizing Glosses: New Perspectives on Late Anglo-Saxon Glossography* (2011).

Joshua Welsh is an assistant professor at Central Washington University (CWU) in Ellensburg, Washington. He teaches rhetoric and professional writing courses in the English department at CWU. His research involves the rhetoric of technology. He is especially interested in how new technologies shape existing modes of communication. Selected publications include "The Rhetoric of Reasonable and NonDiscriminatory: Conflicting Visions of Innovation in the Smart Phone Patent Wars" (*Journal of Contemporary Rhetoric*) and "Common Sense and the Rhetoric of Technology" (*Journal of the Project on the Rhetoric of Inquiry*).

Introduction

Mary R. Lamb

This edited scholarly collection offers strategies for teaching reading and writing that highlight the possibilities, opportunities, and complexities of digital literacies. Most people intuitively connect reading and writing, and instruction in both is a longstanding component of education in America. However, in colleges and universities, a one-hundred-year scholarly discussion differentiates the two practices, largely brought about by disciplinary changes at the postsecondary level, including the need for specialization and academic departments. Currently, composition scholars acknowledge a renewed interest in the intersection of these activities. For example, in 2003, Marguerite Helmers edited *Intertexts: Reading Pedagogy in College Writing Classrooms*, which offered chapters on various ways to teach a facet of critical reading to students in writing classes. In *College English*, in 2012, Mariolina Rizzi Salvatori and Patricia Donahue observed a "revival" in the scholarly interest in reading in composition studies (199). They advocated for "the production of new ideas about how to teach reading, writing, and their interanimation" (205). They note that "theories of reading in the 1980s and early 1990s . . . shifted the conversation away from what to read to how to read" (206). Alice Horning and Elizabeth Kraemer's reference book *Reconnecting Reading and Writing: Reference Guide to Rhetoric and Composition* (2013) offers historical accounts of the scholarship on the subject and demonstrates persuasively that reading and writing should be taught concurrently. Ellen C. Carillo in *Securing a Place for Reading in Composition* focuses on strategies to teach reading processes (2015) that, she argues, will enable students to apply their knowledge in other areas. Carillo urges us to "articulate more concretely what [we] mean by reading, which activities would fall under this category, and how [we] imagin[e] reading's relationship to writing" (152). Indeed, the premise that reading and writing are integrally linked in some way is a given in most composition studies; scholarship on how to teach these skills is ever evolving. This book continues this line of inquiry by building on composition scholarship that has examined reading processes in the context of writing instruction and extends the conversation by including digital media. Working in digital spaces has complicated even further the discussion of how and why students read and blurred the disciplinary and conceptual lines between reading and writing. What is emerging is new theories and practices of reading in both print and digital spaces—theories that account for how diverse student readers encounter and engage digital texts. This collection contributes to this work by offering strategies for sustaining reading and cultivating writing in this landscape of changing digital literacies.

This introduction acquaints readers with a brief outline of pertinent scholarship on reading in composition studies as a framework for those who wish to do further reading. Next, it posits reading practices as collaborative in digital spaces.

Brief History of Reading in Composition Studies

Scholarship on reading in composition generally casts reading as a problem of some sort. For example, in 1943, George S. Wykoff characterized students' poor reading as a "problem" that composition teachers needed to solve since "reading is a primary or supplementary aid in teaching composition" (245). Horning and Kraemer's 2013 review of scholarship suggests that "students [still] do not read as well as they could and should to be successful in writing classes and elsewhere in college" (20). Wykoff notes the main purposes for reading in composition classes: "reading for pleasure, reading for understanding, reading for information, and reading in order to write better" (246). The pleasure reading is "to break the monotony of assignments in grammar, punctuation, spelling, diction, and writing" (246), which may have been true in early writing instruction. Reading to understand is what we'd call reading comprehension, but also for literary understanding (246). He breaks reading to write better into separate purposes: for ideas; for "models of types of writing;" to learn about and develop style; to expand vocabulary; as examples of grammatical and syntactical choices available to writers; for mechanical, formal characteristics of certain genres; and to practice proofreading skills (246). Writing instructors, Wykoff argues, lack the skills to address students' reading deficiency since they lack deep knowledge about the "reading-for-writing purpose" beyond an acknowledgement that writers often benefit from "conscious imitation of models" (250). He suggests that instructors gain training in pedagogy and learn from reading research in psychology and education, and he argues for further research into outcomes when reading is used to teach writing (253) in order to test "the assumption that the more effectively a student reads, the more effectively he writes" (254). While his article reduces reading instruction to addressing remedial needs, his outline of the purposes for reading and his call for better teacher training echo through subsequent scholarship. It's fair to say that scholars have been engaged in the work he advocates in various forms during the seventy-five years that followed his publication.

Other researchers note the problem is the instructor's lack of knowledge of how to teach reading processes (Newkirk, *Only Connect*; Helmers). Marguerite Helmers asserts that "traditional and institutional notions of reading as 'belonging' to courses in literature, teacher education, or even remedial programs are academic constructions that have been naturalized in professional discourse and must be revisited and revised" (5). The work to do so has remained a steady concern in scholarship. For example, Marilyn S. Sternglass, in her 1976 "Composition Teacher as Reading Teacher," draws on Frank Smith's *Psycholinguistics and Reading* (1973) to argue for sentence-combining as a way to increase students' syntactical choices (381) and teach "two skills for the price of one" (382).

Reading has also been portrayed as a problem for writing teachers when it distracts from the work of teaching writing. This is due to a variety of reasons, namely the fact that English departments were establishing themselves, and that teaching writing was consistently subordinated to the study of literature. David Joliffe names this anxiety over teaching reading as "'the reading problem': the failure of the field in general to interrogate the roles that reading plays in high school and college writing and to recognize the paucity of theories, methods, and materials teachers have in both settings to develop more informed perspectives about themselves as teachers of reading" (3). Indeed, Edward P. J. Corbett warned that the "siren song of literature" would lure otherwise practical instructors and writers away from their task of teaching and learning writing. This disciplinary anxiety about the field of rhetoric and composition appeared in scholarship that sought to demarcate the subject of composition courses from courses in literature. Even as teachers recognized the value of using texts to teach writing, disciplinary configurations, pedagogical disagreements, and culturally laden power grabs (Miller), separated the aims of literature (reception) and writing (production) courses. In this context, a debate ensued about including literature in the composition classroom, demonstrated by Gary Tate's call to include it and Erica Lindemann's argument against it (*College English* 1993), and then Peter Elbow's plea to end the debate (*Rhetoric Review* 1993). Elbow's article, in typical Elbow both/and style, offers ways for both composition and literature teachers to teach both processes, including his wonderful suggestion of including "rough drafts of reading" when we approach texts with students (22). Most recently, Helmers reminds us that "reading does not [only] refer to the novel, or the passive consumption of aesthetic literature, but to a process of investigation and articulation" (22), and recent scholarship does reflect this understanding. Helmers cites Donna Qualley's description of reading as an "essayistic, ethnographic venture . . . a form of hermeneutic inquiry into texts" (61 qtd. in Helmers 22). In this volume, Qualley further argues how we not only read in order to write, but how writing in digital spaces encourages further critical reading since the nature of reading has become collaborative and interactive in digital spaces.

No doubt the literature vs. writing debate affected scholars' work in exploring reading and writing connections beyond just reading literary texts, which I'll return to below. But first, I'll note a couple of additional main players in the debate. Winifred Horner's (1983) *Composition and Literature: Bridging the Gap* was an apologia of sorts, which grew out of an MLA panel with Wayne Booth in which she tried to validate composition research and squelch the subordination of the field ("Foreword" ix). Her collection offered a set of essays that each explored a facet of her argument against the false dichotomy of reading and writing as separate fields of study. Twenty years later, Linda S. Bergmann and Edith M. Baker published *Composition and/or Literature: The End(s) of Education* (NCTE, 2006). In Horner's "Foreword" to it, she notes the dichotomy remains, but does so in part because composition has established itself as separate programs (x). I note this book because the chapters are offered as "models for such ongoing conversations about the institutional and theoretical relations between composition and literary studies" (3). While our collection doesn't attempt to posit the aims of higher education and English's institutional role in those aims like Bergmann and Baker's, the chapters in this collection do offer strategies that cross—and blur—some of the same disciplinary lines and animate how the discipline might move forward during a digitized age when writing, reading, and literature are mediated in ways that push academic boundaries.

As composition scholarship turned away from textual analysis of formal features, the purported realm of literature teachers, it turned to the writer's processes, and the treatment of reading in composition followed suit. For example, reading played a role in Donald Murray's "student-centered" approach to teaching writing in "Teaching the Other Self: The Writer's First Reader" published in 1982. He posits the writer as a "monitor" and reader of his own evolving text with skills that can be taught and cultivated, which he also discusses in "Reading While Writing," a chapter in Newkirk's *Only Connect*. He, along with Peter Elbow, focused more on the students' internal reading and writing processes rather than the student's relationship to source texts, cultural situations, and rhetorical aims.

Some scholars seeking to understand the process of reading and interpretation, and the role that played in writing, turned to literary reader-response theories. Louise Rosenblatt's 1938 *Literature as Exploration*, out of kilter with the current New Criticism of that decade and the ascendancy of professional literary interpretation and English departments' disciplinary professionalization, nevertheless had wide influence later. In 1978, her *The Reader, the Text, and the Poem: The Transactional Theory of The Literary Text* distinguishes efferent reading (for information to take way) from aesthetic reading (focusing on the process and experience of the literature). Reader response appealed to the current expressive and process-orientated composition scholars in the 1960s and 1970s for its focus on writers and their interaction with the text. For example, Sally

Barr Reagan explains a course based on David Bleich's *Readings and Feelings*. Her "reader response course is sequentially structured and requires personal research, but does not teach the modes . . . [it] helps students gain understanding of how they use language and how language illustrates self" (17). Reading portrayed here is a relationship or transaction between the reader and the text, the reader who becomes the writer constructing meaning.

Scholarship continued to focus on the process of reading even as the "problem" of how to teach reading, and if we should be teaching reading, especially literary interpretation, in composition simmered in the scholarship. Three books published in 1986 exemplify scholarship that portrays reading in the composition classroom as interactions between the student and texts she was reading: *Convergences: Transactions in Reading and Writing*, edited by Bruce T. Peterson; *Facts, Artifacts, and Counterfacts: Theory and Method for a Writing Course*, by David Bartholomae and Anthony Petrosky; and *Only Connect: Uniting Reading and Writing*, edited by Thomas Newkirk. In Newkirk's collection, Carol Batker and Charles Moran draw on reader-response theory in "The Reader in the Writing Class." For these scholars, the subject of writing should be the student and his interaction reading and interpreting texts.

Rhetorical reading is a particular way composition scholars viewed the way readers react to texts and act on them through writing. This approach is exemplified in the textbook, *Reading Rhetorically: A Reader for Writers*, by John C. Bean, Virginia A. Chappell, and Alice M. Gillam, first published in 2001 and currently in its 4th edition and by Maxine Hairston's "Using Nonfiction Literature in the Composition Classroom," in Petersen's *Convergences* (1986). In Doug Brent's *Reading as Rhetorical Invention: Knowledge, Persuasion, and the Teaching of Research-Based Writing*, published in 1992, the potential reader imagined as audience becomes a heuristic for writers as they develop their persuasive strategies.

Similarly, Christina Haas describes "rhetorical reading" as "attention to the motives and contexts of both writers and other readers" (24). When readers read rhetorically, they "use or infer situational information— about the author, about the texts' historical and cultural context, about the motives and desires of the writer—to aid in understanding the text and to judge the quality and believability of the argument put forth in it" (24). Haas opposes rhetorical reading with the strategies students bring to first-year writing, strategies that see texts as "bodies of information or collections of facts, rather than as complex social and rhetorical acts" (24). Rhetorical reading, on the other hand, requires interpretation about "the author's identity and 'agenda,' the response of others to the argument, other texts with similar or diverse perspectives" (24). First responses focus on the content and personal responses, but Haas argues that students should be taught to assess the rhetorical situation (Haas 26). Haas' later work, *Writing Technology: Studies on the Materiality of Literacy* (1996), studies the cognitive changes we experience reading and writing online and with electronic technology. When I began teaching college writing after teaching high school students around 1999, I was excited to apply these rhetorical reading strategies in my courses since those skills weren't being taught in the literary secondary curriculum I'd taught. Over the course of the next decade or so, I noticed the reverse in college students: they had skills in rhetorical reading of nonfiction, but less experience reading literature. In fact, the Common Core State Standards focus on nonfiction, argumentation, and rhetorical features of texts. Sullivan, Tinberg, and Blau credit rhetorical reading's popularity in college classrooms with its inclusion in the CCSS (xviii). Indeed, in classrooms and in popular culture, teachers and the general public note the narrowing of types of reading students do in and out of the classroom, the lack of reading skills students demonstrate, and the lessening of reading overall.

Rhetorical Readers and Digital Curators

In contrast to this view, we are in a period of the most pervasive, widespread circulation of information as ever before. Screens displaying words, images, and texts pervade every aspect of our lives, so even as we aren't reading books, we are reading (Baron 10–12). Our premise in this book is that as "digital reading" has become more "productive" and active, the lines between reading and writing blur in ways that require teaching both in writing classes. If early scholarship on digital, electronic writing worried about these changes or treated this literacy as an "add-on" to the primacy of alphabetic print, that fear has been outpaced by the mere reality of the current age of electronic information and networks. Indeed, published twenty-five years ago, George P. Landow's work in literature and hypertext argues that "we must abandon conceptual systems founded upon ideas of center, margin, hierarchy, and linearity and replace them with ones of multilinearity, nodes, links, and networks" (5). Even in light of this reality, Cynthia L. Selfe argues that writing teachers "continu[e] to privilege alphabetic texts over texts that depend on visual elements, I believe, because such texts present familiar forms, forms with which we have developed a comfortable, stable, intellectual relationship" (71). Indeed, a majority of teachers were trained in graduate school in mostly print and alphabetic literacy. While other digital forms of communication and narrative dominate our lives outside the classroom, and increasingly within our workplace, we have yet to wholly make the disciplinary transition to including them in our courses.

The disruption of roles of writer/reader has been praised by scholars, notably Jay David Bolter, who argues the authority of the author is diminished in digital texts. In "The Database and the Essay: Understanding Composition as Articulation," Johndan Johnson-Eilola applies this digital and postmodern logic to writers and authorship, suggesting that the emerging work of writers isn't to create "original" texts but rather the "ability to understand both users and technologies, [in order to] brin[g] together multiple, fragmented contexts in an attempt to broker a solution" (201). In this sense, "writers—or designers, more accurately—actively map fragments back into contexts recursively" (226). Some go so far as to argue that the visual is now ascendant to print. For example, Gunther Kress, in *Literacy in the New Media Age*, published in 2003, argues that writing is becoming "subordinated to the logic of the visual in many or all of its uses" (7). This results in a different role for readers since reading images departs from the meaning-making work of reading text: "The imaginative work in writing focuses on filling words with meaning—and then reading the filled elements together, in the given syntactic structure. In image, the imagination focuses on creating the order of the arrangement of elements which are already filled with meaning" (4). The writer gives up some power to the reader. For example, Kress argues that textbooks are not "careful development of complex coherent structure" that ask readers for "deliberate carefully reflective engagement with these pages" (21). Rather, many have become "collections of worksheets" that require readers to "work with, to do things with, to act with and often to act on." (21). Kress explains that our written stories have "a reading path, both literally, along the lines of writing, from top to bottom, from left to right, as well as in its simple sequential unfolding" (152). James Sosnoski offers an apt summary of these differences in "Hyper-readers and Their Reading Engines," published in 1999. His schematic of digital reading has changed in scale but not in kind in the past decade. He quotes Geoffrey Sirc's account of reading hypertext: "Material is chosen not because it's a privileged text, a 'difficult' masterpiece from the 'history of wring,' but because it's easily available. It's whatever you notice out of the corner of one's eye from the endlessly shifting screen in front of you" (9 qtd. in Sosnoski 163). He notes that hyper-reading "allow[s] writers to invent and/or map relations among bits of information to suit their own needs" (163). Other scholars also address the visual aspect of digital media. Kristie S. Fleckenstein, Linda Calendrillo, and Demetrice Worley in *Language and Image in the Reading-Writing Classroom: Teaching Vision* encourage teaching visual literacy but haven't totally ceded to print. In their 2002 collection they offer "explicit and specific strategies for integrating imagery into their pedagogy" but treat imagery and language on equal par, not subordinating one to the other. Scholars in this collection continue this work: Catherine Gabor and Riley Nelson examine the concept of authorship in digital spaces, and to examine design as part of composition, Molly E. Daniel's chapter demonstrates strategies for design as a way to cultivate active readers.

Scholarship has also lamented—or at least noted the difference—in the experience of reading digitally, including hypertext but also PDFs that are searchable, but lack hyperlinks. Some note the difference as a matter of fact: James Sosnoski argues that readers dominate hypertext in their research: "there is no doubt that the reader is in charge and that the text is subservient to the reader's wish. This can be most readily seen when hyper-readers abandon reading book length e-texts or articles from beginning to end and query them for data relevant to their research" (169). Many others worry about the experience of reading online and the type of reading skills being produced in digital environments (Carr, "Is Google Making Us Stupid?," 2008, and *The Shallows*, 2010; Baron *Words Onscreen*, 2015; Birkerts). Naomi S. Baron explains that in one study of reading a short story digitally vs. print, digital readers found the story "jumpy" and "[not] flowing properly" (173). David W. Chapman argues against approaches that supplant print literacy and cautions us not to produce "technicians" instead of writers (256). Baron offers a more measured view and acknowledges that print and digital platforms both have advantages and disadvantages. Anne Wysocki welcomes this increased awareness of the medium and argues, "these results of digitality ought to encourage us to consider not only the potentialities of material choices for digital texts, but for any text we make, and that we ought to use the range of choices digital technologies seem to give us to consider the range of choices that printing-press technologies (apparently) haven't" (10). As readers increasingly experience digital texts because of convenience, they come to expect these features, including shorter texts. Indeed, Baron notes that "deep reading and rereading, uninterrupted reading, and tackling longer texts are seen by fewer and fewer people as part of what it means to read" (231).

This collection argues that we should no longer focus on whether or not we should include digital literacy, analogous to the decades old debate of whether or not we should include reading and literature in writing classes. Rather, as Michael Knievel argues, we "must confidently assert a fundamental, inseparable relationship between technology and the humanities" (245). This relationship "move[s] beyond a cosmetic makeover of our view of technology [and] offers a real role for English studies in an evolving technology narrative, and a thoroughly humanistic narrative at that" (245). Indeed, we assume that digital writing permeates all aspects of our lives. Thus, we argue that digital spaces have changed readers' approaches to all texts, included print ones, in popular culture. Indeed, even print books are being shaped by the digital media. This is the latest cultural iteration of people's relationship to books. Alberto Manguel chronicles how people first read aloud since "written words . . . were meant to be pronounced out loud, since the signs carried implicit, as if it were their soul, a particular sound" (45). Next, he describes St. Augustine's shock at stumbling upon Ambrose's silent reading (50). Silent reading seems obvious to current readers, yet digital media are making that practice increasingly social and collaborative. Publishers capitalize on social media, television, and the Internet to publicize their books and to create immediacy and audience-interaction that print-based books alone lack. Of course the text in books themselves is digitized through database subscriptions and online projects like Project Gutenberg. But print books are increasingly accompanied by extratextual lives in digital media, including reviews and recommendations. Amazon and every bookstore website curates lists that are created by staff and public readers. Apps such as Goodreads offer online communities of readers to read and discuss books. The book alone seems to be not enough—readers crave additional interaction in the form of interviews with the author and discussion questions at the back, fan sites online, blogs, etc. In academics, the professor chooses and curates the reading lists; in popular culture, readers gravitate toward like-minded reading groups or celebrities for their recommendations. The most well-known late twentieth-century mediator of popular reading is Oprah's Book Club, founded in 1996. It ran fifteen years until 2011 and included seventy books. As I noted in 2005, her book club "demonstrates that rather than thwart print literacy, electronic media might simply shape what properties of reading are emphasized, in this case the social, rhetorical aspects of reading" (Lamb 256). Popular press articles note the renewed interest in book clubs and the social rather than solitary aspects of reading (Hall; "New Leaf"). Toni Morrison, appearing in 1998 on the Oprah Winfrey episode discussing her novel *Paradise*, the second Morrison novel chosen for the club, responds to Winfrey's insecurity about the necessity of a study group to understand the novel. She succinctly states: "Novels are for talking about and quarrelling about and engaging in some powerful way. . . . Reading is solitary, but that's not its only life. It should have a talking life, a discourse that follows" ("Book" 9). Once one of a kind, the celebrity book club now stands in a crowded field of reading-list-curators that range from country music stars to past presidents, and these extratextual activities are no longer optional but rather part of the reading and literary landscape of print publishing.

Of course there have always been reference resources for readers to drawn on, such as encyclopedias and dictionaries, and readers have long created marginalia in books. Today, there is an increased reliance on and use of what I dub here "parareaders." I take the Greek *para* to mean "at or to one side of, beside, side by side" or "beyond, past, by." Note also one use of the word implies roles that are ancillary or subsidiary of others, as in "paralegal" or "paraprofessional." I also like the implication of this prefix's usage in chemistry as "pertaining to or occupying two positions." Thus, I argue that the devices, enhancements, online communities, and computer-assistance programs constitute parareading, a collaboration between reader, text, and other readers and experiences, including multiple online and face-to-face sites, videos of author interviews, television films of the book, blog discussions, discussion boards, texts, and Tweets, and face-to-face or Web-based book clubs. All these digital experiences we read with, through, and into become part of the source text, even print books. This digital and mediated paraphernalia are increasingly not only *adding to* our reading experience but becoming *essential to* it. In 1986 Alexander Nehamas, in "What an Author Is," notes that "this process [of interpretation] has no end. Interpretation ends when interest wanes, not when certainty, or an ultimate meaning, is reached" (688). So the author may be dead, but the critic-reader is more important than ever, especially in digital spaces. This rhetorical situation in digital environments is full of self-selecting pop-up ads and such so that the reader's context is partially the function of an algorithm. Students reading in digital environments, or in print with access to digital sources, are partially creating their textual experiences as they read, based on the additional sources they incorporate. In this collection, Joshua Welsh brings these algorithms to the forefront, challenging us to teach the students how to handle reading online that is driven by algorithms and crowded with extratextual media.

This popular reality hasn't been fully addressed in scholarship that still views academic effective reading as solitary, rhetorical, reflective, and analytic. I am suggesting that we need additional theories and models for helping students account for all these extratextual experiences they have with texts, and that theories of teaching reading in writing classrooms should acknowledge these collaborative reading practices. For example, one way I have noticed that parareading is changing our notions of literacy is how instructors approach students' texts. Increasingly, teachers who a decade ago might have required hard copies (or earlier, handwritten essays) are now requiring that students submit essays online, through a classroom management platform. These come from institutional site licenses, such as WebCT, Blackboard, or Desire2 Learn, or from commercial publishers and software, such as Turnitin.com. Teachers for the most part still expect students to continue reading source texts and writing about and with them, in a rather solitary, linear way. Yet teachers increasingly outsource our own reading to computer software to "adjudicate" student's originality for us. We avail ourselves of all the collaborative possibilities of online submissions, including hyperlinks, embedded video, direct links to sources, video and audio responses to students, submission records, and the ability for students to collaborate. As we discuss "originality" percentages with students, perhaps we should develop assignments for students to more fully cite and discuss all the extratextual tools they used in their reading and curating of sources.

In this sense, readers are collaborative writers of the texts (in the reader-response sense and in the material, digital sense). Collaborative learning and collaborative writing are well-established practices in writing classrooms (LeFevre; Ede and Lunsford), and many have noted the collapse of reader-writer distinctions in many digital environments. For example, Johndan Johnson-Eilola notes the collapse of reader/writer distinctions when reading a literary hypertext: "Individual readings . . .

develop out of interactions between the multiply structured hypertext and the specific navigational actions of the reader. Users of literary hypertexts can come to realize their power as reader-writers whose actions appear to determine fundamental characteristics of the story" (195). Indeed, I argue that this quality now extends to other, non-hypertext, linear texts, both print and online.

One way future research might nuance our understanding of the digital collaborative reader is through theories of collaborative writing. Lisa Ede and Andrea Lunsford trace the "death of the author" à la Barthes and Foucault to illustrate theories that bring the "reader" into prominence (87). Next, they illustrate how the role of "author" works in professional and academic settings when writers collaborate. They note two types of collaboration, dialogic and hierarchical. Dialogic shares all the tasks of writing equally but hierarchical divides tasks, often according to the power structure of the group. Collaborative authorship was also discussed by Keith D. Miller and Elizabeth A. Vander Lei's "Collaboration, Collaborative Communities, and Black Folk Culture." They note three types of collaboration: historic, similar to allusions and intertextuality; communal: where the speaker and audience are indistinct, and work together to produce the text; and call-and-response, where the speaker and audience are distinct, but physically together creating a partially new text. I'm drawn to their explanation of how authorship varies according to the needs of the audience and the needs of the speaker, but the primary effect of the collaboration is a renewed sense of community rather than a unitary author.

These collaborative authorship theories account for the cultural work that happens when creating texts, thus portraying collaboration as a complex system that can be positive rather than negative, arising from the fact that the writer "needs help." Similarly, these theories might help students and teachers recast extratextual material in positive ways that extend their experience and complicate their interpretations, rather than as shortcuts to "true meanings" or as "cheating." Johnson-Eilola notes that even theorists open to "nonlinear conceptions of reading and writing" have been slow to link "the social and individual aspects of literacy to its technological aspects," even while cautioning us against "totalizing" and simplifying these processes (203). Similarly, collaborative authorship theories may shed light on the digital and extratextual material that readers/writers bring to meaning making and productively complement the work of literary and rhetorical scholars. Numerous scholars have written extensively about how the reader, text, and "interpretive communities" (Fish) or Bahktin's "dialogism" engage to make meaning through language. Reception studies offer interpretations of the cultural work of texts that harness the full rhetorical situation (Mailloux; Radway, 1984, 1997; Schweichart and Flynn). In digital landscapes, the "student-critic-reader" is more active than ever, inviting other texts into the context, engaging all the various texts and extra-textual-paraphernalia, and sometimes dealing with uninvited intrusions. Developing similar reception studies may offer insights into how we teach reading and writing in digital landscapes.

The chapters in this collection all share the premise that reading is collaborative—readers using parareaders for various purposes as they read—and that writing instruction should help students understand and reflect on this process. This type of reading is simply not the linear reading earlier generations did, where we read, make interpretive guesses, learn new information, adjust our hypothesis, in a recursive process. In current reading practices, both reading printed texts with phone in hand and reading online, the recursive process happens simultaneously in interaction with the source text. The chapters in this collection offer ways to help students understand this process and become reflective about it, similar to what Kathleen Blake Yancey discusses in *Teaching Literature as Reflective Practice*, when she distinguishes the "experienced/lived curriculum" from the "delivered curriculum" to theorize ways to acknowledge all the ways students experience texts (58). Our students' "experienced/lived curriculum" is far more crowded and expansive than the one we are delivering to them, and this collection demonstrates ways to open our classrooms to make room.

Overview

Part 1 Collaborative Reading: Approaches to Reading in Crowded Digital Spaces, approaches theories of reading and writing that happen digitally. Part 2 Collaborative Digital Reading and Writing Pedagogy focuses on strategies for the classroom by applying reading theories, design principles, and rhetorical concepts to writing instruction. Chapters address the particular challenges and opportunities of reading and writing online. In Part 3 Implications and Institutional Contexts, the authors consider disciplinary and institutional implications of this pedagogy. We hope this collection expands both our imagination and our ideas of what reading and writing can do and be in our students' lives.

Works Cited

Bahktin, Mikhail M. *The Dialogic Imagination*. Edited by Michael Holquist, Translated by Caryl Emerson and Michael Holquist, University of Texas Press, 1981.

Baron, Naomi S. *Words Onscreen: The Fate of Reading in a Digital World*, Oxford University Press, 2015.

Bartholomae, David, and Anthony Petrosky. *Facts, Artifacts, and Counterfacts: Theory and Method for a Writing Course*, Boynton/Cook, 1986.

Batker, Carol, and Charles Moran. "The Reader in the Writing Class." *Only Connect: Uniting Reading and Writing*, edited by Thomas Newkirk, Boynton/Cook, 1986, pp. 198–208.

Bergmann, Linda S., and Edith M. Baker, editors. *Composition and/or Literature: The End(s) of Education*, NCTE, 2006.

Birkerts, Sven. *The Gutenberg Elegies: The Fate of Reading in an Electronic Age*, Faber and Faber, 1994.

Bolter, Jay David. *Writing Space: Computers, Hypertext, and the Remediation of Print*, Lawrence Erlbaum Associates, 1991.

"Book Club: Toni Morrison." *The Oprah Winfrey Show*, ABC, 6 Mar. 1998, Transcript.

Brent, Doug. *Reading as Rhetorical Invention: Knowledge, Persuasion, and the Teaching of Research-Based Writing*, NCTE, 1992.

Chapman, David W. "Brave New (Cyber) World: From Reader to Navigator." *Teaching Writing: Landmarks and Horizons*, edited by Christina Russell McDonald and Robert L. McDonald, Southern Illinois University Press, 2002, pp. 249–58.

———. "A Luddite in Cyberland; or, How to Avoid Being Snared by the Web." *Computers and Composition*, vol. 16, no. 2, 1999, pp. 247–52.

Corbett, Edward P.J. "Literature and Composition: Allies or Rivals in the Classroom?" *Composition and Literature: Bridging the Gap*, edited by Winifred Bryan Horner, Chicago University Press, 1983, pp. 168–84.

Ede, Lisa, and Andrea Lunsford. *Singular Texts/Plural Authors: Perspectives on Collaborative Writing*, Southern Illinois University Press, 1990.

Elbow, Peter. "The War between Reading and Writing: And How to End It." *Rhetoric Review*, vol. 12, no. 1, Autumn 1993, pp. 5–24.

Fish, Stanley. *Is There a Text in This Class? The Authority of Interpretive Communities*, Harvard University Press, 1980.

Fleckenstein, Kristie S., Linda T. Calendrillo, and Demetrice A. Worley, editors. *Language and Image in the Reading-Writing Classroom: Teaching Vision*, Lawrence Erlbaum Associates, 2002.

Haas, Christina. *Writing Technology: Studies on the Materiality of Literacy*, Lawrence Erlbaum Associates, 1996.

Haas, Christina, and Linda Flower. "Rhetorical Reading Strategies and the Construction of Meaning." *On Writing Research: The Braddock Essays 1975–1998*, edited by Lisa Ede, Bedford, 1999, pp. 242–59.

Hall, Brian. "The Group: When Did Reading, Once a Solitary Pursuit, Start to Attract a Crowd?" *New York Times Book Review*, 6 June 1999, pp. 22–3.

Horner, Winifred Bryan, editor. *Composition and Literature: Bridging the Gap*, University of Chicago Press, 1983.

———. "Foreword: A Reflection on Literature and Composition, Twenty Years Later." *Composition and/or Literature: The End(s) of Education*, edited by Linda S. Bergmann and Edith M. Baker, NCTE, 2006, pp. ix–xvi.

Horning, Alice S., and Elizabeth W. Kraemer, editors. *Reconnecting Reading and Writing*. Reference Guides to Rhetoric and Composition, edited by Charles Bazerman, Mary Jo Reiff, and Anis Bawarshi, Parlor Press, 2013.

Johnson-Eilola, Johndan. "The Database and the Essay: Understanding Composition as Articulation." *Writing New Media*, edited by Anne Frances Wysocki, Johndan Johnson-Eilola, Cynthia L. Selfe, and Geoffrey Sirc, Utah State University Press, pp. 199–235.

———. "Reading and Writing in Hypertext: Vertigo and Euphoria." *Literacy and Computers: The Complications of Teaching and Learning with Technology*, edited by Cynthia Selfe and Susan Hilligoss, MLA, 1994, pp. 195–219.

Joliffe, David A. "'Learning to Read as Continuing Education' Revised: An Active Decade, But Much More Remains to Be Done." *Deep Reading: Teaching*

Reading in the Writing Classroom, edited by Patrick Sullivan, Howard Tinberg, and Sheridan Blau, NCTE, 2017, pp. 3–22.

Knievel, Michael S. "(Re)defining the Humanistic: Making Space for Technology in Twenty-First Century English Studies." *Transforming English Studies: New Voices in an Emerging Genre*, edited by Lori Ostergaard, Jeff Ludwig, and Jim Nugent, Parlor Press, 2009, pp. 229–48.

Lamb, Mary R. "The 'Talking Life' of Books: Women Readers in Oprah's Book Club." *Reading Women: Literary Figures and Cultural Icons from the Victorian Age to the Present*, edited by Janet Badia and Jennifer Phegley, University of Toronto Press, 2005, pp. 255–80.

Landow, George P. *Hyper/Text/Theory*, The Johns Hopkins University Press, 1994.

LeFevre, Karen Burke. *Invention as a Social Act*, Southern Illinois State University Press, 1982.

Lindemann, Erika. "Freshman Composition: No Place for Literature." *College English*, vol. 55, no. 3, Mar. 1993, pp. 311–16.

Mailloux, Steven. *Rhetorical Power*, Cornell University Press, 1989.

Miller, Keith D., and Elizabeth A. Vander Lei. "Collaboration, Collaborative Communities, and Black Folk Culture." *The Right to Literacy*, edited by Andrea A. Lunsford, Lelene Moglen, and James Slevin, MLA, 1990, pp. 50–60.

Miller, Susan. *Textual Carnivals: The Politics of Composition*, Southern Illinois University Press, 1991.

Murray, Donald. "Reading While Writing." *Only Connect: Uniting Reading and Writing*, edited by Thomas Newkirk, Boynton/Cook, 1986, pp. 241–54.

———. "Teaching the Other Self: The Writer's First Reader." *College Composition and Communication*, vol. 33, no. 2, May 1982, pp. 140–8.

Nehamas, Alexander. "What an Author Is." *The Journal of Philosophy*, vol. 33, no. 11, Nov. 1986, pp. 685–91.

Newkirk, Thomas, editor. *Only Connect: Uniting Reading and Writing*, Boynton/Cook, 1986.

"New Leaf: The U.S. Is Seeing a Boom in Book Festivals." *Atlanta Journal-Constitution*, 26 Apr. 2000, p. C1.

Peterson, Bruce T., editor. *Convergences: Transactions in Reading and Writing*, NCTE, 1986.

Radway, Janice A. *A Feeling for Books: The Book-of-the-Month Club, Literary Taste, and Middle-Class Desire*, The University of North Carolina Press, 1997.

———. *Reading the Romance: Women, Patriarchy, and Popular Literature*, The University of North Carolina Press, 1984.

Rosenblatt, Louise M. *The Reader, the Text, the Poem: The Transactional Theory of the Literary Work*, Southern Illinois State University Press, 1978.

Salvatori, Mariolina Rizzi. "Conversations with Texts: Reading in the Teaching Composition." *College English*, vol. 58, no. 4, April 1996, pp. 440–53.

———. "Reading and Writing a Text: Correlations Between Reading and Writing Patterns." *College English*, vol. 45, no. 7, Nov. 1983, pp. 657–66.

Salvatori, Mariolina Rizzi, and Patricia Donahue. "What Is College English? Stories about Reading: Appearance, Disappearance, Morphing, and Revival." *College English*, vol. 75, no. 2, Feb. 2012, pp. 199–217.

Schweickart, Patrocinio P., and Elizabeth A. Flynn, editors. *Reading Sites: Social Difference and Reader Response*, MLA, 2004.

Selfe, Cynthia L. "Toward New Media Texts: Taking Up the Challenges of Visual Literacy." *Writing New Media*, edited by Anne Frances Wysocki, Johndan Johnson-Eilola, Cynthia L. Selfe, and Geoffrey Sirc, Utah State University Press, pp. 67–110.

Sosnoski, James. "Hyper-Readers and Their Reading Engines." *Passions, Pedagogies, and 21st Century Technologies*, edited by Gail E. Hawisher and Cynthia Selfe, Utah State University Press/NCTE, 1999, pp. 161–77.

Sullivan, Patrick, Howard Tinberg, and Sheridan Blau, editors. *Deep Reading: Teaching Reading in the Writing Classroom*, NCTE, 2017.

Tate, Gary. "A Place for Literature in Freshman Composition." *College English*, vol. 55, no. 3, Mar. 1993, pp. 317–21.

Wysocki, Anne Frances. "Opening New Media to Writing: Openings and Justifications." *Writing New Media: Theory and Applications for Expanding the Teaching of Composition*, edited by Anne Frances Wysocki, Johndan Johnson-Eilola, Cynthia L. Selfe, and Geoffrey Sirc, Utah State University Press, 2004, pp. 1–41.

Yancey, Kathleen Blake. *Teaching Literature as Reflective Practice*, NCTE, 2004.

Part 1

Collaborative Reading

Approaches to Reading in
Crowded Digital Spaces

1 How Digital Writing and Design Can Sustain Reading, or Prezi Is Not Just for Presentations—Well, Now, Maybe It Is

Donna Qualley

We have all heard it. We may have even said it to ourselves and our students. Good readers make good writers. You must know how to read before you can write. Reading sustains writing in the same way that air sustains life. No air, no life. No reading, no writing. The idea that reading is foundational to writing seems pretty unshakeable—even when the research calls this relationship into question.

In her 2015 book, *The Rise of Writing: New Directions in Mass Writing*, Deborah Brandt makes the bold claim that writing is now conditioning how and why we read. And this "ascendancy of writing-based literacy create[s] tensions in a society whose institutions were organized around a reading-based literacy" (3). We have seen these tensions play out in the many books (and teacher anecdotes) lamenting the loss of deep, intensive, focused reading practices, supposedly brought on by the shift from print to digital technologies. In his oft-cited 2008 *Atlantic* article, "Is Google Making Us Stupid?" Nicholas Carr bemoaned that with internet reading, "our ability to interpret texts, to make the rich mental connections that form when we read deeply and without distraction, remains largely disengaged." And we have seen these tensions play out in our classrooms. Our own field's "Citation Project" (see Howard, Serviss, and Rodrigue, 2010) reveals the challenges that students have in accurately reading, summarizing, and paraphrasing outside source material. One of the key findings of this research—that students typically quote from the first paragraphs or pages of a source—would seem to support the belief that students don't read or can't read or just won't read in the careful, deliberate ways we expect.

But perhaps, suggests Brandt, people are reading in ways we don't expect. Today, more people, especially in the workplace, are reading to support their habit of writing. In her 2014 essay, "Deep Writing: New Directions in Mass Literacy," Brandt notes that there is a tendency for "routine reading" to take place "within acts of writing." In other words, individuals, both inside and outside of school, may be showing "a loss of appetite" for reading on its own, for reading outside of the realms of writing (19). If Brandt's observations have merit, and more reading is happening in the service of writing, then could writing—specifically, digital forms of writing—become a way to nourish and sustain certain kinds of reading? If I find myself discouraged by students' reading practices, how might I devise ways to use digital writing and design to reengage them in reading? This is the question I posed for myself in the fall of 2016.

I regularly teach an upper-level course in literacy studies, which is part of our writing studies minor. Of all the writing studies courses I teach, this one is the most content heavy. Students read, view, and/or listen to a range of theoretical, narrative, and visual print and online texts. Almost all the reading will either be unfamiliar or contradict what students assume literacy is and what literacy does. To help students sustain their reading of all this new information about literacy, I designed a quarter-long digital curation and design project using Prezi. My aim was for students to gradually come to a more complex historical, cultural, social, political, and personal understanding of literacy. Over the years, I have experimented with different print and digital production projects to help students synthesize this material so that they can construct more robust understandings of what literacy is and what literacy does, but none have worked as successfully as I would have liked.

Why Prezi?

Although Prezi[1] is typically used as a platform for formal presentations, it is also a good tool for personal information management, invention, and connection-making. Prezi does not lock users into a linear format like word processing does, and it's easier to continuously move things into different shapes and configurations that enable users to visualize relationships between ideas. The blank and infinitely revisable screen allows users to put information anywhere on the Prezi canvas and rearrange it later using the Prezi tools (e.g., frames, shapes, colors, sizes, lines, symbols, fonts, and zooming and tilting capabilities) to highlight (or "code") information into categories. It's also easy to insert images, YouTubes, and website links. Prezi was the only digital site that I could find that offered users the opportunity to invent, arrange, and experiment with their own designs and linkages without relying on predetermined templates.

In her 2010 essay, "The Rise of the Template, The Fall of Design," Kristin Arola shares her concerns about how the steady growth and use of templates in Web 2.0 technologies. When users "post within preformatted templates designed by the site's creators," they are prevented from making their own "purposeful choices and arrangements." More importantly, templates separate form from content. (6). As Arola notes, "Even though we can choose a template . . . we are not producing design ourselves" (7). Using templates to teach writing is not new to the field. We are all aware of ubiquitous templates such as the five-paragraph essay and Gerald Graff and Cathy Birkenstein's set of "They Say, I Say" templates for teaching academic arguments.

Decisions about design choice and arrangement are obviously important rhetorical decisions for writers, but could these design decisions also be important for readers of both print and online texts as well? Certainly, the use of familiar template formats on the web can ease the burden of both *excess* of available information and *access* to that information by making certain forms of digital reading more efficient and speedy (such as foraging to see what is available), as Daniel Keller suggests in his book, *Chasing Literacy: Reading and Writing in the Age of Acceleration.* However, templates can work against readers who are trying to *do* or *produce* something with the information that they read. Relying on templates in the era of digital production can forestall invention and deter readers and writers from discovering new links and relationships between ideas. In order to use digital writing to sustain and deepen reading or to curate content in such a way that individual readers can readily make connections, they need a more flexible platform. I thought I had found this flexible platform in Prezi.

In the rest of this essay, I will first describe the project that I devised using Prezi—not as a presentation platform, but as a curation and connection-making affordance to sustain students' reading (and rereading) throughout the course. I then offer a kind of cautionary tale about the dangers of relying on proprietary software before closing with a brief discussion of two students' projects from the second time I taught this course.

The Prezi Literacy Curation Project

First, what do I mean by curation? A curator (*cura* from the Latin meaning "care") is a "content specialist," a person who gathers (or "aggregates"), organizes, and interprets information on a specific subject. Traditionally, curators were associated with heritage collections (galleries, museums, libraries, or archives). With the explosion of information on the internet and the rise of social media, digital, curators are in demand. These are people who select, organize, and bundle information into categories so it is easily accessible to others. But curation, which has been called an "emerging" twenty-first-century information literacy, can also serve as an aide for one's own continuous learning.

How It Worked

For each of the assigned texts, students put information that struck them as interesting or important anywhere on their Prezi screens, either as they were reading or soon after they finished. Their content might include concepts, definitions, explanations, examples, memorable points, personal connections, questions, or other commentary. For some readings, students might include a lot of content and for other readings, not so much. They could group information into tentative clusters as they went along—or they could wait until they had collected information from several texts. With each reading, students frequently found themselves reorganizing earlier information as they encountered the new content, often adding ideas they had neglected or overlooked the first time or deleting stuff that seemed less useful or critical to them in hindsight. Or they simply chose to reconnect the "dots" into new configurations for aesthetic reasons. In every case, students' initial bundles and categories changed over the quarter. See Appendix 1A for a version of this assignment.

Backtracking and Side Excursions

I have long touted the importance of building our reading and writing courses in spirals rather than linear progressions so that students return to earlier work from their (supposedly more informed) positions later in the course. In practice, this continual looping back hasn't always cemented or deepened my students' understanding of the course material as much as I anticipate it will. I finally realized I needed to make these loops and spirals explicit in the formal structure of the course and not simply a class assignment. If I simply asked my students to "reflect" on Q or re-read X from the position of Y (where Y might be a text, a concept, a theory, an activity, an experience), it was just too easy for them to engage in "pretend rereading" by doing a single fly by over the material. So, I wanted to try something different. On my course schedule, I set aside specific days for "Backtracking and Side Excursions." On these days, students could "backtrack" through the reading we had done thus far to anchor the ideas more firmly in their minds or look for connections between readings. They could also take a side trip into one of the concepts or topics that they would have liked to have read more about. Canvas, my course LMS site, contained additional articles and videos for every required reading. These class days also gave me an opportunity to sit with each student in this 20-person class and make observations and answer their questions about their developing designs.

And because our class met in a computer lab, students always had access to their Prezis and could refer to them during our class discussions of the reading. Many students added information to their Prezis that emerged during our class discussions. The nice thing about being in the lab is that students could write a quick note on their Prezis in class and later, elaborate on it and decide where the information fit. I have never experienced students using their "class notes" so productively.

Seeing Other People's Prezi Projects in Process

On the backtracking and side-excursion days, students also had the opportunity to see what information and how much information their colleagues included on their Prezis. They noticed the kinds of connections their peers were making between different concepts, and sometimes borrowed and copied each other's ideas for arranging their information. For example, after seeing one student's use of speech bubbles, speech bubbles began to emerge everywhere. The more experienced Prezi users offered tips and suggestions to the less experienced users.

I should add that I also did this project along with my students. Initially, I shared strategies that I had stumbled across such as using the same

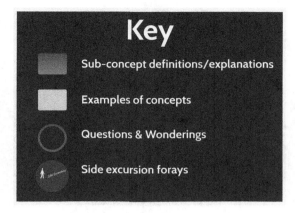

Figure 1.1 Donna's Prezi key

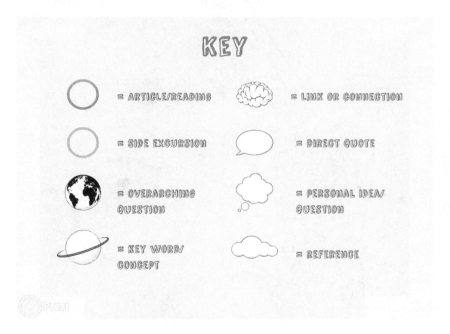

Figure 1.2 Hanna's Prezi key

color, shape, or symbol for similar forms of information (e.g., definitions, examples, questions, side excursions). Figure 1.1 illustrates the very simple key I devised for myself. It consisted of different colored rectangles for definitions/explanations and examples, circles for questions, and a walking figure encased in a colored circle for side excursions.

Figure 1.2 shows a more complex key that Hanna Hupp, one of the students in this course, developed. Hanna used different colored circles

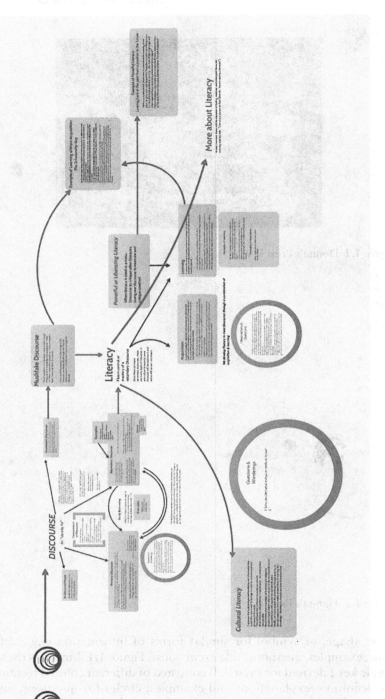

Figure 1.3 Donna's week three version of Prezi

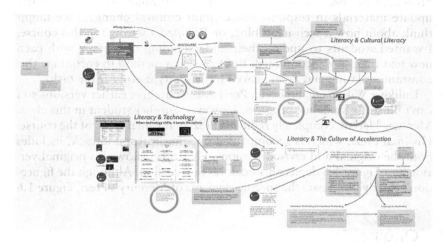

Figure 1.4 Donna's week seven version of Prezi

for readings and side excursions and different kinds of speech bubbles for direct quotes and personal ideas and questions. She used images to show the connections she was making (a brain), her overarching questions (the world), and key words or concepts (a satellite).

I also made a copy of my early Prezi configurations so I could demonstrate how my initial "draft" was changing with the addition of new information. Figure 1.3 shows my beginning Prezi and Figure 1.4 shows a more elaborate, recategorized, and reconfigured Prezi. Figure 1.3 depicts my initial grouping and connection-making at the end of week three. The class had read two chapters from James Paul Gee's *Social Linguistics and Literacies*, Richard Rodriguez's chapter, "The Achievement of Desire," from *Hunger of Memory*, and had just begun examining articles on cultural literacy. Figure 1.4 shows my more robust version of Prezi at the end of week seven. In addition to containing more information, my content has been reconfigured into four large categories: Discourse, Literacy and Cultural Literacy, Literacy and Technology, and Literacy and the Culture of Acceleration. I was beginning work on a fifth category, Affinity Spaces and the New Media Literacies. This Prezi now includes several side excursions, a few images, and some YouTube links in its path as well.

A Regenerative Remix

In many ways, this project works like a regenerative remix. Remix scholar Eduardo Navas defines a regenerative remix as the juxtaposition of "two or more elements that are constantly updated, meaning that they are designed to change according to data flow." The remix continually "regenerates" because there is a need to continually re-aggregate and update materials in response to constant cultural change. (We might think about how a website, a blog, or *Wikipedia* works.) In this course, I wanted students to update their understanding of literacy with each new text that they encountered. But I needed a method to encourage this constant updating and Prezi proved to be pretty useful for the task.

Unlike a Wiki page, however, Prezi doesn't archive earlier versions so I can't illustrate students' progress. However, another student in this class, Mercury Herlan, completely redid his Prezi in the final week of the course. His final Prezi, which is accompanied by a musical soundtrack, includes both the original and revised versions. Figure 1.5 shows his original version and Figure 1.6 depicts his final, revised version. Although the figures don't clearly illuminate the specific elements of Mercury's Prezi, Figure 1.6

Figure 1.5 Mercury's original Prezi

Revised Prezi

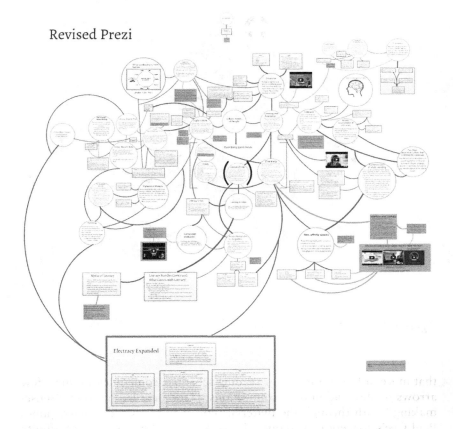

Figure 1.6 Mercury's revised Prezi

clearly indicates a more detailed canvas with a different arrangement. The Prezi contains more links between information (as indicated by the lines criss-crossing the canvas) and more commentary (denoted by the shaded rectangles).

Hanna Hupp's Final Prezi

Hanna's final Prezi appears in Figure 1.7. She opted to focus on specific information and the overall design and aesthetic of her Prezi. Her Prezi consists of 84 slides that tilt and whirl and zoom in and out across the canvas. The order of her final path reveals how she is connecting information together, and a few arrows denote additional connections between ideas and concepts. Although many students in this class created a path

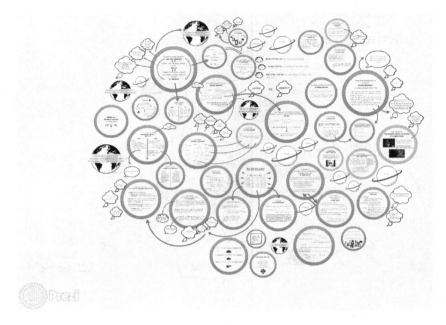

Figure 1.7 Hanna's completed Prezi

that more or less followed our reading schedule, sometimes adding a few arrows to show additional connections, Hanna carved her own "sense-making" path through the material. For example, we discussed James Paul Gee's concept of Discourse in week one and his concept of affinity spaces in week eight. In most of the other students' Prezis, Discourses and affinity spaces were slides apart because their paths closely followed the order in which they first encountered the material. Hanna followed her initial three slides on Discourse with a definitional slide on affinity spaces to contrast the two concepts. Sometimes, she puts information from two readings on the same subject side-by-side to show differing perspectives. For example, one circle entitled "Cultural Literacy: Then and Now" contains bullet points from E. D. Hirsch on one side and bullet points from Eric Liu's 2016 *Atlantic* essay that calls for a crowd-sourced, ever changing list of "what every American needs to know." As she moves from slide to slide, she punctuates the movement with "big" questions in her world images such as the ones that follow her Hirsch and Liu slide: "Is there a universal knowledge we should all have? Who are the cultural gatekeepers of such knowledge?" She follows this slide with a speech bubble containing her own questions and wonderings: "How practically possible would it be to make a list à la Hirsch and Liu without marginalizing or alienating some subset of people? Does this make such a list inherently flawed? How necessary is it to have that kind of universal knowledge?"

Unlike most of the other students in this class whose final slides coincide with our final readings, Hanna's Prezi culminates with the key question of the course: "So what is literacy?" Drawing on the course texts, her side excursions, and class conversations, she answers this question with a series of questions of her own that reveal her awareness of the tensions surrounding differing conceptions of literacy (see Figure 1.8). She then follows this slide with an answer, illustrated with images from social media (see Figure 1.9).

Hanna's final two slides reveal her own understanding of the political and ideological issues swirling around definitions and discussions of literacy. Figure 1.10 depicts Hanna's culminating question and Figure 1.11 reveals her thinking at the end of her Prezi.

Hanna's and the other students' Prezis are the digital writing and design that sustains and deepens their reading and learning all quarter. This digital platform allows them to work visually and recursively through the material and blur the lines between (re)reading, (re)writing, and (re)designing. Students are more apt to try different configurations and paths before settling on a final design. Revision is easy! Using the color, shape, and size features of Prezi, students can denote linkages and add commentary in ways that would

Figure 1.8 Hanna's culminating questions about literacy

OR MAYBE A COMBINATION OF THEM ALL...

A CONSTRUCTION THAT DEEPLY INFLUENCES WHO WE BELIEVE OURSELVES TO BE AND HOW WE ARE PERCEIVED BY OTHERS.

NOT JUST READING AND WRITING, BUT A PATTERN OF BEHAVIOR, THE FUNDAMENTAL BUILDING BLOCKS OF COMMUNICATION.

Figure 1.9 Hanna's answer to her questions

HOW CAN WE MAKE LITERACY MORE...

INCLUSIVE, DIVERSE,
REPRESENTATIVE, POWERFUL,
ENGAGED, ACTIVE,
RELEVANT, EQUITABLE?

Figure 1.10 Hanna's culminating question

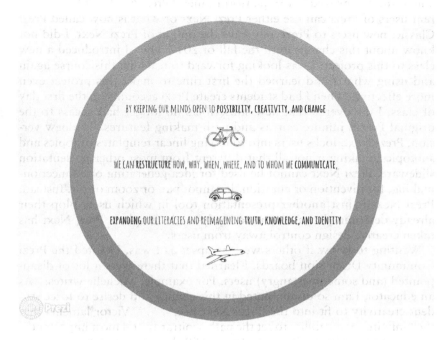

Figure 1.11 Hanna's final answer (for now)

have been much more difficult if working in print alone. Because they are continually manipulating the concepts and theories (individually and in the company of others), they deepen their comprehension of the material. Their work of constantly piecing together information, making connections, (re-)designing, and asking questions reveals their active and collaborative reading and rereading of the material. Their writing indeed sustains their reading. Peter Elbow noted years ago that students "will put more care and attention into reading when they have had more of a chance to write what's on their minds and when they have been given more opportunities to assume the role of writer" (10). For far too long, he says, "reading tends to imply, 'sit still and pay attention,' whereas writing tends to imply, 'get in there and do something.'" (10). My students have gotten in there and done something with their reading. As a result, their reading did something for them.

My Jubilation Is Short Lived, or the Dangers of Relying on Proprietary Software

Unfortunately, dear reader, I have just described a project that you will never be able to duplicate or adapt—unless you already signed up for a Prezi account prior to April 25, 2017. On that day, the company unveiled a new and "improved" Prezi platform called "Prezi Next." Whereas current users of Prezi can use either Prezi Next or what is now called Prezi Classic, new users to Prezi only have the option of Prezi Next. I did not know about this change until the fall of 2017 when I introduced a new class to this project. I was looking forward to teaching this course again and using what I had learned the first time to make this project even more effective. When I had students create Prezi accounts on the first day of class, I discovered that new subscribers no longer had access to the original Prezi's infinite canvas and path making features. The new version, Prezi Next, locks users into following linear templates of topics and subtopics, making it not all that different from most other presentation slideware. Prezi Next cannot be used for idea-generating or connection-making, for invention or curation. It cannot pan or zoom or tilt. Instead, Prezi Next is just another presentation tool in which users plop their already determined content into a ready-made template. Prezi Next has taken creative design control away from users.

Wanting to know if others were as upset as I was, I visited the Prezi Community Discussion boards. I learned that there were a lot of disappointed (and sometimes angry) users. For example, Michelle writes: "As an educator, I am so disappointed in this change and desire to force student creativity to fit into the 'Prezi Next Box' . . . " Victor laments that the "infinite zoom, ability to set the path arbitrarily and most importantly, the ability to spin the frame to 90 or 180 degrees is what made Prezi absolutely revolutionary." Bethany explains that

> [b]eing able to insert an image and make that into my next slide, edit the path, and use infinite zoom were all the tools that gave my presentations depth and additional illustration and meaning. (Imagine an image of the brain, then as I describe a specific part of the brain, we zoom to it! Magical! Then I describe the neurochemicals inside that part, and we zoom again the neurochemicals! Brilliant!). I can't even double click on an image to zoom to it anymore.

Ivana's post captures much of the sentiment:

> Overall the program is a watered-down version of the original Prezi, making it simple for non-creative people to make "interesting presentations" with template based design. . . . I think a lot of the people complaining here liked Prezi for the freedom it offered. . . . You hooked everyone with a great program then completely changed its core function. I can only assume the feedback you used to guide your decision making was "There's too many options!" and "It's too complicated!" These people should have stuck to PowerPoint and you could have left the rest of us with the unmolded clay that was Prezi Classic.

In contrast, Paul's response show's his disinterest in having a platform of "unmolded clay" if it is going to lead novices to create poor presentations. His focus, like many in the business world, is on the bottom line—the final product: "Prezi Next is more user-friendly for non-specialists AND superbly built for presenting your company in a sales conversation. . . . Prezi Classic had 'too much' freedom for many people out there on the internet, leading to an incredible amount of poorly designed Prezis." Of course, the ability to create with "unmolded clay" is the very reason that so many teachers, writers, and designers liked Prezi Classic.

The title of post on the website *Prezijedi: Presentations Designed* captures the rift pretty accurately: "Prezi Classic vs. Prezi Next: A Story about How Utility Wins Over Possibilities." The post goes on to sum up the good news and the bad news about the change. Some of the bad news is that "the ideation ability that a free and open canvas gave you to first visualize your ideas in a mind-map, only to then refine your ideas into sections in a certain order—is gone from Prezi. All that ideation and content structure forming needs to happen outside of Prezi." The post astutely notes that users must have "a clear vision prior to starting" with Prezi Next, which seems to be just another version of that old adage: "Think about what you want to say before you say it." And of course, this is the problem with all the digital templates that Kristin Arola is talking about.

A Somewhat Happy Ending to My Cautionary Tale: The Workaround

In the end, I was able to find a way to repeat this project with my 2017 course, and the students produced even more impressive results. I created 20 new Prezi Classics on my site and invited each student to collaborate with me on one of them. Their Prezi accounts allowed them to use the Prezi Classic tools with this one Prezi. I also repeated this process with a graduate course in 2018. Although my workaround allows students to utilize Prezi Classic in my course, I wrestle with the ethical questions of giving students access to a tool that they will not be able to use and adapt in other situations. Some people from the Prezi Community Discussion Board have suggested that people look on the web for "reusable" Prezi Classics to download. Supposedly, this gives them access to the editing tools for Prezi Classic. They can then delete everything in the Prezi and start afresh. But surely, it would be much better for users and for the company to bring back Prezi Classic!

I close this chapter by sharing work from two students from my 2017 course. Many of these students made prodigious use of meaning-based images and arrangements that demonstrated the very concepts they were discussing. Some students also linked their information by creating narrative threads that pulled all of it together. We need more technologies that leave the thinking and design work to users so that they can find their own

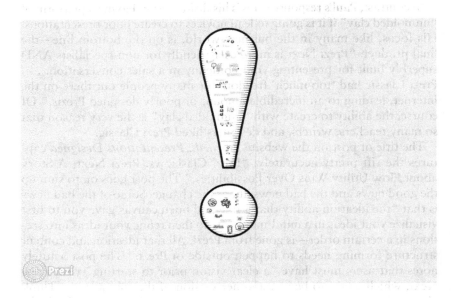

Figure 1.12 Claire's Prezi

available means for making sense of what they read, representing their knowledge, and communicating it to others.

Claire Phelan depicted her Prezi as an exclamation point. The image in Figure 1.12 is deceptive because it hides the 236 slides that comprise it. The point contains 172 slides specifically focused on literacy and the 64 slides in the period capture ideas from a new apparatus that Gregory Ulmer in his many publications has christened "electracy."

In her path, Claire tells her own "story" of literacy by linking the different sections with narrative commentary that summarize what she has just presented or uses questions to propel viewers into the next section. For example, after discussing Gee's chapter on the "The Literacy Myth" and John Szwed's essay, "The Ethnography of Literacy," she summarizes: "Basically, if we want to understand the importance of literacy, we have to observe its functions with various cultures. Different people have different uses for reading and writing, and we can't just say that reading and writing is 'important' because its importance varies depending on the context in which it is used." This summary is followed by a question that launches her into a discussion of Gee's concepts of Discourses: "But why do we need literacy? Well, in order to operate properly within our Discourses of course"! After moving through Gee's concepts of primary and secondary Discourses, learning, acquisition, early borrowing, and mushfaking, she sums up again: "We are all part of Discourses in one way or another. We begin as part of our primary Discourse, and then we

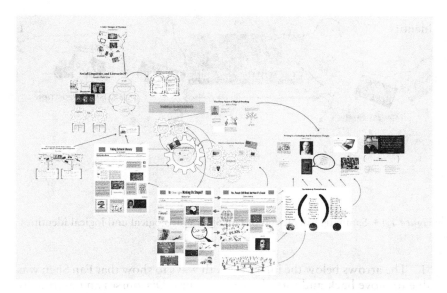

Figure 1.13 Samnang's Prezi

incorporate various secondary Discourses from there." Claire continues to build her narrative in this fashion throughout her Prezi. Her narrative thread really demonstrates the depth of her understanding of how all the pieces of the course fit together for her. She is writing and designing, but then rereading and summarizing the gist of each section.

Samnang Than's 193 slide Prezi depicts the work he did in finding and creating visual images. Looking at Figure 1.13, we can see at a glance the many pictures and images he used in constructing his Prezi. Some of the online articles that we read are depicted as three newspaper and magazine webpages: Karl Taro Greenfield's "Faking Cultural Literacy" and Stephen Johnson's "Yes, People Still Read" essays from *The New York Times* and Nicholas Carr's essay "Is Google Making Us Stupid" from *The Atlantic*. At the top of the Prezi, information from Richard Rodriguez's chapter "Credo" from *Hunger of Memory* appears within a map of the United States and Mexico.

On the far left in the middle of the canvas next to Greenfield's "Faking Cultural Literacy" page is a cluster of images that is not discernible in Figure 1.13. It represents a detailed image discussion of a 1989 *College Composition and Communication* essay by Fan Shen that describes his process of learning "English composition." Figures 1.14 shows a close up of this slide. As he did with Rodriguez, Sam illustrates Fan Shen's native and new cultures with maps of the counties. The countries are connected with an image of the Chinese collective "we" and the English individual

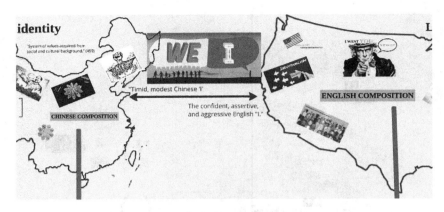

Figure 1.14 Samnang's depiction of Fan Shen's ideological and logical identities

"I." The arrows below the image go both ways to show that Fan Shen was able to move back and forth between cultural Discourses and eventually perform in either. Uncle Sam is clearly visible in the United States map and readers should just be able to make out a picture of Mao Tse Tung in the China map. Samnang's visible representation of the two cultural Discourses also enables him to return to two of Gee's concepts, "dominant groups" and "dominant Discourses," and better understand the distinctions. Like all these students' Prezis, this slide contains multiple layers of images and information, making it difficult to represent accurately in a two-dimensional format. I use this slide as an example of how one student uses the visual capabilities of Prezi to "show" as well as "tell" how he is understanding the material.

Can digital forms of writing and design help sustain students' reading? The work my students produced in these classes suggests that digital writing and design may not only blur the boundaries between these literacy practices but also dismantle the binaries. In some cases, reading may begin the dance, but writing and designing sustains its movement and development.

Appendix 1A
Curating Literacy Project: Building Your Regenerative Remix Archive

About Curation

Today, a curator is a "content specialist," a person who gathers (or "aggregates"), organizes, and interprets information on a specific subject. The word comes from the Latin *cura*, meaning "care." The word "curator" also goes back to the word *curatus*, which meant, "spiritual guide," or "one responsible for the care of souls." Over time, curation has morphed into an intense care and love for a subject or set of artistic works. Traditionally, curators were associated with heritage collections (e.g., for a gallery, museum, library, or archive). With the explosion of information on the internet and the rise of social media, digital curators are in demand. These are people who gather, organize, and bundle information into categories so it is easily accessible to others. But curation, which has been called an "emerging" twenty-first-century information literacy and an example of "combinatorial creativity," can also serve as a "tool for continuous personal learning."

The Curation Project

As a way of managing your own learning and building a more robust understanding of course content, you will become content curators, designers, and information architects for this project. Working in Prezi (Classic), you will construct and curate a literacy archive, gradually categorizing and connecting (and reconnecting) information from the course in ways that become meaningful to you.

Archive building is an ongoing, recursive, and nonlinear process; archives are always under construction. Gradually, you gather information, filter it through the lenses of your own intellectual and aesthetic sensibilities, and forge a path for others to follow. But this archive will not be static. It will be an archive that works like a web page that is always being updated.

So, Why Prezi?

Prezi is typically used as a platform for formal presentations (as an alternative to PowerPoint). And yet, Prezi Classic (sans templates) is also an excellent tool for information management, invention, and connection-making.

Prezi lets you represent ideas and connections visually, and it's easier to continuously move things into different shapes, configurations, and alignments that enable you to discover new relationships between ideas. The blank and infinitely revisable screen allows you to put information down in any order and rearrange it later using the Prezi tools (frames, shapes, sizes, lines, symbols, colors, fonts, zooming capabilities) to highlight (or "code") information into categories. It's also easy to insert images and links if you wish. Over the quarter, you will find yourself adding, deleting, reorganizing, and moving stuff around into different configurations as new information comes in and new kinds of linkages occur to you.

So, How Does It Work?

As you are "reading" (or soon after you finish) each of the assigned "texts," write down information anywhere on your Prezi canvas that strikes you as important. While it is beneficial for you to get the raw information from the reading onto your Prezi before we discuss the texts in class, there may be times when this tactic is not always possible. Still, don't wait too long, because you will lose some of the learning benefit.

Your content will likely include concept definitions, key points and explanations, memorable quotes and examples, personal connections and illustrations, and your own commentary and questions. You can begin connecting the dots and grouping information into tentative categories as you go—or you might wait until you have collected information from several texts. Expect that your initial bundles and categories of information to change throughout the quarter as you discover new ways to signify and arrange your information.

Prezi Invites Backwards and Sideways, Spiraling Movement Through Content

Prezi allows you to represent both the vertical and horizontal dimensions of learning: the widening out as you accumulate more knowledge and practice and the deepening in as your general knowledge becomes more precise and specialized. The image of circling loops in a spiral depict the gradual and recursive nature of learning. Learning doesn't happen in a straight line. With each new level, we continually circle back over the territory that we have just inhabited. In practical terms, this means that you may not own each idea or concept when you first encounter them. However, as you revisit and work with this material in light of later learning, you gradually acquire a deeper understanding. That's the goal anyway!

Your "finished" Prezi will:

• Include a "Key" to your Prezi that explains your categorizing decisions.

- Incorporate accurate information from all required readings (definitions, explanations, memorable quotes, and/or examples of key concepts and theories, and so on).
- Make use of different Prezi tools and capabilities (e.g., grouping frames, shapes, color, arrows, lines, images and/or other clip art, links, zooming, tilting).
- Have a final "path" for moving through the information in your Prezi that makes sense to you and ensures that each slide in your path focuses on the idea or connection you are trying to illuminate (without too much intrusion from other slides).
- Include some of your own commentary and/or "wondering" questions.
- (Ideally) capture some of your own side-excursioning into the additional texts I have provided on Canvas.

Note

1. When I use the term, "Prezi," I will be referring to what the company now calls "Prezi Classic." I will use "Prezi Next" to denote the new Prezi platform.

Works Cited

Arola, Kristin. "The Design of Web 2.0: The Rise of the Template, the Fall of Design." *Computers and Composition*, vol. 27, no. 1, 2010, pp. 4–14, doi:10. 1016/j.compcom.2009.11.004.

Bethany, Love. "Is It Still Possible to Join Prezi Classic as a New User?" *Prezi Classic Community*, 5 June 2017, www.preziclassic.community/t/is-it-still-possible-to-join-prezi-classic-as-a-new-user/65807/67. Accessed 15 July 2018.

Brandt, Deborah. "Deep Writing: New Directions in Mass Literacy." *Vernacular Literacies: Past, Present, and Future*, edited by Anne-Catrine Edlund, Lars-Erik Edland, and Susanne Haugen, Umeå U/Royal Skyttean Society, 2014, pp. 15–28, www.umu.diva-portal.org/smash/record.jsf?pid=diva2%3A736804&dswid=903. Accessed 13 July 2015.

———. *The Rise of Writing: Redefining Mass Literacy*, Cambridge University Press, 2015.

Carr, Nicholas. "Is Google Making Us Stupid?" *The Atlantic*, July/Aug. 2008, www.theatlantic.com/magazine/archive/2008/07/is-google-making-us-stupid/306868/. Accessed 14 July 2018.

Elbow, Peter. "Writing First!" *Educational Leadership*, vol. 62, no. 2, Oct. 2004, pp. 8–13.

Gee, James Paul. *Social Linguistics and Literacies: Ideology on Discourses*. 5th ed., Routledge, 2015.

Graff, Gerald, and Cathy Birkenstein. *They Say/I Say: The Moves That Matter in Academic Writing*, W.W. Norton, 2006, 2009, 2014.

Greenfield, Karl Taro. "Faking Cultural Literacy." *The New York Times*, 14 May 2014, www.nytimes.com/2014/05/25/opinion/sunday/faking-cultural-literacy. html. Accessed 14 July 2018.

Herlan, Mercury. Unpublished Prezi, 2006.

Hirsch, E. D. *Cultural Literacy: What Every American Needs to Know*, Houghton Mifflin, 1987.

Howard, Rebecca Moore, Tricia Serviss, and Tanya K. Rodrigue. "Writing from Sources, Writing from Sentences." *Writing & Pedagogy*, vol. 2, no. 2, 2010, pp. 177–92.

Hupp, Hannah. Unpublished Prezi, 2016.

Ivana_Monson. "Is It Still Possible to Join Prezi Classic as a New User?" *Prezi Classic Community*, 10 Oct. 2017, www.preziclassic.community/t/is-it-still-possible-to-join-prezi-classic-as-a-new-user/65807/67. Accessed 15 July 2018.

Johnson, Steven. "Yes, People Still Read, But Now It's Social." *The New York Times*, 19 June 2010, www.nytimes.com/2010/06/20/business/20unbox.html. Accessed 14 July 2018.

Keller, Daniel. *Chasing Literacy: Reading and Writing in the Age of Acceleration*, Utah State University Press, 2013.

Liu, Eric. "What Every American Should Know: Defining Common Cultural Literacy for an Increasingly Diverse Nation." *The Atlantic*, 3 July 2015, www.theatlantic.com/politics/archive/2015/07/what-every-american-should-know/397334/. Accessed 14 July 2018.

Michelle_Axmear_Rock. "Is It Still Possible to Join Prezi Classic as a New User?" *Prezi Classic Community*, 18 Sep. 2017, www.preziclassic.community/t/is-it-still-possible-to-join-prezi-classic-as-a-new-user/65807/67. Accessed 15 July 2018.

Navas, Eduardo. "Remix Defined." *Remix Theory*, www.remixtheory.net/?page_id=3. Accessed 14 July 2018.

Paul_Naveau. "Is It Still Possible to Join Prezi Classic as a New User?" *Prezi Classic Community*, 6 Nov. 2017, www.preziclassic.community/t/is-it-still-possible-to-join-prezi-classic-as-a-new-user/65807/67. Accessed 15 July 2018.

Phelan, Claire. "What Is Literacy?" Unpublished Prezi, 2017.

"Prezi Classic vs Prezi Next: A Story about How Utility Wins over Possibilities." *Prezijedi: Presentations: Designed*, www.prezijedi.com/prezi-classic-vs-prezi-next. Accessed 15 July 2018.

Rodriguez, Richard. *Hunger of Memory: The Education of Richard Rodriguez*, Bantam, 1983.

Shen, Fan. "The Classroom and the Wider Culture: Identity as a Key to Learning English Composition." *College Composition and Communication*, vol. 40, no. 4, Dec. 1989, pp. 459–66.

Szwed, John. "The Ethnography of Literacy." *Writing: The Nature, Development, and Teaching of Written Communication*, edited by Marcia Farr, Lawrence Erlbaum Associates, 1981, pp. 13–23.

Than, Samnang. Unpublished Prezi, 2017.

Victor, Zdanowicz. "Is It Still Possible to Join Prezi Classic as a New User?" *Prezi Classic Community*, 1 Aug. 2017, www.preziclassic.community/t/is-it-still-possible-to-join-prezi-classic-as-a-new-user/65807/67. Accessed 15 July 2018.

2 Developing Information Literacy Through Critical Reading and Writing

Alice Horning

The Elephant in the Room

If you look up the phrase "the elephant in the room," Google or some other search engine will tell you the elephant refers to a problem too big to ignore. Teaching and learning information literacy (IL) is just such a problem, much too big to ignore. IL is an integral aspect of critical literacy, or the ability to use higher-order thinking skills (analysis, synthesis, evaluation, application) when dealing with information in written texts on pages or screens. The more time we all spend on screens, the more important this aspect of critical literacy becomes. A clear understanding of current students' weaknesses in IL and reading further reveals the scope of the problem. To help solve it, a rigorous definition of academic literacy creates a clear goal, and a model based on case studies with novice and expert readers and writers offers the component awarenesses and skills needed to reach that goal. Inquiry-based research and writing assignments can help students develop the needed abilities; these should be an essential component of every course across the curriculum, drawing on resources available through faculty librarians as well as those of reading and writing scholars.

Experts and Novices: A Model of Academic Critical Literacy, and a Goal

My own work with novice and expert readers has led me to propose a definition and a model of academic critical literacy. These offer a clear goal that instructors should be aiming for in all courses. It is not that any individual course or instructor is going to make students expert readers, but that this goal should inform all postsecondary instruction. It is also not the case that the librarians can "fix" students' IL skills any more than writing teachers can solve all first-year students' writing problems. The point here is that all faculty members can and should be working on these goals; librarians can offer expertise in IL, while writing instructors can offer expertise in writing and rhetoric, and disciplinary instructors can offer their specialized knowledge of their field and its discourse in a range of texts. An elephant-sized problem calls for this kind of collaborative team effort.

The definition of academic critical literacy that I have created arises from IRB-approved case study research with novices and experts (Horning, *Reading*). My research has shown that experts have awareness of text structure, context, and language as well as the key skills of analysis, evaluation, synthesis, and application. As the latest ACRL analysis suggests, experts read for main ideas and details, evaluate critically (ACRL, *Framework*), and can synthesize two different texts on the same topic, recognizing similarities, differences, and other points of connection. Finally, experts can use what they read for their own purposes. These awarenesses and skills lead to a straightforward definition of academic critical literacy:

> Academic critical literacy is best defined as the psycholinguistic processes of getting meaning from or putting meaning into print and/ or sound, images, and movement, on a page or screen, used for the purposes of analysis, synthesis, evaluation and application; these processes develop through formal schooling and beyond it, at home and at work, in childhood and across the lifespan and are essential to human functioning in a democratic society.
>
> (Horning, *Reading* 14)

This definition creates a goal every instructor should be trying to achieve in every class in every discipline.

The definition of academic critical literacy fits together well with the newly revised IL definition proposed by the Association of College and Research Libraries (ACRL), which is as follows:

> Information literacy is a spectrum of abilities, practices, and habits of mind that extends and deepens learning through engagement with the information ecosystem. It includes.
>
> • understanding essential concepts about that ecosystem;
> • engaging in creative inquiry and critical reflection to develop questions and to find, evaluate, and manage information through an iterative process;
> • creating new knowledge through ethical participation in communities of learning, scholarship, and civic purpose; and
> • adopting a strategic view of the interests, biases, and assumptions present in the information ecosystem.
>
> (ACRL, *Framework*)

Taken together, these definitions make clear the knowledge, abilities, and skills students need to be successful in college and in their personal and professional lives. The issue then, is to understand the nature of the problem and create strategies to work effectively toward helping students develop the reading and IL skills they need in every course.

The IL Problem

Accumulating piles of data point to the IL problems of current students. The pertinent data comes not only from studies that focus specifically on the IL skills enumerated by the ACRL *Framework for Information Literacy for Higher Education* but also on data from students' attempts at research and from studies of their reading abilities (Head). Those findings are worth examining briefly because they reveal the elephantine scope of this problem. The development of the SAILS (Standardized Assessment of Information Literacy Skills) instrument is described in detail by Joseph Salem and Carolyn Radcliff, two faculty members involved in the test's creation. Recent results reported on the SAILS website (www. projectsails.org) as presented in 2015 (Radcliff et al.) suggest that only about 50% of students can find, analyze, evaluate, cite, and use appropriate sources found through online searching, whether through library databases or common search tools; skills in evaluating sources are notably weak. Results from different tests of these skills show similar results (Hill, Macheak, and Siegel 32; Katz; Katz and Elliot).

A qualitative study of first-year students' responses to research assignments shows similar difficulties with IL (Head). This study, one of a series of research studies done by Project Information Literacy, a nonprofit based at the Information School of the University of Washington, draws on several types of information. It includes an analysis of library resources in high schools and colleges, in-depth interviews with a small group of first-year students, and an Internet-based survey of almost 2,000 students. The main findings show that beginning students had trouble finding, reading, analyzing, and evaluating source materials from the library, actually or virtually (Head 3–4). The problem, it should be clear, is not only an IL problem but also a reading problem; both are components of academic critical literacy.

The Reading Problem

The reading facet of the problem has been measured by standardized tests and other instruments. Perhaps the king of all standardized instruments measuring reading ability is the reading section of the ACT. This portion of the ACT is a 35-minute multiple-choice test, requiring students to read four passages and answer 10 questions on each one. In 2006, ACT released a study in which it reported the results of tracking 563,000 students for three years, looking at scores on the reading portion of the ACT and success in college. Success was defined by ACT as a 2.0 GPA and returning for a second year of postsecondary study. Only 51% of students earned ACT's criterion score of 21 (scale 0–36) and were successful by its definition. ACT claims there is a causal relationship between reading ability and success (ACT 23–25). A stronger definition of success yields a much larger percentage of students who do not have the skills needed. More recent studies by ACT from 2016 show declining results on the Reading portion.

Admittedly, the measures discussed thus far are standardized tests, and while the IL tests are untimed, the ACT is a timed test and is on paper. It entails reading short passages given the time constraints. Various studies have suggested that results on standardized tests like the ACT and SAT reflect overall academic background as well as socio-economic status. However, qualitative studies of various kinds (such as Jolliffe and Harl) also reflect students' inability to read, analyze, synthesize, evaluate, and use texts for their own purposes. For example, the Citation Project (Jamieson and Howard; Jamieson) and Haller's case studies of three students also make clear students' difficulties using qualitative kinds of data (Haller; see also Laskin and Haller).

These quantitative and qualitative studies show clearly that most students not only don't have sufficient IL skills to find and evaluate sources for possible use in a paper, but also they don't read well enough to carry out the kind of rhetorical reading and source connections expected in research writing. So, what to do? Teaching higher-level reading and IL skills is the obvious answer, but the situation demands a deeper response. To get students where they need to be, the detailed working definition of academic critical literacy presented at the outset can provide a starting point. This definition leads to a useful model of expert reading and writing that offers a goal toward which to work. With the model in hand, sample assignments and teaching strategies can provide options for instruction in every course and at every level in postsecondary institutions of all kinds.

Getting There: Approaches to Teaching Academic Critical Literacy

Some work on reading is already going on, of course. Librarians have been doing this work in their IL instruction; their standards have been in place for more than 10 years. Among a number of good books on IL instruction is one by Joanna Burkhardt which contains a large set of exercises to help students develop the skills enumerated in the *Framework* document. These exercises are keyed to and thus especially useful for helping students develop the relevant skills. Not only does the book present the *IL Standards*, but it ties each of the exercises specifically to sections of that document so their usefulness and applicability is clear. Other ideas and approaches can be found in Linda Nilson's *Teaching at Its Best*, which has chapters devoted to teaching strategies in many disciplines; a second resource that includes the work of librarians and faculty members who have worked closely with librarians is my edited collection with my library colleague Beth Kraemer, called *Reconnecting Reading and Writing*. This book, which can be downloaded without charge, contains several chapters by librarians focused on IL issues. For suggestions across the disciplines, see the work of Alison Gregory and Betty McCall McClain and by Francia Kissel and a group of her colleagues (see also my edited collection with Gollnitz and Haller). From the standpoint of research assignments, work is needed to integrate IL with analysis, evaluation, synthesis, and application. The assignment that follows (see Appendix 2A) offers a generic kind of approach that can draw on IL instruction, leading to better reading, fuller engagement with source materials (both primary and secondary), and higher quality student work. This task is one that I have used in various modified forms in both discipline-based courses (in Linguistics, for example) and skill-based courses (in Business Writing, for example). It works equally well in either realm. The task I set in this example is for an inquiry project in a course on the history of literacy (see Appendix 2A).

Unlike a research project that relies exclusively on secondary sources, this task entails a "hands-on" aspect that requires students to make use of a primary source such as an observation or interview. The work with printed sources, though, focuses their attention on reading for analysis, evaluation, synthesis, and application. The analysis comes about through reading notes that require enumerating five main ideas presented in the source. Students can also be challenged to prepare 25-word summaries of sources (Bazerman), a process that demands close reading. The evaluation section requires that they think through the criteria set in the ACRL *IL Framework*, but drawn from the earlier *IL Standards* document: authority, accuracy, currency, relevancy, bias, and appropriateness. The Burkhardt book provides exercises for students to learn how to make these judgments before they do so in their own projects. The synthesis skill comes as students compare and contrast each source with the others they have found, looking to see how the sources relate to one another, so that when they come to the work of making use of their sources in their report, they are able to do so appropriately.

In the appendices, I offer some samples of how students responded to the assignment. These samples are used with students' express written consent given in an IRB-approved process of data collection (see Appendix 2B). A careful look at these student samples will show how this task plays out. Both students' notes on their sources reflect a careful reading and understanding of main points the author(s) make on their topics. The evaluation notes are particularly revealing of how the students completed this task. All the students who submitted their research materials to me set up the evaluation work in a similar fashion.

In the Case A notes, it is clear that the student has read a portion of the book dealing with reading to children. The notes capture five points that the student incorporates into the literature review section of the paper. In addition, at a later point in the paper when the student is discussing a primary source interview with a working teacher, she comes back to the source, integrating one of those key points into the discussion to support the point she is trying to make about the value of early reading experiences. Case B shows a somewhat more superficial approach in the notes, but the discussion in the literature review excerpt makes clear that the student was able to make use of key ideas from this source to frame her discussion of the literacy problems of autistic children and to focus on the positive input autistic students can have in class.

While the Case B student does not fully probe all the ACRL aspects of evaluation, it is clear that both students did give some thought to the quality of the material they chose. The evaluation of sources is especially important. It is a key part of the IL work the ACRL recommends in its Authority Frame and elsewhere. It can and should be taught to students explicitly. One of the all-time best handouts ever created for this part of the work appears in Appendix 2C. Careful application of the ACRL criteria will help students see for themselves how useful appropriate evaluation can be.

In the students' notes for synthesis, their plans to use the sources in their reports, and in the brief examples of the written reports, these cases show that the required work in the research notebook produced a deeper engagement with the source material. Instead of what Rebecca Moore Howard and her colleagues refer to as "quote mining" (Howard, Rodrigue, and Serviss), these students looked at and made note of how their sources contributed to the points they wanted to make, and how they related to other source materials that they had reviewed for their projects. The assignment requires students to engage the sources at a deeper level; their analyses, syntheses, and evaluations lead to specific plans for how to deploy the material in their reports. It is the kind of work that draws on the skills my model suggests that experts have and most students need to develop. Their perception of the connections among their sources moves in the direction of contextual awareness I have found among expert readers. While it is not likely or reasonable to expect that undergraduates in a beginning course would have the wide-ranging textual, contextual, and linguistic awarenesses of experts, the students' comments suggest the beginnings of the development of some contextual awareness. The more we use assignments like this one, the more we help students develop their expertise not only as information literate readers but also as academically critically literate readers and writers.

Looking Forward

By a variety of measures, both large-scale standardized test instruments or more qualitative case studies and other detailed approaches, reading is a huge problem, an elephant. As calls for accountability and justification of postsecondary education grow and as students and parents express concern about the usefulness of college given steadily escalating costs, there is increasing need to make clear what it is that we do. Instruction in IL as part of academic critical literacy can respond specifically to these real concerns. The findings presented on students' reading problems on pages and screens shows just how big the elephant in the room really is. We cannot make them experts, but with a clear definition of academic critical literacy and a model of expertise, every instructor can and should be working on reaching this goal. Careful use of the ACRL *IL Framework*, in particular, can help students read and use sources more appropriately. The exercises and work described here in the sample assignment require students to analyze, evaluate, synthesize, and apply material they have processed using IL skills. These skills apply equally to material found online as they do to material found on old-fashioned paper pages. As students learn to apply the ACRL knowledge practices, they also become academically critically literate; these skills will be essential to success in every course and every discipline in their education, as well as beyond school, in their personal and professional lives.

Works Cited

ACT. *The Condition of College and Career Readiness*, www.act.org/content/dam/act/unsecured/documents/CCCR_National_2016.pdf. Accessed 21 June 2017.

———. *Reading between the Lines: What the ACT Reading Test Reveals about College Readiness*, https://forms.act.org/research/policymakers/pdf/reading_summary.pdf. Accessed 21 June 2017.

Association of College and Research Libraries. *Framework for Information Literacy for Higher Education*, Chicago, IL, ACRL, https://acrl.ala.org/ilstandards/wp-content/uploads/2014/11/Framework-for-IL-for-HE-draft-3.pdf. Accessed 21 June 2017.

———. *Information Literacy Competency Standards for Higher Education*, www.ala.org/acrl/standards/informationliteracycompetency. Accessed 21 June 2017.

Bazerman, Charles. *The Informed Writer*, Houghton Mifflin, 1995. Reissued by WAC Clearinghouse, 2011. https://wac.colostate.edu/books/informedwriter/. Accessed 1 Oct. 2015.

Burkhardt, Joanna. *Teaching Information Literacy Reframed: 50 Framework-Based Exercises for Creating Information-Literate Learners*, Chicago, ALA/Neal Schuman, 2016.

D'Angelo, Barbara J., Sandra Jamieson, Barry Maid, and Janice R. Walker. *Information Literacy: Research and Collaboration across Disciplines*, WAC Clearinghouse, 2017.

Gregory, Alison S., and Betty L. McCall. "Building Critical Researchers and Writers Incrementally: Vital Partnerships between Faculty and Librarians." D'Angelo, et al., pp. 371–86.

Haller, Cynthia R. "Toward Rhetorical Source Use: Three Student Journeys." *WPA: Writing Program Administration*, vol. 34, no. 1, 2010, pp. 33–59.

Head, Alison J. Learning the Ropes: How Freshmen Conduct Course Research Once They Enter College. (Project Information Literacy Passage Studies Research Report). Seattle, WA: University of Washington, www.projectinfolit. org/uploads/2/7/5/4/27541717/pil_2013_freshmenstudy_fullreportv2.pdf. Accessed 22 June 2017.

Hill, J.B., Carol Macheak, and John Siegel. "Assessing Undergraduate Information Literacy Skills Using Project SAILS." *Codex: The Journal of the Louisiana Chapter of the ACRL*, vol. 2, no. 3, 2013, pp. 23–37.

Horning, Alice S. *Reading, Writing and Digitizing: Understanding Literacy in the Electronic Age*, Cambridge Scholars Press, 2012.

Horning, Alice S., Deborah-Lee Gollnitz, and Cynthia R. Haller. *What Is College Reading?*, WAC Clearinghouse/University of Colorado P, 2018, https://wac. colostate.edu/books/collegereading/. Accessed 22 Sep. 2017. [Note: free download].

Horning, Alice S., and Elizabeth W. Kraemer, editors. *Reconnecting Reading and Writing*, Parlor P/The WAC Clearinghouse, 2013, https://wac.colostate.edu/ books/reconnecting/. Accessed 1 June 2017. [Note: free download].

Howard, Rebecca Moore, Tanya K. Rodrigue, and Tricia C. Serviss. "Writing from Sources, Writing from Sentences." *Writing and Pedagogy*, vol. 2, no. 2, 2010, pp. 177–92, www.researchgate.net/publication/228480887_Writing_ from_Sources_Writing_from_Sentences. Accessed 22 June 2017.

Jamieson, Sandra. "What the Citation Project Tells Us about Information Literacy in College Composition." D'Angelo, et al., pp. 115–38.

Jamieson, Sandra, and Rebecca Moore Howard. *The Citation Project*, https:// citationproject.net. Accessed 22 June 2017.

Jolliffe, David J., and Allison Harl. "Texts of Our Institutional Lives: Studying the Reading Transition: From High School to College: What Are Our Students Reading and Why?" *College English*, vol. 70, no. 6, 2008, pp. 599–617.

Katz, Irwin R. "Testing Information Literacy in Digital Environments: ETS's Iskills Assessment." *Information Technology and Libraries*, vol. 26, no. 3, 2007, pp. 3–12.

Katz, Irwin R., and Norbert E. Elliot. "Information Literacy in Digital Environments: Construct Mediation, Construct Modeling, and Validation Processes." D'Angelo, et al., pp. 93–114.

Kissel, Francia, Melvin R. Wininger, Scott R. Weeden, Patricia A. Wittberg, Randall S. Halverson, Meagan Lacy, and Rhonda K. Huisman. "Bridging the Gaps: Collaboration in a Faculty and Librarian Community of Practice on Information Literacy." D'Angelo, et al., pp. 411–28.

Laskin, Miriam, and Cynthia R. Haller. "Up the Mountain without a Trail: Helping Students Use Source Networks to Find Their Way." *"Meta": Random House Unabridged Dictionary*, edited by Barbara J. D'Angelo, Sandra Jamieson, Barry Maid, and Janice R. Walker, WAC Clearinghouse, 1966, pp. 237–56.

Nilson, Linda B. *Teaching at Its Best: A Research-Based Resource for College Instructors*. 3rd ed., Jossey-Bass, 2010.

Project SAILS (Standardized Assessment of Information Literacy Skills), Kent State University, 2000–2017, www.projectsails.org.

Radcliff, Carolyn, Megan Oakleaf, and Michele Van Hoeck. "So What? The Results & Impact of a Decade of IMLS-Funded Information Literacy Assessments." In *Proceedings of the 2014 Library Assessment Conference: Building Effective, Sustainable, Practical Assessment*, Washington, DC, Association of Research Libraries, 2015.

Salem, Joseph A., and Carolyn J. Radcliff. "Using the SAILS Test to Assess Information Literacy." *Building Effective, Sustainable, Practical Assessment: Proceedings of the Second Library Assessment Conference*, Charlottesville, 2006, pp. 131–7, www.libraryassessment.org/bm~doc/proceedings-lac-2006.pdf. Accessed 22 June 2017.

Appendix 2A
Inquiry Project Assignment

Inquiry Project Assignment

In your inquiry project, you will need to begin as with all research projects, with a question or series of questions to which you want to know the answer. Your question should focus on some aspect of the history of literacy that is of interest to you; it should be tied to the core question in the course: what are the lessons from history that can help us understand contemporary literacy practices? There are several possible general directions you may find of interest, but keep in mind that this project should have some kind of "hands-on" component: interview, case study, observation/ethnography, experiment, etc. Two different options are to consider literacy issues for a different language or literacy issues in a different country. Overall, I hope you will choose some aspect of our topic that you find personally engaging. We can set up individual meetings on topic choices if you like.

The first step will be to decide on the question(s) you want to answer. You may want to arrange a research consultation in the library to get some help with finding sources in print and online. For some topics, government documents will be an important resource. We will have a library lecture with Beth Kraemer (to be discussed in class), and she can be of help to you individually, or you can consult any other reference librarian.

You must keep a research notebook for this project. The notebook should contain both a running commentary on your work as your project unfolds and a compilation of your source materials. You will want to write down your question(s) and preliminary sources in your research notebook, and you should plan on bringing your notebook to class every day from now to the end of the project. If you keep the notebook electronically, you'll need your gizmo, and you will need to print out the notebook to submit with your final report. For at least three of your sources, in your research notebook, you will need to complete a process designed to help you read and understand the sources fully and make effective use of them in your report.

The Process Is as Follows

1. Choose your three sources carefully; only sources that have citations and a Reference or Works Cited list should be used.
2. Evaluate each source for these issues: authority, accuracy, currency, relevancy, bias, appropriateness. We will discuss how to make these judgments.
3. Read the source carefully and present in a few paragraphs or pages a summary of at least 5 key ideas relevant to your topic. These can be your notes on your reading of the source.
4. Compare and contrast the ideas presented in each source with other material you have examined. Enumerate two similarities or differences between this source and your others.
5. In 100–200 words, write out your plan for deploying this source in your paper.

Follow this process for at least three of your sources and include your notes in your research notebook. [Assorted directions and requirements follow, omitted for length . . .]

Annotated Bibliography

For this assignment, you are to prepare an annotated working bibliography of all sources collected thus far for your inquiry project. My intention is for this task to help you move forward on the project and also to get you to begin preparing your Works Cited or Reference list entries even before you have begun drafting the paper.

For each item you cite, give the full citation in proper form in the format you are using. Then, in fifty (50) words or less, describe each source in terms of whether it is primary or secondary, in terms of its content, and in terms of how it answers your research question.

You should have a minimum of eight (8) sources on your annotated bibliography; there is no maximum. Remember that not everything you include in this working bibliography will necessarily be cited in your paper or appear in your final report. This Annotated Bibliography will be reviewed and returned and must be included with your Research Notebook and folder of materials for the project when you turn in your paper.

NOTE: You cannot receive credit for the inquiry project unless you submit the annotated bibliography and all other parts of this project as required.

Appendix 2B
Sample Student Work

Case A: Preparing for and Encouraging Literacy in Young Children

Source Evaluation #2: Literacy's Beginnings: Supporting Young Readers and Writers *(Print)*

1. Reading Notes: The portion of this book that is relevant to my topic makes some points about what books and reading to children can do for their literacy. The authors highlight five key benefits of reading to children. It instills in them that reading is pleasurable. When children are read to, they are more likely to play with books on their own and see it as an enjoyable experience. The book also points out that children will sit and look at books for longer than they will other toys, which is essential to foster positive feelings toward books and encourage reading in the future.

    Reading to children also shows them how to properly handle books. They learn how to hold books right side up, how to turn pages, and that we read from left to right. Eventually, children will move past the physical aspects of books and understand that they offer more than just the opportunity to turn pages; they also offer stories and knowledge.

    Children also eventually learn that the pictures in books are symbols and not just pretty things to look at. They learn that the pictures convey meaning based on what is being read to them and what is written on the page. They learn that not only are pictures interesting to look at, but are representations of real things.

    Being read to fosters a sense of closeness and routine with those reading to children. Although this is not entirely relevant to my research question, it is important if a parent is wondering what reading to their child could do in the short term as well as in the long term. Book-sharing instills that reading is a shared experience with family and underlines its importance. Moreover, it keeps showing children that reading is a way to be close to family members and share activities.

In a broader sense, when read to, children learn that books communicate meaning. Learning that things have deeper meaning is crucial in many aspects of life, not just reading. It is essential to understand the constant messages we encounter in everyday life and also to effectively communicate our messages to others. From books, children learn to use these written language skills to make crucial connections to spoken language clues.

2. Source Evaluation: This book was written by Lea M. McGee and Donald J. Richgels and this third edition was published in 2000 by Pearson Education Company.

   a. Authority: McGee and Richgels are textbook authors, researchers, and observers of teachers, as well as parents.

   b. Currency: This book is used for education courses and has six editions, the most recent published in 2011. The third edition was the latest edition carried by our Educational Resource Library at Oakland University

   c. Relevancy: This book is relevant to my research topic because it focuses on the support that adults and educators need to provide children to support literacy, which is one of my research questions.

   d. Accuracy: This book offers a references list, mostly consisting of studies conducted by researchers on children and education. These sources could be conducted to determine the accuracy of the information.

   e. Objectivity/Bias: The information contained in this book seems to be presented objectively. It uses sources to back up claims and exercises, since this is a textbook. However, the authors pointed out in the preface that some of their experiences with children were not in a research setting but with their own children, and pointed out that their children's experiences should serve as norms against which to compare other children. Also, they point out that not all children of all backgrounds will respond the same way to the techniques they describe in this book, but they have researched many different children and all can benefit from some support.

   f. Appropriateness: This book appears to be a good source of information for educators and students and also for my research purposes. The theories and techniques mentioned are cited with sources from studies of children and the exercises are also backed up and explained. This book is also used as a textbook for education, with more of a focus on what educators can do to support young readers.

3. Application: I plan to use this source in my paper to back up the reasoning that reading to children at a young age can help to ensure literacy later. In particular, this source highlights the physical understanding of books that being read to can instill in a child, like the

proper orientation of a book and how the sentences are arranged on a page. I plan to use it in a paragraph about phonological awareness because I believe that topic relates to the physical understanding of books in that they are both basic precursors to learning to read. Also, I plan to use this source to back up the point (also mentioned in another source) that books and print convey meaning.

4. Comparison: This source offers many of the same ideas as the book *Literacy Development in the Early Years: Helping Children Read and Write* by Lesley Mandel Morrow. Both books were written to *be* used in a higher education setting for individuals studying early childhood education, so it makes sense that there would be some overlap. In particular, reading is essential in early childhood education, and I doubt any educator would disagree. For that reason, both books include sections about how reading to children helps them learn to read in the future, including the fact that books communicate meaning and foster positive relationships and attitudes toward reading.

Excerpts from Paper:

In scholarly literature, many researchers of young children have offered their own answers to these questions. A few works detailing this research include those written for college students studying literacy development in young children and how sign language can benefit hearing children's literacy. . . . Similarly, *Literacy's Beginnings: Supporting Young Readers and Writers* by Lea M. McGee and Donald J. Richgels offers more ways that teachers and parents can prepare for literacy in young children . . .

(In section reporting interview with a teacher) From being read to in particular, a child can learn how to hold a book the correct way and the way words and sentences are arranged, like how to read from left to right (McGee and Richgels 34). . . . In addition to teaching a familiar structure, books communicate meaning to children. Early experiences foster a crucial understanding that books tell us a message through their words (McGee and Richgels 35).

Case B: The Autism Label and Learning Literacy

(Reading notes set up as an outline of sorts; first page of article provided)

I. Evaluation
    A. Authority: Yes
    B. Accuracy: Yes; citations by many other researchers and they did their own case studies (3 different participants).
    C. Currency: Fall 2002 (fair) [Note: article page indicates 2009 pub]
    D. Relevancy: Yes; provides key points to my project
    E. Bias; yes that the PECS is a good tool to use for those learning with an autism label

    F.   Appropriateness: Yes; this is *how* (one way) autistically labeled children learn to communicate and be literate

II. Key ideas (summary)

    A.   Efficacy of PECS program assessed in terms of the amount of training needed for the mastery of PECS skills by children with autism.

    B.   Collateral effects of PECS training on several behaviors

    C.   Collateral effects on social-communicative behavior and problem behavior

    D.   Spoken language in terms of spontaneous speech

    E.   Ancillary gains that have been reported following PECS literacy
Marginal note: pages 214–215 for "the purpose of my study"

III. Compare and contrast (with my other sources)

    This source was a little hard to get through because there was so much information that was being covered. With that said, however, it does provide a lot of useful information about why the PECS is able to help with behavior problems.

IV. Plan for paper

    This will be included in the literature review section and it will provide information relating to an outcome of the PECS.

Literature review opening paragraph:

   The subject of literacy and autism has been around since the mid 1950s, which is around the same time that Hans Asperger gave a name to the disorder. Along with the overall topic of literacy and autism as an umbrella, there are several subtopics as well. Chandler-Olcott and Kluth (2009) wrote an article about how children with autism can be beneficial in a classroom for the teacher and the other children in the classroom. Chandler-Olcott and Kluth researched on how the autistic child can provide classroom cues to the instructors as to how they are teaching, and giving cues for other social events that happen within the classroom. They also mention how an autistic child can help the other children in the classroom develop their symbolic understanding and physical cue interpretations (i.e., hand signals, body movement and body language). Chandler-Olcott and Kluth state that having children with the autistic label in the inclusive classroom, "offers everyone rich possibilities for collaborative, inquiry-based literacy learning," (Chandler-Olcott and Kluth, 2009, 552). In their study they describe four ways as to why autistic children can help a classroom: conceptions of literacy expand for the other children, multiple ways of participating in classroom life are valuable for the autistic children, instructional planning focuses on outcomes instead of activities, and the instructors are positioned as inquirers (Chandler-Olcott and Kluth, 2009). In sum, they found that autistic children can help expand the knowledge of other children and help teachers expand their techniques.

Appendix 2C
Evaluating Sources Handout

Oakland University Kresge Library Pathfinder: Evaluating Websites

1. **Authority:** Who is the author/developer of the website? What qualifications does s/he have for creating this site/page? What organization/company/person hosts the page (i.e., where is it located)? (If you're unsure, try shortening the page's URL to determine the organization or company that's hosting the site.)
2. **Currency:** Is the page or site current? Maintained regularly? When was it last updated?
3. **Relevancy:** Is the information relevant to your topic?
4. **Accuracy:** What facts can you check to ensure that the information contained on this website is correct?
5. **Objectivity/Bias:** Is the information presented objectively? What kind of bias do you think the author(s) of this page may have?
6. **Appropriateness:** In your opinion, is this site a good source of information? Is it a scholarly source? Would you use it in a paper? Why or why not?

S. Lombardo; updated 9/01

3   Arguing with Ourselves

Rhetorical Reading and Algorithms on the Web

Joshua Welsh

Algorithms are everywhere. They control Wall Street, they evaluate teachers, they make the Internet work. In recent years, some of the effects of algorithms on various aspects of society have come under scrutiny. For example, Cathy O'Neil describes the process by which some algorithms run amok in *Weapons of Math Destruction*. O'Neil argues against some kinds of algorithms, especially those that rely on proxies and do not include a way to learn from past mistakes. Certainly, we should be wary of these kinds of algorithms and the ways they can work to further marginalize poor people and communities. But when it comes to algorithms and reading, the stakes may be even higher. When algorithms shape reading choices, they are in some ways deciding what is *worth* reading and, therefore, worth *knowing*. Yet, given the closed nature of these kinds of algorithms, readers are often unaware that such systems stand between them and what they read.

In many ways, questions involving reading are intimately bound up with those involving writing. Christina Haas investigates writing and technology in *Writing Technology: Studies on the Materiality of Literacy*. Haas outlines a long history of scholarship on writing and technology, from Plato's famous critique of writing in *The Phaedrus* to Walter Ong's claims that writing itself transforms human consciousness in fundamental ways. Most interesting for questions about algorithms is Haas's compelling justification for connecting technology to studies of writing itself. Following Vygotsky, Haas points out that "writing has the potential for even more profound transformations of humans [than purely material tools such as the hoe] because it operates on both [the psychological and the physical] levels—both its psychological (semiotic) aspect and its material-technological aspect have the potential to transform" (16). Furthermore, Haas argues that "Technology studies must focus in an exacting way on technology itself" (32). Researchers cannot satisfy themselves with looking "through" a given technology to find its consequences. We must study the technology itself. However, studying technology does not require us to focus on a single black box, instead technology "must be examined broadly, in all its cultural, historical, and material manifestation" (32).

For the purposes of better understanding how algorithms affect reading, the next section provides a necessarily brief overview of reading technologies writ large, including those technologies that offer to read our students' work for us.

When confronted with the phrase "reading technology," many people will focus first on-screen reading (as opposed to reading printed books). For example, scholars such as Naomi Baron have argued quite convincingly that screen reading works to diminish the cognitive benefits that reading paper books brings. Much of this boils down the distractions afforded by on-screen reading, especially when compared to the textually isolated nature of the printed word (chap. 8). Although Robert Clowes has questioned the methodological rigor of several studies that connect screen reading with so called shallower reading, Baron points to a range of research that indicates reading on screen negatively impacts readers' attention spans, ability to focus, and comprehension. However, Clowes does provide an important counter to overly deterministic concerns that sometimes dominate the debate surrounding screen reading and cognitive development. As Clowes puts it: "Our tools do not simply impact upon our minds, but are themselves part of a constantly evolving, cognitive ecology" (Clowes 14). In other words, if we view screen reading as something that can re-wire our brains without our awareness or our consent, then we risk seeing screen reading technology as overly deterministic, with its own pre-ordained ends.

Teachers of writing, when confronted with the term "reading technology," may find themselves considering the various technologies that offer to read—and evaluate—our students' writing for us. Jinhao Wang and Michelle Brown compared one particular computer automated scoring system with human ratings of the same student writing samples. They found that the computer grading system rated the writing samples "significantly higher" than the human graders did (20). In a similar vein Doug McCurry investigated the ability of machine scoring to evaluate "broad and open writing tests" and compared machine scores of such tests to human scores, finding ultimately that "essay marking software cannot score an open writing task as reliably as human markers" (McCurry 127). Nevertheless, Wilson and Czik conducted an empirical study that found that students who receive computer feedback reported higher motivation in writing, but that the final quality of the writing was no different than students who only received teacher feedback on their work (105).

Perhaps the most familiar reading technology comes in the form of plagiarism detection software such as *TurnItIn*. Lucas Introna analyzes the relationship between algorithms (i.e., code) and governance. One aspect of governance and algorithms is the desire to govern the algorithm itself. A recent example of this is found in the "right to be forgotten" decision that "allows EU residents to request the removal of search results that they feel link to outdated or irrelevant information about themselves"

(Gibbs). Introna finds such efforts to govern algorithms "helpful," but like Clowes warns that such attempts "tend to overemphasize the agency of the algorithms and do not appreciate sufficiently the embeddedness of these sociomaterial practices, and more importantly, the performative nature of these practices" (Introna 29). A second aspect concerning governance and algorithms involves the efforts to use algorithms "*to enact governance*" (29), that is, to control people's behavior. One example might be a system which uses algorithms to find suspects through facial recognition systems or to detect credit card fraud.

The third aspect of government and algorithms sees algorithms as tied up in Foucault's concept of "governmentality," which involves the use of "*calculative practices*" that are involved in constituting "expertise and subjects" (Introna 30). Introna points to *TurnItIn* as one example of this type of governance. *TurnItIn* uses algorithms to look for matches between a student essay (for example) and a database of source texts. Without taking a stand on the somewhat controversial aspects of plagiarism detection software, Introna points out that, viewed through the lens of governmentality, *TurnItIn* may fall short of many users' goal of ferreting out plagiarism in student writing, noting instead that "what the algorithms often detect is *the difference between skillful copiers and unskillful copiers*" (Introna 36). Regardless of whether one finds *TurnItIn* to be an indispensable tool for teaching writing or an infringement on students' rights, the software does illustrate just how intertwined algorithms have become in the teaching of writing.

TurnItIn also helps demonstrate that teachers of writing should be keenly interested in algorithm studies. Because of their ubiquity, algorithms have a dangerous potential to seem invisible. As Christina Haas puts when debunking the myth that technology can be invisible, "The danger of the transparent technology assumption . . . is that when it is operative there is no need for inquiry about technology: If technology is 'immaterial,' so to speak, there is no need to study it at all" (34). But as I have tried to argue above, understanding how algorithms shape reading is of crucial importance to teachers of writing. As Doug Brent puts it, reading and writing "are inseparable and reciprocal acts" (1). This is as true in 2017 as it was 25 years ago. However, algorithmically driven reading codifies the connection between reading and writing in computer code—code which is either inscrutable to the layperson or intentionally hidden in proprietary "black boxes." Writing teachers may not be able to pry open these boxes themselves, but we can teach our students to be critical of these technologies and their consequences.

What Is an Algorithm?

Early in my research for this chapter, I was watching a TED talk about computer algorithms in finance. I found the talk to be quite terrifying; the gist of it is that such algorithms are programmed to react to stock market changes with such speed and at such volume that a single algorithmic decision can move the entire stock market up or down by significant margins (Slavin). Towards the end of the video, my seven-year old son waked in and, ever the precocious student—asked "What are algorithms?" I stammered for a few seconds, before finally answering, "Algorithms are decisions that computers make that affect people." Although such a definition is probably deficient in terms of explaining the math or the computer science that undergirds such computer-made decisions, it is not far off from a definition that puts the concept within grasp of those people whose lives are impacted by them, which is to say, everyone.

Very early in the development of electronic computing, the people developing computers saw the future of human-computer interaction in somewhat utopic terms. One early example is Edmund Berkeley, who worked on some of the earliest digital computers during World War II (Longo 3). In 1949, Berkeley wrote *Giant Brains or Machines That Think*. Much of this book attempts to explain the inner workings of the computing machines of the time, but Berkeley also imagines ways that computers might solve problems in the future. He suggests that computers in the future will be able to solve problems of several types, including "Problems of control": "Probably the foremost problem which machines that think can solve is automatic control over all sorts of other machines. This involves controlling a machine that is running so that it will do the right thing at the right time in response to information" (Berkeley 188).

In the late 1960s, J.C.R. Licklider and Robert Taylor wrote their influential essay "The Computer as a Communication Device" (1968). Amidst canny descriptions of the future workings of the Internet and overly optimistic predictions concerning the impact that networked computers would have on unemployment, Licklider and Taylor suggest that the computer as a communication device will do more than simply make it easier to send messages to one another. The authors describe a "a complex of computer programs and data that resides within the network and acts on behalf of its principal, taking care of many minor matters that do not require [the user's] personal attention and buffering [the user] from the demanding world" (Licklider and Taylor 38). Licklider and Taylor call this system an "on-line interactive vicarious expediter and responder," or OLIVER:

> At your command, your OLIVER will take notes (or refrain from taking notes) on what you do, what you read, what you buy and where you buy it. It will know who your friends are, your mere acquaintances. It will know your value structure, who is prestigious in your eyes, for whom you will do what with what priority, and who can have access to which of your personal files. It will know your organization's rules pertaining to proprietary information and the government's rules relating to security classification.

Some parts of your OLIVER program will be common with parts of other people's OLIVERS; other parts will be custom-made for you, or by you, or will have developed idiosyncrasies through "learning" based on its experience in your service.

(38–9)

Although much of Licklider and Taylor's essay has shown its age, the interaction between software, data, and "learned" values seems especially telling in the algorithm-driven world of today.

Since Licklider and Taylor's time, other computer scientists have labored to define algorithms for practitioners in their own field. For example, Kowalski (1979) refines the idea of computer control with his opening statement: "An algorithm can be regarded as consisting of a logic component, which specifies the knowledge to be used in solving problems, and a control component, which determines the problem-solving strategies by means of which that knowledge is used" (424). Kowalski goes on to dive deep into the logical structures that can be used to shape such control. However, he doesn't provide a sense of what or whom such logical components might actually be used *to* control. Ultimately, for the purposes of understanding how algorithms shape the lives of ordinary people, it may be more helpful to concentrate on what algorithms do.

Tarleton Gillespie helps shape this perspective nicely, especially in terms of understanding how algorithms impact readers in the digital age: "Algorithms play an increasingly important role in selecting what information is considered more relevant to us, a crucial feature of our participation in public life" (Gillespie, "Relevance" 168). In essence, algorithms are doing exactly what Licklider and Taylor predicted they would. When it comes to the algorithms that shape much of our online reading, algorithms "learn" from our past actions—what we have read, what we have "liked," what we have purchased—and they strive to show us other items that we will read, like, or want to purchase.

Algorithms Shape the World We Live in

Taken as mere recommendation systems, algorithms may seem unimportant. After all, what harm can there be in simply helping me find a movie that will delight me in the same way that previous movies have delighted me? And why should we take the enjoyment out of a service that helps me discover lesser-known bands that create music I love? However, scholars in the nascent field of critical algorithm studies are arguing persuasively for the importance of understanding and critiquing the ways that algorithms shape the totality of what we view, hear, and (I would argue) most importantly read. "That we are now turning to algorithms to identify what we need to know is as momentous as having relied on credentialed experts, the scientific method, common sense, or the word of God" (Gillespie, "Relevance" 168). Couple this quiet epistemic sea change with the tentacle-like nature of algorithms (they seem to be shaping a wide swath of the media we are presented with online), and Gillespie's concept of "algorithmic entanglements" starts to take shape: Paraphrasing Nick Couldry, Gillespie argues that "algorithms are built to be embedded into practice in the lived world that produces the information they process, and in the world lived of their users" (Gillespie, "Relevance" 183). Thus, Gillespie argues, "we must consider not their 'effect' on people, but a multidimensional 'entanglement' between algorithms put into practice and the social tactics of users who take them up" (Gillespie, "Relevance" 183). For Gillespie, these entanglements are a decidedly two-way street: users unconsciously and consciously shape the algorithm through their use of it. We do this unconsciously when we click or tap to read a particular news story and the algorithm that determines our news feed records that as a vote in favor of that kind of news. We do this consciously when we install browser extensions designed to disrupt marketing based on previously entered search terms. Nevertheless, algorithmic entanglements are so ubiquitous and so nearly instantaneous (operating in the realm of milliseconds), that many of us affected by algorithms are unaware of the web of data and decisions into which their actions are woven.

In fact, McKelvey refers to Robert Gehl's argument that algorithms act so quickly that "users may be affected without ever being informed" (McKelvey 603). However, just as important as the question of whether or not users recognize that algorithms are shaping what they read on the Web is the question of the consequences of such entanglements. McKelvey argues convincingly that "algorithmic control has significant social consequences," including the "troubling assumptions about users" that some algorithms seem to make (598). Pointing to a well-known example of an algorithm that associated Grindr (a dating app for gay men) with a Sex Offender search app in the Google Play store, McKelvey and others have raised questions about whether the algorithm that put these two apps in the same set of results was wrong, or whether this association simply revealed troubling things about the people that use the algorithm. In other words, did the algorithm reinforce negative stereotypes on its own, or based on the input of the public using the algorithm?

Regardless of how one answers that question, the fact remains that algorithms shape the public sphere in less controversial, but equally important ways. McKelvey points out that media and information technologies help form the foundation of public life in much of the world and that algorithms shape the flow information (in the form of bandwidth distribution) and the kind of information that is delivered to readers (in the form of monitoring intellectual property usage and shaping the kinds of content that are offered to readers in news feeds and other curated content streams).

Furthermore, since the work of these algorithmic entanglements is done at nearly instantaneous speeds and leave little trace of the inputs and decisions that affected the results, it becomes extremely difficult to discern and critique the values that are shaping the results. Postman has argued that any dominant technology ("technopoly" in Postman's terms) "eliminates alternatives to itself. . . . It does not make them illegal. It does not make them immoral. It does not make them unpopular. It makes them invisible" (48). However, dominant technologies themselves fade into invisibility through the ubiquity. We only notice the power system and high-speed Internet access when these systems stop working. But invisibility and opaqueness seem to play a crucial role in the very functioning of algorithms. Algorithms *must* hide their inner workings in order to function. If a user can see how an algorithm works, then users can "game" the algorithm, and the algorithm itself will stop functioning as its design intended (Gillespie, "Relevance"). Gillespie also points to the "Google bombing" trend of the early 2000s and sex-columnist Dan Savage's redefinition of the word "Santorum" as examples of algorithm gaming ("Algorithmically Recognizable"). However, it is precisely the hidden inner workings of algorithms that makes them problematic. Any algorithm that hides its inner workings seems to be anti-democratic by definition. Yet any algorithm that reveals itself may stop functioning altogether.

Algorithmic Invisibility and the Myth of Algorithmic Neutrality

The invisible nature of algorithms also makes "algorithmic awareness" very difficult on the part of users. Between algorithm-driven search results, news feeds, and recommendation systems, it's difficult to imagine any piece of reading that begins or ends on the World Wide Web that is not affected by an algorithm. Even a cursory search for a basic "fact" such as the definition of Bernoulli's principle (which describes the lift experienced by paper airplane wings and Frisbees) is likely to be filtered through at least one search algorithm, a spell-checking algorithm, an auto-complete algorithm, and some sort of recommendation algorithm before the user finally chooses a document or video to help explain the concept. Yet unless the user stops to look for them, most of those algorithms will not make themselves known, and the document or video will be chosen in the matter of seconds.

Researchers trying to measure algorithmic awareness have come to conflicting conclusions. For example, Eslami et al. conducted a study on Facebook users' algorithmic awareness. They found that most of the people in their study were not aware of the impact that algorithms have on what they read. "We suspect that users are not aware of most curation, even when the presence of a filter appears to be obvious to those with a background in computing" (161). The authors also point to the implications of this lack of algorithmic awareness, even the seemingly banal area of Facebook friends: "Users incorrectly concluded that friends had dropped them due to political disagreements or the unappealing behavior. In the extreme case, it may be that whenever a software developer in Menlo Park adjusts a parameter, someone somewhere wrongly starts to believe themselves to be unloved" (161). Eslami et al. argue for some sort of alert system that lets users know when an algorithm has filtered what they are seeing on the Internet, but given the ubiquitous nature of algorithms, it seems as though these alerts would quickly fade into the background noise of daily life.

By way of contrast, Rader and Gray studied Facebook users' awareness of what they call the "algorithmic curation" of the News Feed. They found that their study of participants' beliefs "ranged widely, from believing the News Feed shows all possible posts from their Friends, to automated filtering by an algorithm" (sec. "Summary of Findings"). Rader and Gray also acknowledge the possibility that algorithmically aware users may try to "reverse engineer" the algorithm in order to "use the mechanisms provided by the system to achieve their goals" (sec. "Reverse-engineering the Algorithm"). It is not clear why people making use of a tool to achieve their own goals is considered something that needs correcting, but nevertheless the authors suggest this problem might be resolvable, since "it may be possible for designers to leave clues for users to help them inadvertently form intuitive theories that may be more friendly to the intended operation of the algorithm—in effect, using the propensity of users to reverse-engineer the system as a mechanism for controlling some of the second order effects created by the feedback loop" (sec. "Reverse-engineering the Algorithm"). In other words, never fear, even if users do manage to wrest control from the system, engineers may be able to outsmart and manipulate those same users to using their newfound power to feed the algorithm just the same. In any case, one key finding these researchers offer is that only 8% of their participants felt that their News Feeds were not being affected by algorithmic control; most people in their study had some sense of algorithmic awareness.

Whether or not users are aware of their algorithmic entanglements, Gillespie argues that people "do not dwell on algorithms." Instead, we "[tend] to treat them as unproblematic tools in the service of a larger activity: finding an answer, solving a problem, being entertained" ("Relevance" 178). Indeed, this way of approaching algorithms suits companies such as Facebook and Google well, since for them, algorithmic invisibility is part and parcel with algorithmic neutrality or impartiality. Gillespie describes the well-known example of Google's initial resistance to changing its search results after sex columnist Dan Savage worked with his readers to "redefine" conservative Senator Rick Santorum's last name in a way that some might find offensive (Gillespie, "Algorithmically Recognizable"). In response to public pressure to change its search algorithm so that users searching for the term "Santorum" would be directed to the Senator's page rather than Savage's page, Google refused, telling a CNN reporter that "We do not remove content from our search results, except in very limited cases such as illegal content and violations of our webmaster guidelines" (Sutter). Of course, others have pointed to cases where Google has indeed altered its search results, for a variety of reasons (see Grimmelmann). But Google's resistance to be seen as willing to alter the algorithm points to the myth of algorithmic neutrality. If Google is willing to allow human intervention every time someone is offended by a search result, then the algorithm will no longer be seen as an impartial calculator, simple serving up what the user has asked for.

However, technology is never neutral. Philosopher of technology Andrew Feenberg argues against viewing technologies as neutral tools that merely do the bidding of the people who use them. Note also that Feenberg is equally skeptical of seeing technology as deterministic, which is the perspective that puts all (or nearly all) agency in technology itself. Instead, Feenberg argues, those interested in technology should take a "critical approach," which views technology as an "'ambivalent' process of development suspended between different possibilities" (15). Additionally, algorithmically driven systems that make recommendations on what to read are specifically designed *not* to be neutral, since we shape our results with every link we click and every news story we "like."

Conceiving technology not as a *thing* but as a *process* that is made by people to do things seems to lie at the heart of Gillespie's own recommendations for understanding algorithms: Gillespie argues that we cannot stop at studying algorithms themselves or the individual impacts they have on people. Instead, "We must study the interaction between providers of information and algorithmic assessors of information, sometimes a confluence of interests and sometimes a contest, and the results that these interacting forces generate" ("Algorithmically Recognizable" 75).

Algorithms, Identity, and Ethos

Early in the history of the Internet, researchers began working to unravel the relationship between computer-mediated communication and identity. Hiltz and Turoff found that early users of pre-World Wide Web computer conferencing systems participated in a "social and psychological process [that differed] from other modes of communication, such as face-to-face meetings, telephone, or letter writing" (76). They concluded that users develop "specialized norms" for communicating via computer (125). Other researchers have described how some users have taken advantage of the affordances offered by these new "specialized norms" to create new identities for themselves, ranging from outright deception (Van Gelder) to identity performances in online spaces (Grabill and Pigg). In many of these cases, users communicating via networked computers use the tools at hand to shape new identities.

However, the rise of social media seems to complicate notions of identity further, as Warnick and Heineman make clear in the 2012 book,

Rhetoric Online. Following Maurice Charland, Warnick, and Heineman take up the idea of "constitutive rhetoric" and the ways that participating in online communication can shape a person's identity: Charland's perspective on constitutive rhetoric allows us . . . to think about identity in social media from a metaperspective. That is, instead of focusing on the ways in which users can create certain kinds of identities for themselves by using the tools of the medium . . . we can instead consider how users' identity *as* social media users is determined in specific was by the "text"—a social networking technology or website—that enables and constrains the ways in which they think about their identity (Warnick and Heineman 104).

Charland's argument draws heavily on Althusser's concept of interpellation, or "the process of inscribing subjects into ideology" (Charland 138). Although Charland makes clear that not every rhetorical act results in an constituted audience, he does argue that audience members play an active (if often unconscious) role in their own interpellation: "Interpellation occurs at the very moment one enters into a rhetorical situation, that is, as soon as an individual recognizes and acknowledges being addressed" (Charland 138).

Algorithmically driven reading amplifies this process. When a reader is presented with content driven by previous reading choices, that reader may see him or herself as an audience member participating in a discourse. In Charland's words, "We . . . cannot say that one is persuaded to be a subject; one is 'always already' a subject" (Charland 141). But since the selection of reading material is largely determined algorithmically, the reader may not recognize the role that technology plays in creating that discourse.

Giving over the selection of what we choose to read to algorithmic systems also creates problems for evaluating the credibility of sources. Of course, questions concerning credibility are nothing new to the researchers of online communication. As early as 2004, Warnick was providing guidelines to help online readers evaluate source credibility. A few years later, Metzger summarized the problem and categorized the suggested solutions: "The Internet has made the need to critically evaluate information more important than ever before while also shifting the burden of credibility assessment and quality control from professional gatekeepers onto individual information seekers" (Metzger 2079). Solutions surveyed by Metzger range from "checklist approaches" (2079) to "a contextual approach to credibility assessment" (2083). Contextual credibility assessment was suggested by Meola in 2004. Meola's critique of the checklist approach is well-founded, and indeed, he argues convincingly that checklists themselves are overly mechanistic (read algorithmic), and are "at odds with the higher-level judgment and intuition that we presumably seek to cultivate as part of critical thinking" (337). Interestingly, Meola's critique of checklist-driven or even automated approaches to judging credibility for student writers applies to algorithm-driven reading selection as well: "If we teach students to surrender evaluation to a mechanical process, we teach them to sacrifice part of their autonomy as learners and knowers" (338). As an alternative, he suggests teaching students to evaluate website credibility using "information *external* to the website in order to evaluate it" (338). Meola argues that instructors should teach their students about the "reviewed resources" available online, and that we should help students hone skills involving "comparison" (339–40) and "corroboration" (341–2) of online sources. Similarly, we must help students recognize and evaluate the contexts that shape what they read online today.

Conclusion and Recommendations

Hopefully it is clear by now that algorithms are tightly bound up with reading and therefore with writing. As such, teachers of writing need to look for ways to account for these entanglements in their teaching. With that goal in mind, I offer the following preliminary suggestions:

First, we must strive to teach students when they are reading something that has been chosen by algorithm. This may be difficult to do, because so much of what we read online is algorithmically selected. However, relatively simple exercises, such as comparing how various search terms create different results on different search engines, can help debunk the myth of technological invisibility.

Second, we can work to teach students that they are entering into a conversation long before they begin a specific search. In other words, much of what is presented to readers is shaped by what they have read in the past. We can ask students to consider the implications of being served up more of what used to delight them. One classroom or short writing activity might be to present students with a list of recommended reading and ask them to analyze the contexts that might have shaped such a list.

Finally, we should teach to raise students' overall algorithmic awareness. In much the same way students are taught to recognize when they are being targeted by advertising and what some of the implications of that targeting can be, writing teachers can help students recognize when an algorithm is shaping a reading choice or a news feed item. At the college level, we could ask students to read articles from the emerging field of critical algorithm studies.

Works Cited

Baron, Naomi S. *Words Onscreen: The Fate of Reading in a Digital World*, Oxford University Press, 2016.

Berkeley, Edmund Callis. *Giant Brains: Or Machines That Think*, Science Editions, 1961.

Brent, Doug. *Reading as Rhetorical Invention: Knowledge, Persuasion, and the Teaching of Research-Based Writing*, National Council of Teachers of English, 1992.

Charland, Maurice. "Constitutive Rhetoric: The Case of the Peuple Quebecois." *Quarterly Journal of Speech*, vol. 73, no. 2, 1987, pp. 133–50.

Clowes, Robert W. "Screen Reading and the Creation of New Cognitive Ecologies." *AI & Society*, Feb. 2018, pp. 1–16. *link.springer.com*, doi:10.1007/s00146-017-0785-5.

Couldry, Nick. *Media, Society, World: Social Theory and Digital Media Practice*, Polity Press, 2012.

Eslami, Motahhare, et al. "'I Always Assumed That I Wasn'T Really That Close to [Her]': Reasoning about Invisible Algorithms in News Feeds." *Proceedings of the 33rd Annual ACM Conference on Human Factors in Computing Systems*, ACM, 2015, pp. 153–62. *ACM Digital Library*, doi:10.1145/2702123.2702556.

Feenberg, Andrew. *Transforming Technology: A Critical Theory Revisited*, Oxford University Press, 2002.

Gehl, Robert W. "The Archive and the Processor: The Internal Logic of Web 2.0." *New Media & Society*, vol. 13, no. 8, Dec. 2011, pp. 1228–44. *SAGE Journals*, doi:10.1177/1461444811401735.

Gibbs, Samuel. "Google to Extend 'Right to Be Forgotten' to All Its Domains Accessed in EU." *The Guardian*, 11 Feb. 2016, www.theguardian.com/technology/2016/feb/11/google-extend-right-to-be-forgotten-googlecom.

Gillespie, Tarleton. "Algorithmically Recognizable: Santorum's Google Problem, and Google's Santorum Problem." *Information, Communication & Society*, vol. 20, no. 1, Jan. 2017, pp. 63–80. *Taylor and Francis+NEJM*, doi:10.1080/1369118X.2016.1199721.

———. "The Relevance of Algorithms." *Media Technologies: Essays on Communication, Materiality, and Society*, vol. 167, 2014. *Google Scholar*, https://books.google.com/books?hl=en&lr=&id=zeK2AgAAQBAJ&oi=fnd&pg=PA167&dq=gillespie+the+relevance+of+algorithm&ots=GngHLUSZui&sig=OnUjYR73Sw1Q2uHQZEki6LezJa8.

Grabill, Jeffrey T., and Stacey Pigg. "Messy Rhetoric: Identity Performance as Rhetorical Agency in Online Public Forums." *Rhetoric Society Quarterly*, vol. 42, no. 2, 2012, pp. 99–119. *Taylor and Francis+NEJM*, doi:10.1080/02773945.2012.660369.

Grimmelmann, James. "The Google Dilemma." *New York Law School Law Review*, vol. 53, 2009, 2008, p. 939, http://heinonline.org/HOL/Page?handle=hein.journals/nyls53&id=941&div=&collection=.

Haas, Christina. *Writing Technology: Studies on the Materiality of Literacy*, Lawrence Erlbaum Associates, 1996.

Hiltz, S.R., and M. Turoff. "Chapter 3: Social and Psychological Processes." *The Network Nation: Human Communication via Computer*. Revised ed., The MIT P, 1993, pp. 76–127.

Introna, Lucas D. "Algorithms, Governance, and Governmentality: On Governing Academic Writing." *Science, Technology, & Human Values*, vol. 41, no. 1, Jan. 2016, pp. 17–49. *SAGE Journals*, doi:10.1177/0162243915587360.

Kowalski, Robert. "Algorithm = Logic + Control." *Communications of the ACM*, vol. 22, no. 7, July 1979, pp. 424–36. *ACM Digital Library*, doi:10.1145/359131.359136.

Licklider, J.C., and R.W. Taylor. "The Computer as a Communication Device." *Science and Technology*, vol. 76, 1968, pp. 20–41. *Google Scholar*, http://gatekeeper.dec.com/pub/DEC/SRC/publications/taylor/licklidertaylor.pdf.

Longo, Bernadette. *Edmund Berkeley and the Social Responsibility of Computer Professionals*. 1st ed., M & C, 2015.

McCurry, Doug. "Can Machine Scoring Deal with Broad and Open Writing Tests as Well as Human Readers?" *Assessing Writing*, vol. 15, no. 2, Jan. 2010, pp. 118–29. *CrossRef*, doi:10.1016/j.asw.2010.04.002.

McKelvey, Fenwick Robert. "Algorithmic Media Need Algorithmic Methods: Why Publics Matter." *Canadian Journal of Communication*, vol. 39, no. 4, 2014. *Google Scholar*, www.cjc-online.ca/index.php/journal/article/view/2746.

Meola, Marc. "Chucking the Checklist: A Contextual Approach to Teaching Undergraduates Web-Site Evaluation." *Portal: Libraries and the Academy*, vol. 4, no. 3, July 2004, pp. 331–44. *Project MUSE*, doi:10.1353/pla.2004.0055.

Metzger, Miriam J. "Making Sense of Credibility on the Web: Models for Evaluating Online Information and Recommendations for Future Research." *Journal of the Association for Information Science and Technology*, vol. 58, no. 13, 2007, pp. 2078–91.

O'Neil, Cathy. *Weapons of Math Destruction: How Big Data Increases Inequality and Threatens Democracy*. 1st ed., Crown, 2016.

Postman, Neil. *Technopoly: The Surrender of Culture to Technology*. 1st ed., Knopf, 1992.

Rader, Emilee, and Rebecca Gray. "Understanding User Beliefs about Algorithmic Curation in the Facebook News Feed." *Proceedings of the 33rd Annual ACM Conference on Human Factors in Computing Systems*, ACM, 2015, pp. 173–82. *Google Scholar*, http://dl.acm.org/citation.cfm?id=2702174.

Slavin, Kevin. *How Algorithms Shape Our World*, TED: Ideas Worth Spreading, 2011. *www.ted.com*, www.ted.com/talks/kevin_slavin_how_algorithms_shape_our_world.

Sutter, John D. "Santorum Asks Google to Clean Up Search Results for His Name." *CNN*, 21 Sep. 2011, www.cnn.com/2011/09/21/tech/web/santorum-google-ranking/index.html.

Van Gelder, L. "The Strange Case of the Electronic Lover." *Talking to Strangers: Mediated Therapeutic Communication*, edited by Gary Gumpert and Sandra L. Fish, Ablex, 1996, pp. 533–46.

Wang, Jinhao, and Michelle Stallone Brown. "Automated Essay Scoring Versus Human Scoring: A Comparative Study." *The Journal of Technology, Learning and Assessment*, vol. 6, no. 2, Oct. 2007. *ejournals.bc.edu*, https://ejournals.bc.edu/ojs/index.php/jtla/article/view/1632.

Warnick, Barbara, and David Heineman. *Rhetoric Online: The Politics of New Media*. 2nd ed., Peter Lang, 2012.

Wilson, Joshua, and Amanda Czik. "Automated Essay Evaluation Software in English Language Arts Classrooms: Effects on Teacher Feedback, Student Motivation, and Writing Quality." *Computers & Education*, vol. 100, Sep. 2016, pp. 94–109. *ScienceDirect*, doi:10.1016/j.compedu.2016.05.004.

4 A Difference in Delivery
Reading Classroom Technology Policies

Jacob W. Craig and Matthew Davis

Introduction

Since the refashioning of the book into the e-book for e-readers, a substantial body of scholarship has emerged considering the effects of reading on screens. Through several frames of reference, including neuroscience (Carr), literary studies (Wolf), and media studies (Baron; Birkerts), there emerges a resounding feeling that print affords a kind of reading that electronic texts cannot and that media-specific differences make digital texts deficient for learning, research, and meaning making when compared to printed texts. These concerns about screen-based reading reflect a persistent cultural anxiety about the use of electronic texts and digital devices for reading, research, and learning that are later passed on to new generations of readers and students when codified in technology statements developed as part of course policy sheets and syllabi.

Such technology statements typically define what devices are sanctioned for use during class meetings and, perhaps more commonly, if and how devices are to be used during class meetings. Statements like the following set collected and circulated by Brown University's Sheridan Center for Teaching and Learning, frequently appear in syllabi:

- I know many of you read online or take notes on your laptops or tablets, however, electronics are a major distraction in class and disrupt class discussion [. . .] But, because we often read online, I will allow them. However, if I find they become distracting, I hold the right to disallow them in class.
- Laptop/tablet use in lectures is not recommended. Using your laptop or tablet to take notes often leads to checking email and social media or browsing the internet. This hinders your learning and has also been shown to distract those around you. Therefore, I highly recommend taking notes on paper [. . .] If you choose to use your laptop or tablet in class, please sit in one of the side sections of the

lecture hall. NO LAPTOP OR TABLET USE IN THE CENTER SECTION OF THE LECTURE HALL.

("Sample")

At face value, these statements are attempts to create a classroom environment hospitable for learning by keeping potential distractions at the periphery of "real learning," that is, learning in print at "the center section of the lecture hall." Rather than understanding the digital devices that students own and bring with them into classrooms for their potential to support student learning, these policies parallel concerns about the presence of digital texts in traditionally print-only environments. In doing so, these policies assume that digital media, devices, and networks can only exacerbate mythologies about today's college students: specifically, their lack of "ability and experience either to concentrate on or to comprehend detailed, complex, and hypotactic texts" (Salvatori and Donahue 315).

In this chapter, we examine what the technology policies contained within syllabi communicate to students about the devices they use to read, write, and learn on their own time, outside of the classroom. We identify that such policies too often fail to support or authorize students' agency over their literate development. We observe that because syllabus policies have the weight of institutional power and may be one of the few instances where students attend to the relationship between their devices and their literate development, they are an important site of technological discourse, the "complex cultural network of discourses, practices, institutions, and power relations" that plays an integral role in the validation and naturalization of new technologies in the cultural sphere (McCorkle 36). Although students encounter a variety of technological discourse—some, like those from the marketplace, emphasize the seemingly endless benefits of buying a new device—the discourse they encounter through course policies informs how they understand the value, function, and effect of their devices in relation to their literate development within academic environments.

In what follows, we provide an analysis of course policy sheets collected in the Spring 2017 academic year from two different institutions: an urban public research university in the northeastern US and a liberal arts college in the southeastern US. Based on our analysis, we argue that in attempting to preserve classroom environments as they have been understood in the late age of print, technology bans also undermine the social nature of literacy and learning while perpetuating myths about students' literacies that have little historical or conceptual basis. Drawing upon our analysis, we conclude by suggesting more productive ways of structuring course policies—and therefore textual interactions—available to students. Our goal in this examination of course policies is to forward possibilities for contextually sensitive, "positive implementations of technology that support and sustain" student learning (McCorkle 17). Although our discussion focuses on the more quotidian instances of technological discourse that reproduce technological anxiety in new generations of readers and learners, there is a wealth of scholarship about e-reading to inform such policies. Thus, to provide a context for our analysis of these policies, we start by examining formal technological discourse about the efficacy of digital reading and digital texts.

Anxious Technological Discourse

Concern about digital devices in classrooms has gained plenty of traction in the public sphere, mirroring the same passions that emerged when it was believed that text message writing (or textspeak) would hinder students' writing development and even diminish the English language itself. In his 2014 *New Yorker* article, Dan Rockmore described his "electronic etiquette policy" that he developed after it became commonplace for students to bring laptops with them into the classroom. His primary concern was the incongruence between "twenty-first-century tools (computers, tablets, smartphones) with nineteenth-century modalities (lectures)," between "play and pedagogy." Anne Curzan echoes Rockmore's point in a *Chronicle of Higher Education* post, similarly emphasizing how networked technologies alter the classroom environment by creating distractions for everyone while reinforcing "*addictive patterns with email, texting, Facebook, etc.*" (italics ours). There is some basis for these policies; for instance, in Pam Mueller and Daniel Oppenheimer's study of note-taking practices in a lab setting, they conclude that longhand note-taking enabled students to recall information better (1164). How these findings play out in real scenes of student learning—real classrooms—remains to be seen.

Ravizza et al.'s more recent study of internet use in a lecture- and test-based introductory psychology class also finds that students who used a computer in class were not necessarily advantaged over those that chose to write in print. Using a combination of test scores and HTTP requests logged through use of a proxy server, Ravizza et al. found that non-academic web use was "inversely related to performance on the cumulative final exam" (177). They also found no correlation between academic web use and improved score on the final exam (167). What is perhaps most relevant to a project-based course like a writing course, however, is the relationship between self-reported data and HTTP logs. Students who reported that the internet had no effect on their classroom learning "showed no relationship between Internet use and final-exam score," and students who identified that the internet was slightly disruptive "had lower exam scores and used the Internet more than the other group" (178). Thus, what Ravizza et al.'s research ultimately indicates is that students understood their internet use and how their internet use affected their learning.

Although studies like Mueller and Oppenheimer's and Mueller's and Ravizza's have strongly influenced course policies and validated anxieties about digital devices and digital texts, perhaps the most relevant to this discussion are Naomi Baron's *Always On* and *Words on Screen* for their attention to the co-evolution of reading, writing, and technology (*Words* 24) and in their attention to the plurality of screens, devices, and platforms on which reading takes place (*Words* 15). While Baron concedes that reading on screen makes sense for short pieces and light content, she is concerned that reading on screen fails to invite serious reading, creating a "critical shift in the way at least some types of readers have encountered books for centuries" (xiv). Baron argues that, instead of facilitating close and rereading of texts, digital reading encourages the same kind of fast and distracted reading that emerged during the paperback revolution of the nineteenth century (95). In the current moment, Baron argues, digital reading mirrors paperback pleasure reading; both are one-off experiences (95). Predicated on the idea that "modern education, especially higher education, is grounded on the assumption that taking your time—with thinking, with reading—is essential for intellectual development," Baron argues that all of the features of reading in a digital culture are eroding the ability of students to engage in serious reading, thought, and research (166). Thus, Baron's primary investment is in making the case that while digital technologies have made texts more convenient and easier to read (particularly when reading across multiple texts), serious/real/ "deep" reading "is a child of" and only possible in print (168).

In relation to educational contexts, these discussions of technology bans, policies, and anxieties function as a network of technological discourse that continues to influence how the larger culture understands—or should understand—the purpose and effects of digital texts and e-reading. As Ben McCorkle shows, technological discourse has historically facilitated the cultural acceptance of new media, functioning as "a mechanism by which an emergent technology gains easier acceptance into culture at large" (28). Unlike other new media that have been a focus of past technological discourse like hypertext, websites, word processors, and graphical interfaces (and in different historical moments: the codex, typescript, pencils, typewriters, TV, and radio, among others), technological discourse about e-reading has not brought about acceptance in academic contexts.

Within the larger body of technological discourse about e-reading, substantial work from scholars as well as device-makers has tried both "emphasizing the benefits or affordances of the new technology over older ones" and "fostering a sense of familiarity and naturalness" between nascent and new technologies (153). For instance, scholars like Richard Lanham and James Sosnoski emphasize the affordances of new technologies by tracing the emergence of a new kind of reader, an electronic reader or a hyper-reader, who shares control over texts with writers by manipulating how texts are displayed (Lanham 267) and navigated "to suit their own needs" (Sosnoski 163).

As Cynthia Selfe has argued, technological literacy involves more than skills and practices like the ability to annotate digital texts or to summarize complex material; technological literacy also "refers to a complex set of socially and situated values" that "become essential parts of our cultural understanding of what it means to be literate," for instance, the notion that the ability to use a computer equates to digital literacy or the belief that digital texts are private, ephemeral, or even owned by the writer when produced in social networks or in cloud-based office suites (11). The technological discourse that too many students encounter about digital texts and digital devices forwards a specific, print-based vision of literacy that not only limits what practices that students can develop or employ, but also does a disservice to their literate development by depicting the act of reading through harmful mythologies about reading as a silent and reverent activity conceptualized as scenes of private study. In contrast to these mythologies, and as scholars working in the history of the book have shown through studies of marginalia, there is a rich history of reading as a social, collaborative, and performative act of meaning-making. For example, in his examination of marginalia and other markings that readers added to books during the Renaissance period, William Sherman shows that the emergence of the print press "did not automatically, or immediately, render readers passive" (9). Centuries after the emergence of the printing press, readers' marginalia practices went well beyond conventional annotation of texts, including: the customization of books by cutting, combining, and rebinding printed materials; the use of marginalia as a medium for conversation among multiple readers; readers' use of blank pages in books for "penmanship exercises, prayers, recipes, popular poetry, drafts of letters, mathematical calculations, shopping lists" and phonetic markings suggesting the use of printed materials to practice pronunciation by reading aloud (Sherman 15). Although, as Sherman notes, "the cult of the clean book" eventually took hold as paper became more affordable and as library systems became important institutional sites for learning, this history of active reading serves as a compelling analog to the current moment (157). Just as readers in the Renaissance were still learning to trust print as a medium, they turned to an extensive set of literacy practices to contextualize, converse with, and use printed texts as part of their daily lives.

Not unlike readers in the current moment who use multiple devices, platforms, and networks to assert authority and identity in backchannels (Mueller) and to access and participate in communities of practice (Pigg, "Coordinating"), and to compose attention (Rivers), readers in the Renaissance employed a range of practices to engage meaningfully with their new medium: printed texts. Thus, banning the possibilities of meaningful engagement with the new medium of this technological era during key moments of student's literate development not only has the effect of perpetuating a specific and limited cultural understanding of what reading looks like but also limits students' opportunities to engage with texts meaningfully in ways that make sense for the current techno-logical-cultural moment.

In the next section, we provide an analysis of course policies about the use of digital devices collected from our own institutions: nineteen from a liberal arts college in the southeast (Southeast) and thirty-six from a public research university in the northeast (Northeast). Among those policies collected, thirty-nine policies were sampled from first-year writing courses (FYW) and sixteen were sampled from second-year and upper-level lit-erature courses (LIT). The sample size differed between policies sampled from Southeast and Northeast because Southeast instructors teaching FYW courses made frequent use of the technology policy developed for the staff syllabus, often copying it verbatim:

> Almost all course materials—including handouts, assignments, the syllabus, policies, and schedule—will be available online through OAKS. You may use laptops and tablets in class so long as you're taking notes, referring to relevant sources, or conducting other class-related work. Texting is not class-related work, so please keep phones put away at all times.

Given the frequency of this policy in our sample and to prevent skewing our sample, we eliminated all but one instance where the staff syllabus policy was copied verbatim. Though our sample is relatively small, total-ing fifty-five individual syllabi, and is limited to first-year and undergradu-ate courses housed within English Departments, we discovered that the policies we collected were comparable between our two different insti-tutional contexts. This comparability suggests to us that our sample is reflective of at least some of the range of technological discourse that students encounter through course documents.

Preserving the Traditional Social Arrangement

In our sample policies developed for discussion- and drafting-focused FYW courses and in lecture-focused LIT courses, most of the policies we collected echoed Dan Rockmore's concern that digital devices and digi-tal texts are incompatible with productive learning environments. Most overwhelming was the tendency to associate device use as a behavioral issue where the use of prohibited devices—most often, cell phones—or the inappropriate use of devices are akin to arriving late, leaving early, interrupting, and chatting. In contrast with the policies about lecture halls circulated by administrators at Brown that offered a pedagogical justification or a strategy for working across media to promote students' comprehension of lecture materials, syllabi from our collected sample were resounding in their treatment of devices strictly as behavioral problems or as prohibited behaviors more generally. For example, one policy collected from a FYW section at Southeast discusses the use of devices as equivalent to other common examples of disrespectful behavior found in syllabus policies: "Please treat the members of this community with respect by avoiding the following behaviors: using cell phones/electronic devices, arriving late, leaving early or in the middle of class."[1] Another collected from a course in Literature at Northeast outlines that if a student is given a dispensation to use a device in an otherwise print-only classroom, that student should "please respect the time and space of the classroom—your time, my time, and the time of your classmates—by using the device exclusively as a reading tool." When not discussing device use as a behavioral issue or a matter of respect, policies tended to blankly prohibit digital devices, stating simply that cell phones, laptops, and e-readers should be turned off and stowed away during class.

Justifications for the prohibition of devices were often linked to a broader attempt to define the social arrangement of the classroom as a space removed from other aspects of daily life and defined by a sustained engagement with a specific text. In such cases, devices are not only distractions but threats to learning environments that one Northeast instructor describes as a "rare space isolated from the electronic and real worlds." Similarly, a Southeast instructor's cell phone policy asks students to imagine that their "social life is subordinate to your academic education." In such formulations of the relationship between school and other domains of life, electronic social exchanges that do not exclusively concern the classroom community and are not authorized by the instructor are understood as secondary and inconsequential to the classroom community.

Related to this issue of student agency, our sample of policies unevenly imagined and narrowly applied prohibitions and limitations on digital technologies, often restricting students' opportunities to make choices about how to read, write, and take notes while instructors exempted themselves from their own policies. In other words, policies went beyond managing the attention of students to prescribing how students are supposed to learn, sometimes even in ways that contradicted the focus of the course. This most often occurred in first-year writing classrooms themed around issues of pop culture and media. The most illustrative of these came in a syllabus developed for a writing class at Southeast themed "New Media and Identity." Students in the course were meant to "work to understand and analyze the meaning of the culture we inhabit and the technology we use, especially how it relates to the increasing globalization of our world. We will explore how space, time and technology influence who we are as people." In terms of policy and in contradiction of the course's theme, the course's technology policy told students to "bring with you the appropriate texts or materials" while negating the possibility that some of those appropriate texts and materials might be online by also instructing students to "turn off cell phones and any other electronic devices, and be prepared to take part in the work of the class." In other words—and despite the theme of the course—the policy suggests that texts made and shared online are neither appropriate nor part of the work of the class. While this course policy is perhaps the most illustrative of the theme, it was common for courses—most often first-year writing courses—that directly included a focus on digital culture to emphasize print, particularly through delivery requirements.

Despite these variances in the degree to which technologies are allowed or prohibited between the two sampled institutions, common across both was the practice of placing delivery requirements on students. These delivery-focused technology policies were mechanisms through which instructors made claims about their authority over the learning environment regardless of whether or not that environment included the study of digital culture. Such delivery requirements included asking students to download and print readings; check email daily; use a wiki or other content management system; submit projects in print; use a Genius annotator; and use specific file names (e.g., YourLast-Name_Project1.doc). For example, it was commonplace for Northeast instructors to distribute syllabi through websites (most often, course wikis) and to share readings online or through an electronic course reserve when not already available as a printed text; these instructors then often required or strongly encouraged students to print materials shared online or through electronic reserves, stating in one case, "You MUST print out all PDFs and come to class with the text(s) carefully read and notes made in detail." Where not required, policies either encourage students to read and annotate in print or emphasize print as the preferred medium for their work. For example, in a FYW course at Northeast the instructor posted course materials through a wiki, instructing students to print their readings "or bring a device on which you can access them." But the instructor also required students to save their work in print for a portfolio project: "Please use one binder to file/organize all the paper we generate over the course of the semester." At Southeast, print is also privileged but to a lesser extent; the policy contained in the staff syllabus, which the majority of FYW instructors use, allows students to read "handouts, assignments, the syllabus, policies, and the schedule" in the learning management system using "laptops, cellphones, and tablets." Among those that did not use the staff syllabus technology policy, all included a technology prohibition (most often, cell phones) and either requiring or insisting that students read and take notes in print.

While the nature of the requirements themselves varied, what was perhaps most surprising was how instructors who implemented print-only

or print-mostly requirements on students also made use of digital technologies to facilitate their own delivery of course content. This disparity
between instructors' ability to deliver texts electronically and students'
accountability to an array of technology policies suggests that technology
policies do not apply to instructors. Even in those courses that attempt
to recreate a microcosm of print culture by prohibiting reading and note-
taking on devices, instructors have license to communicate electronically
with students and hold them accountable to checking their email frequently. Thus, even where the preservation of a learning environment
closed-off from outside influence is not the justification for the use of
a technology policy, technology policies become mechanisms through
which instructors extend their authority beyond the classroom, influencing how students read and write in preparation for class, and at the same
time, limiting students' agency over their reading, writing, and learning
inside the classroom.

Instances of technological discourse that attempt to preserve the social
arrangement of the classroom as a space removed from the "real world"
and establish it as a place where print is still the dominant medium
work to reinforce anxieties by suggesting that print is the medium most
appropriate for learning and that only those with expertise in print—
particularly, instructors—can effectively attend to their choices of media
and use of digital devices. These anxieties exacerbated by the association
of device use with behavioral issues that disrespect and disrupt communities focused around the study and production of texts, suggesting
that digital devices and digital spaces are about disruption rather than
student learning.

Defining Academic Work

In addition to monitoring students' behavior and learning, even in some
cases in ways that were antithetical to the content of the course, we
observed that course policies also consistently imagined digital devices
as anathema to academic work. Most often, students' devices and their
functions were imagined as attention traps that exclusively and necessarily distract students. In particular, these course policy sheets state that
the presence of digital devices ultimately causes students to engage in a
range of destructive behaviors: "surfing the web," checking email, engaging with social media, texting, "accessing pornography," and making up
excuses for late work while in class. In other words, these policies narrowly imagine what students are doing onscreen, suggesting students are
not using the required course management software, not accessing the
course website, not reviewing readings, not visiting the websites professors provide for additional resources (e.g., the OWL at Purdue). Some
policies provide self-justification, outlining how the devices work against
the goals of the course: "Again: studies show that multi-tasking in class

will probably lower your performance. We don't want that." (The irony here is that no such studies are listed.)

Even courses in which digital delivery is specifically described as integral to the academic work of the course—in the course focus, readings and content, research requirements, or supplementary resources—often prohibit the use of delivery devices that could access digital materials or accomplish digital tasks. When digital devices are allowed, their possible productivity is almost always about reading, note-taking, or looking things up quickly. None of the course policies described meaningful, sustained engagement with digital technologies during the class meetings, and very few mentioned the use of devices, platforms, software, or texts as having potential for drafting, workshopping, revising, peer reviewing, researching, discussing, or analyzing. (As we collaboratively write this article online, and given how much writing takes place online generally, this strikes us as an especially ironic omission among the policies.) For instance, one instructor at Southeast did mention that laptops could be "handy" for workshops without an indication of why or how, before mentioning that the pen and paper, or the "old fashioned way," is also permissible, suggesting—at best—digital technologies are capable of replicating print.

Most surprising were course policies developed for courses where digital media and digital culture were topics in the course and/or where a digital environment (for example, a wiki, a blog, or another CMS) figured prominently in the course. In these cases, course policies overwhelmingly reinforced the idea that learning happens in print and face-to-face while digital technologies are only useful for accessing readings, note-taking, and communicating with the instructor outside of class, thus narrowly imagining what academic work entails. Among the six sampled syllabi that were distributed online or were developed in courses where digital and contemporary culture are foci, all six recommended or required students to read in print. For instance, in a course on culture and technology, wherein the primary objective was to "explore how space, time and technology influence who we are as people," the technology statement read simply: "turn off cell phones and any other electronic devices and be prepared to take part in the work of the class." A generous reading of these policies might identify the underlying pattern of positioning of digital devices as impeding learning as being undergirded by the idea that digital devices and digital texts are only useful for academic work outside the classroom; in more extreme cases, the belief seems to be that they are not capable of contributing to academic work at all.

Conclusion

As composition studies has increasingly taken up pedagogies that emphasize writers' choices (for example, Shipka's *Composition Made Whole*), this sample of course policies suggests that students consistently lack the opportunity to make meaningful choices in how they read, write, and learn. Rather than offer choice, support, and reasoning, we have found that these technology policies consistently prescribe practices while imagining reading, writing, and learning within a microcosm of print culture, obscuring the reality that much of the serious work students do outside of class occurs in a material- and media-rich scene of literate action. As Stacy Pigg has shown, students develop sophisticated sets of habits both onscreen and in social space to negotiate the challenges of living and working in a hyper-networked attention economy by "combining shared social spaces and personal technologies to support learning processes over time through informal but sustained writing processes" ("Emplacing" 269). As Pigg shows, students understand that their attention is a commodity, and much like the students' part of Ravizza et al.'s study, they are aware of what they need to do and not to do to pay attention. By limiting the devices they use to read, learn, and write—and along with them, the strategies and practices they find helpful—prescriptive policies deny students opportunities to develop and practice literacy with materials that they regularly use as part of their academic work outside of class.

While policies may attempt to guide students to processes and practices that can productively sustain their academic work by providing models of good academic behavior, we also observe that they occlude possibilities for student engagement with delivery technologies in ways that are productive—and maybe even experimental—and for students' cultivation of the ability to manage their own attention (in the same ways professors assume for themselves). Part of this work of making new possibilities available to students involves imagining attention as a limited but not static resource that is gained and lost depending on the devices present in the room but as composed. As Nathaniel Rivers has argued, attention is an important resource that is not possessed but is formed through relations between students, devices, texts, and a range of other materials. As he argues, "Moving forward in digital rhetoric, the task is not just to measure a new digital tool against 'attention' but to slowly trace the very composition of attention in action, each and every time." This notion of attention as composed is a compelling starting point for imagining what student learning might best look like from behind the podium because it suggests possibilities for students to consider what devices and media are most conducive to their academic work.

In short, there is substantial research that would bolster thinking through careful limitations on digital device use in the classroom. However, we find little of that thinking—and none of that research—mentioned or reflected in the course policies discussed here. Instead, instructors use technology policies as a locus of control for defining acceptable behavior and delimiting the possible ways that academic work can be productively accomplished. What we identify in the course policies, then, is expressive of anxiety and a desire for control—of community, classroom, attention—and as willing to exact punitive measures to ensure that control. Some versions of that control orient themselves to device specificity: circumscribing the use of tablets, USB drives, cords and cables, printer cards, earbuds/headphones, cloud storage, and even device charging. The flouting of these behavioral norms is variously punished by shame (it's "disrespectful"), by docking grades via participation, by requests to leave, the applications of the absence policy, or by formal charges before a university honor board.

Given these issues: how we might write course policy statements to more productively shape the discourse surrounding the use of technology in English classrooms? Instead of boiler plates and justifications of policy, what ways forward might we pursue in thinking about policies as sites of productive technological discourse about digital delivery? Below, we suggest an approach to developing course policies: one focused on the goals of the course and the other acknowledging the realities of living in a networked culture where the lines between the curriculum and the extracurriculum are all but completely dissolved. Accompanying these approaches, we also suggest a possible assignment for each designed to help instructors systematically support the inclusion of print and digital technologies in classroom.

This approach to policy-writing involves taking stock of what students are ultimately expected to be able to do by the end of the course and what technologies can support those goals. Such an approach involves not only recommending platforms but also recommending specific ways of using those platforms. To begin to imagine what platforms might be constructive for use in the class, we recommend asking students: what technologies (media, devices, platforms, and software) they have used in the past to read, write, research, and learn; what they did with those technologies; and whether or not—they were effective. Such a list might be generated on the first day of class based on a version of the following.

1. List the technologies (for example: pens; notebooks; laptops; annotation software; e-readers) you have used to read in the past. For each, note whether or not it was effective and why.
2. List the technologies (for example, pens; notebooks; Powerpoint; Google Docs camera phone) *you have used to take notes* in the past. For each, note whether or not it was effective and why.
3. List the technologies (for example: pens; notebooks; Google Docs; Microsoft Word; Pages; markdown or distraction free word processors; blogs; discussion boards) *you have used to write* in the past. For each, note whether or not it was effective and why.
4. List the technologies (for example: double-entry notebooks; books; notebooks; reference software like RefWorks; Google Drive; blogs) *you have used to research in the past.* For each, note whether or not it was effective and why.

After students help generate this list of technologies and their possible productive uses, a compilation of their responses might be shared with them to suggest what academic work looks like using a combination of print and digital media. Based on this list, a policy might be circulated to emphasize what the primary work of the class entails and what technologies can best support that work based on their own responses. Ultimately, this approach involves offering students a set possible best practices that suggest how they might use print and digital technologies to support specific literacy tasks.

Although not always reflected in course policies, students read, write, and learn in a rich media landscape: rich in the range of technologies available to them; rich in demands on their time and attention; and rich in potentials for meaning making. Although research (e.g., Pigg) suggests that students can become adept at navigating this landscape by developing productive habits and preferences, it *is* the case that not all students have had opportunities to develop such habits—in part, because of a persistent idea about what learning should look like.[2] Insofar as classrooms are spaces where students read and write, they are also spaces where students find support for *becoming* better readers and writers—not in isolation from but in tandem with the other contexts where they develop literacy. To acknowledge that students use a range of media outside the classroom and to allow those uses within the classroom gives them license to do what works as well as allows them opportunity to develop new practices with writing technologies: both familiar and unfamiliar.

Notes

1. It may be the case that device-use is understood as bad classroom behavior in order to ease the transition from a highly regulated high school environment to college, but this motive is not reflected in the policies themselves, and is, therefore, beyond the scope of this study.
2. It might be the case that Southeast and Northeast students' economic backgrounds and histories of access have made it difficult to form productive habits in online environments, but whether or not the policies collected and analyzed as part of this study attempt to help students develop such habits is not reflected in the policies themselves, and is, therefore, beyond the scope of this study.

Works Cited

Baron, Naomi S. *Always On: Language in an Online and Mobile World*, Oxford University Press, 2008.
———. *Words Onscreen: The Fate of Reading in a Digital World*, Oxford University Press, 2015.
Birkerts, Sven. *The Gutenberg Elegies: The Fate of Reading in an Electronic Age*, Farrar, Straus and Giroux, 2006.
Carr, Nicholas. *The Shallows: What the Internet Is Doing to Our Brains*, W.W. Norton, 2010.

Curzan, Anne. "Why I'm Asking You Not to Use Laptops." *The Chronicle of Higher Education*, 25 Aug. 2014.

Lanham, Richard A. "The Electronic Word: Literary Study and the Digital Revolution." *New Literary History*, vol. 20, no. 2, *Technology, Models, and Literary Study*, 1989, pp. 265–90.

Mueller, Derek. "Digital Underlife in the Networked Writing Classroom." *Computers and Composition*, vol. 26, no. 4, 2009, pp. 240–50.

Mueller, Pam A., and Daniel M. Oppenheimer. "The Pen Is Mightier Than the Keyboard: Advantages of Longhand over Laptop Note Taking." *Psychological Science*, vol. 25, no. 6, 2014, pp. 1159–68.

Pigg, Stacey. "Coordinating Constant Invention: Social Media's Role in Distributed Work." *Technical Communication Quarterly*, vol. 23, no. 2, 2014, pp. 69–87.

———. "Emplacing Mobile Composing Habits: A Study of Academic Writing in Networked Social Spaces." *CCC*, vol. 66, no. 2, 2014, pp. 250–75.

Ravizza, Susan M., et al. "Logged In and Zoned Out: How Laptop Internet Use Relates to Classroom Learning." *Psychological Science*, vol. 28, no. 2, 2016, pp. 171–80.

Rivers, Nathaniel. "Paying Attention with Cache." *Enculturation*, vol. 23, 2016.

Rockmore, Dan. "The Case for Banning Laptops in the Classroom." *The New Yorker*, 6 June 2014.

Salvatori, Mariolina Rizzi, and Patricia Donahue. "Unruly Reading." *Deep Reading: Teaching Reading in the Writing Classroom*, edited by Patrick Sullivan, Howard Tinberg, and Sheridan Blau, Urbana, IL, NCTE, 2017, pp. 313–38.

"Sample Syllabus Policies on the Use of Mobile Technology in the Classroom," Sheridan Center for Teaching and Learning, Brown University, www.brown.edu/academics/digital-teaching-learning/explore/example/classroom-mobile-device-usage.

Selfe, Cynthia L. *Technology and Literacy in the Twenty-First Century: The Importance of Paying Attention*, Southern Illinois State University Press, 1999.

Sherman, William H. *Used Books: Marking Readers in Renaissance England*, University of Pennsylvania Press, 2008.

Sosnoski, James. "Hyper-Readers and Their Reading Engines." *Passions, Pedagogies, and 21st Century Technologies*, edited by Gail E. Hawisher and Cynthia L. Selfe, Utah State University Press, 1999, pp. 161–77.

Wolf, Maryanne. *Proust and the Squid: The Story and Science of the Reading Brain*, New York, Harper Perennial, 2008.

Part 2

Teaching Writing and Reading in Digital Spaces

5 The Past, Present, and Future of Social Annotation

Amanda Licastro

It is easy to assume that the practice of annotating texts is a dying art. Take, for example, this claim by poet and literary critic William Logan: "[t]hose who read with pen in hand form a species nearly extinct. Those who read the marginal notes of readers past form a group even smaller. Yet when we write in antiphonal chorus to what we're reading, we engage in that conversation time and distance otherwise make impossible" ("Mrs. Custer's Tennyson," *The New Criterion*). But perhaps this conversation would shift if we explored annotation practices that spanned beyond pen and paper. Consider this screenshot from the Kindle app on my phone taken in the summer of 2017 (Figure 5.1).

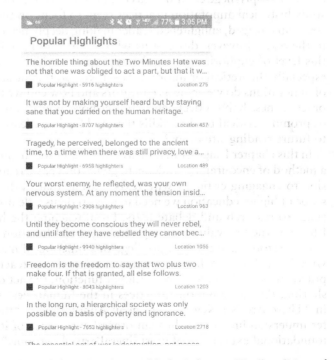

Figure 5.1 A screenshot of the "Popular Highlights" from a Kindle edition of George Orwell's *1984*.

This screenshot captures evidence that 9,940 people highlighted the Kindle edition of George Orwell's *1984*. While *1984* is a popular novel, it is still considered a literary text as well. Of those digitally "highlighting" (to use Kindle's terminology) Orwell's text, a small percentage must be students, but I cannot imagine all 9,940 readers were required to use this particular Kindle edition for a class assignment. Rather these are readers who are in engaged in the very same "conversation time and distance otherwise make impossible" whose loss Logan laments. It would be easy to gather evidence across Amazon's corpora to prove that millions of people annotate texts every day, and that they do so on a public platform. Therefore, the claim that readers do not annotate may not be the central problem. However, it is important to consider what types of annotation we value, and how those values translate into our teaching practices. Therefore, the real question is how and why we should teach students to annotate.

Following that opening quote in Logan's article, he contradicts himself by voicing his displeasure at the discovery of annotations found in a physical book of poems he has purchased online. Logan deduces that these marks were made by a college student, and chastises the anonymous reader for using the margins to identify archaic terms that are unfamiliar and to define words such as "patronizing." Despite the palpable irony, this accusation reveals that Logan—and perhaps many academics and educators—privilege certain kinds of annotations over others. Those who study historical annotation practices seem to focus on those that demonstrate an engaged, enlightened reader making deeply personal connections to the text. However, those of us who teach reading skills may find that this level of euphoria may not be appropriate when assigning—perhaps especially theoretical or informative—texts. So the question is what type of annotations do we value as educators and how can we teach students to practice these habits effectively? Furthermore, how can we use annotation to promote critical reading skills that will facilitate learning and transfer to future reading situations?

In this chapter I suggest that instructors adapt social annotation tools as a method of encouraging students to go beyond basic reading comprehension to engaging critically with texts. I argue that in the changing landscape of higher education we need to give students a flexible, collaborative space to research and debate texts. From teaching the history of media I have learned to value the longstanding social function of annotations, and therefore have come to privilege this function of marginalia. I agree with Jason Jones—who has written extensively on teaching annotation practices—that it is the conversational function, the act of discovery and sharing, that we align our practices in the humanities. As Jones argues in "There Are No New Directions in Annotations," "the notion of better understanding a text through others' experience of it is arguably the foundational experience of most liberal arts classrooms" (*Web Writing*).

In this view, marginalia is not just a personal act, but a public act that can and should be archived and shared. This argument parallels practices in both composition and digital humanities pedagogy which stress student-centered and project-based learning. As Paul Schacht contends in the chapter on "Annotation" for *Digital Pedagogy in the Humanities*

> The participatory ethos of social annotation aligns it with the promise of radical democracy: free expression, common ownership, mutual commitment; liberty, equality, fraternity. The promise stands in marked opposition to those aspects of higher education pedagogy and scholarship that remain, even in democratic societies, hierarchical, exclusive, proprietary, and competitive.
>
> (par. 6)

It is the creation of a communal learning space that can challenge and expand our understanding of a text that I contend is valuable in the act of using social annotation tools to mark a text. By giving students an open digital space to share their thoughts on a text, they can learn from each other through what Cathy Davidson thoughtfully terms "collaboration by difference" (original citation in *Now You See It*, or see updated discussion on HASTAC post "Collaboration by Difference, Yet Again"). Extending reading practices into an online space shifts the focus from the instructor as the authority to a model in which students can discuss their perspectives on a text through thoughtful dialogue. However, in order to teach our students to engage in conversational marginalia it is helpful to provide models.

The Historical Perspective

Demonstrating that marginalia has been used for centuries as instruments of instruction and catalysts for public debate could reframe the act of annotating for students. We can see examples of marginalia that were written with the intention of being read in texts such as the Talmud, early modern Book of Hours, and through the archives of famous authors whose annotations are fetishized by those who study literature. These annotations range from directions to the readers and definitions meant to serve as explanations, to editorial notes and personal anecdotes that reveal how the reader internalized and comprehended the meaning of the text. Scholars use marginalia to historicize and contextualize a text, as well as to study the changing nature of reading across time. Marginalia demonstrate that reading has historically been a public act. In fact, researchers working at MIT's Comparative Media Studies to develop the tool "Annotation Studio" argue that:

> Indeed, the impulse to make marks on a page is so widespread and deeply rooted that it seems to reflect not a cultural formation, as

is writing itself, but rather a natural one: the kinesthetic dimension of learning. In this respect, annotation is intuitive—a practice that readers would follow even without prior historical direction, and therefore wanders across the timeline of the humanities with irregular bursts and continuities.

(Paradis et al.)

Depending on the time period and texts studied, the social nature of annotation is shared between lovers, family members, and communities across space and time. That said, some of the marginalia studied by scholars may not have been intended for an audience outside of these predetermined communities. In some ways, our appropriation of these annotations is an invasion of that privacy, and therefore we should consider carefully how we use the material found in the margins of texts. Similarly, when creating new spaces for social annotation, privacy settings should be clear to the users and adjustable based on the needs of a community.

We can also see the focus on social reading in depictions of the future. Prescient visions of thinkers like Vannevar Bush and Doug Engelbart predicted the need for a network of associated texts. These examples have been explored in great depth elsewhere, but I propose using them in the classroom to demonstrate to students the power and endurance of public annotation. For example, reading Bush's (1945) *Atlantic* article "As We May Think" with students provides a clear example of how visionaries called for a system that would afford easy and open access to information, including the ability to interact with these texts collaboratively, which is precisely what projects such as Book Traces, HathiTrust, and Project Gutenberg (to name only a few) are doing. Showing students that past societies coveted the affordances technology has made possible for us brings a certain allure to using digital annotation tools.

There is considerable research to back up the anecdotal evidence I observed when using this approach in my classes over the past five years. Researchers have conducted numerous quantitative studies coding student writing in the form of social annotations. For example, in "The Affordance of Anchored Discussion for the Collaborative Process of Academic Texts," van de Pol, Admirall, and Simons compare student comments in a discussion forum (using Blackboard) to those anchored in the margins of a text, and conclude that the annotations consistently referred more frequently to the text when composed in the margins than in the discussion board posts. The annotation tool was also more effective at sustaining a continued discussion on one point or topic (353). Studies have also shown that students who read the text collaboratively using social annotation demonstrated considerable improvement in their reading comprehension skills (Johnson, Archibald, & Tenenbaum; Su, Yang, Hwang, & Zhang). There have also been studies that examine not just *if* or *why*, but *what* students write when composing social annotations.

In the article "Case Study of Using a Social Annotation Tool to Support Collaboratively Learning," Fei Gao uses Dillenbourg and Scheider's eight mechanisms of collaborative learning and the Pena-Shaff and Nicolls coding schema to analyze a series of 122 comments across multiple sections of an undergraduate teacher training course and finds that not only did most students post far more comments than required by their instructor, but that the comments were directly relevant to specific sections of the reading with little digression. Furthermore, in "A Case Study in Social Annotation of Digital Text," Alan Reid discovers that students self report a "significantly higher level of motivation" while reading the text when using social annotation tools compared to a control group (12). Based on this research, it is evident that using annotation tools drives students to read closely and engage in relevant discussion about a text. Taken together, the research demonstrates that the use of social annotation tools supports student engagement with texts at a deeper level than other methods, such as discussion board posts or other forms of response divorced from the text. In order to show students the relevance of writing directly in the margins—rather than in a separate space—I turn to historical examples through the Book Traces project.

Book Traces in the Classroom

For the past three years I have invited my students to actively engage in the Book Traces project as a way to substantiate the long-tail of social annotation practices. Book Traces "is a crowd-sourced web project aimed at identifying unique copies of nineteenth- and early twentieth-century books on library shelves" (booktraces.org). Sponsored by NINES at the University of Virginia and led by Andrew Stauffer, Book Traces specifically gathers evidence of nineteenth-century readership practices through finding and documenting marginalia made in texts published before 1923. This time period represents a unique moment when printing was cheap—therefore we have many copies of the same text in circulating libraries—however readers of the time still shared copies of books with family and friends, making texts communal property. Because there are multiple copies of these texts, they are often marked to be moved to offsite storage or destroyed when libraries are faced with tough decisions regarding the capacity of their circulating collections. Similarly, once one copy of a text is digitized and provided electronically, the remaining print copies may be seen as no longer useful. Therefore, the Book Traces project is meant to engage "the question of the future of the print record" in light of these sometimes necessary moves that make original copies of nineteenth-century texts unavailable to researchers (booktraces.org). By demonstrating the rich material that can be found in the marginalia of these "extraneous" copies, Book Traces argues that each text should be examined and studied before it is destroyed. Furthermore, crowdsourcing these efforts shifts the burden off librarians and administrators to students who can learn from the experience.

For example, when teaching at New York University (NYU), I took first-year writing students to Butler Library at Columbia University to search the stacks for pre-1923 texts featuring marginalia from nineteenth-century readers as part of the Book Traces project. Attending the Book Traces event gave students the opportunity to think about the purpose of libraries. This may or may not surprise you, but many college students are intimidated by libraries—especially university libraries where the size and scope dwarf those in their home towns or high schools. They are also unfamiliar with old books. Digging in the stacks gives them a chance to get their hands dirty. This is one thing students comment on the most—the smell, feel, and look of dilapidated books. While searching for annotations, students often inquire about how the texts are stored, preserved, and organized. All these are essential information literacy practices students may not learn elsewhere.

By participating in a Book Traces event students are also exposed to a wide range of annotation types, all of which provide unique information to the viewer. For example, seeing annotations such as dedication pages or acquisition histories familiarizes students with legacy print collections, providing a sense of history and provenance for the offerings available to them as students with access to a university library. Suddenly, the role of the library expands from a convenient place to study, to a resource that serves the greater purpose of maintaining rare collections of invaluable research materials. Or, when students find family genealogies handwritten over decades inside a cover, or a lock of hair preserved between pages, they see books as historical artifacts that capture more than the stories printed inside. These discoveries lead to discussions about what counts as meaningful evidence in the marginalia they find.

When students discover interesting artifacts, a team of librarians and professors help them assess and decipher their findings. For example, if the annotation appears in red ink, it was most likely created by a contemporary author, and therefore is deemed not relevant for the Book Traces project. However, a hand drawn illustration dated before 1923 may be valuable to scholars, and is photographed or scanned to the Book Traces website. Even these small acts of evaluating and categorizing archival ephemera teaches students critical thinking skills. Furthermore, actively participating in the process of digitizing their finding opens the conversation to the future of the humanities at large. How can we make old forms of media accessible to a wider audience? When uploading items students fill out the basic fields provided by the Book Traces site, such as the author, date, and location of their finding. In this act of cataloging, students learn what data we value in the field. Not only does this Book Traces exercise serve as an introduction to textual studies, it is also an introduction to digital humanities. Students move from simply consuming content, to evaluating and repurposing content for a greater goal.

While Columbia and NYU have considerable resources compared to many institutions of higher education, it is possible to replicate this experience at a smaller college. At Stevenson University, my current institution, our library does not have the volume of pre-1923 texts that Columbia holds in their collections. However, Andrew Stauffer gave a talk as part of our Distinguished Speaker Series and brought several examples with him. There are many rare book collections that offer traveling or virtual exhibitions as well. Even a limited engagement with the materials had a huge impact on my students. As you can see in this excerpt from a sophomore student's reflection post, participants were able to recognize and articulate the wider implications of the annotations they examined.

> The social function and form of annotation as a type of communication similar to a modern day email was very cool. Notes to lovers and friends were scrawled on pages or passages that reminded people of each other. [. . .] The major role of books within people's lives during the Victorian-era was put into perspective as a result of Stauffer's work. Books were not just educational, religious or recreational, they were major social tools as well. Book traces [sic] open-source accessibility is a wonderful layout for a really intriguing project.
>
> (Ryan Roche, student at Stevenson University)

As Ryan Roche demonstrates, students can and should make connections between the nineteenth-century annotation practices and the digital reading practices modern readers engage in now. I want students to capture their newfound knowledge of social reading and translate it into their own reading practices.

Reading in Print Versus Reading Online

To start this process, I ask students to read and write about the differences between reading online versus reading in print from a variety of perspectives. In the past I have used "The Deep Space of Digital Reading," by Paul LaFarge, in which the author argues that "[c]ritics like to say the Internet causes our minds to wander off, but we've been wandering off all along." The article models the historicization of contemporary arguments that the Internet is rotting our brains by citing Socrates' worry that "writing would weaken human memory, and stifle judgment" alongside publications making similar claims about digital technology published in the past decade (LaFarge). I pair LaFarge with articles that take on the opposing viewpoint, such as those by Nicholas Carr, providing students with a range of perspectives and entry points to the conversation. Students collaboratively annotate these articles in a meta-exercise in which they are both considering and engaging in different forms of reading, which I will describe in more depth below. Note that I update these readings often to keep these voices fresh and relevant, and that I provide guidance through the process of reading and comprehending the content in today's ever evolving digital context.

I scaffold this assignment by leading students through a series of four activities. First, students track their "attention blindness" by making a tally mark every time they are distracted while reading an article in print. "Attention blindness" is a term borrowed from Cathy Davidson, whose research connecting neuroscience to the humanities reveals that we are learning to multitask in the digital age (2). Many students have 15–20 tally marks in the 15 minutes of reading time provided in class. After they make their tally marks during the 15-minute reading exercise, they are asked if they could complete a short quiz on the content. Most readily admit they would fail. As Davidson argues in her book *Now You See It*, the ability to productively multitask is a vital twenty-first-century skill, and one that should be taught in school. Students read excerpts from Davidson's text to engage with these concepts at a deeper level, and to compare Davidson's approach to the other articles presented previously. Whereas most authors condemn multitasking as a distraction that students must control and avoid, Davidson embraces multitasking as a desirable ability that provides the audience with a unique perspective. By making students aware of their own attention blindness in the classroom, and presenting this as an opportunity rather than a curse, they are more open to experimenting with tools that work with—not against—their natural inclinations to bounce from one task to the next. Second, the students read the same article while annotating using a writing utensil on paper. We then discuss what strategies they used to mark the text and create a list of possible types of annotations the students can incorporate in the future. Even after these first two steps the students' confidence increases markedly when asked to answer comprehension questions. This is important because we want students to engage with texts intentionally and reflect on how they read and process information online and in print. The lesson is simple: active reading helps students comprehend content.

Social Annotation Tools

The third step is to move the exercise into the digital realm by having students read an article on the same topic online using digital tools to create their annotations. The following description is intended to be a pedagogical practice that can translate to any tool—including ones yet to be created. The tool serves as an example, not the only option. After testing several platforms, including Annotation Studio and Google Docs, I am most impressed with hypothes.is. All three tools achieve the same goal: allowing students to collaboratively annotate a document using text, multimedia, and links. However, with both Annotation Studio and Google Docs, the instructor must create a group and upload a version of a text to that private space. While this offers some degree of control and privacy, which is often desirable for the purposes of student work, these platforms do not retain the original formatting and features of a born-digital site. If an instructor wants students to engage with a site specifically in order to comment on aspects of web design such as information architecture, layout, usability, or media and hyperlink inclusion, these platforms do not suffice. Therefore, when teaching my students to navigate webtexts, I prefer to use hypothes.is, which is essentially a layer of tools that do not obstruct or interfere with the integrity of the original web design. It also allows for the option to create private groups or engage in public annotation; an affordance that lends itself to civic engagement and public humanities lessons. Furthermore, hypothes.is a nonprofit and the tool is free to use and open source (read more about their ethical practices here: https://web.hypothes.is/about/).

Many instructors may already be aware of hypothes.is since it is similar to Genius.com. Genius—formerly Rap Genius—is a popular site for annotating music lyrics. For this same reason, students tend to be familiar with the basic premise of this tool. While students may not have experience marking the margins of an Emerson poem, many have added their voice to the comment threads on "Becky with the Good Hair" (a lyric in a Beyonce song). Genius capitalizes on what social media does best—it provides a space to offer an opinion on a popular text using multimedia. Dan Whaley and a team of developers partnered with a former English professor and founding member of the Genius team, Jeremy Dean, when creating hypothes.is with higher education in mind. With this tool users can annotate practically any web-based document, including websites, PDFs, and other formats that can be viewed in a browser. Of course, as with any tool, there are drawbacks and shortcomings.

My goal in utilizing any annotation tool in the classroom is to teach students to read closely and look up information that might help them comprehend and evaluate the text. When employing social annotation tools, the ultimate objective is to have students share their insights and findings in order to create a dialogue about the text. The social aspect harkens back to the nineteenth-century marginalia students studied in their investigation of Book Traces materials. This prepares students to compose comments with the intention of having others read their annotations and respond. For initial interactions with the tool, or with new students, it may be best to restrict the use to only participants in the course, or shared with several sections of the same course. Having students post publicly can be scaffolded in later during the term or in upper-level courses once students are familiar with the process and more confident in their reading comprehension.

Once a user selects a document using the "Paste a Link" or browser plugin, the hypothes.is toolbar will appear on the right-hand side of the screen. From there, the hypothes.is user simply selects a passage in the text and can then either click highlight or annotate. In the dialogue box users can add comments, links, photos, and videos, and the user can determine if the comment should be private, public, or viewable to a pre-set group. If the post is viewable to other users, then the community can respond. This is perhaps the most important function of this tool for the purposes of teaching social annotation. Students should compose annotations with the intention of sharing knowledge and starting conversations with the class. Definitions, research, and reflections serve as catalysts for discussion, much like posts on social media.

Pedagogical Applications

I typically require students to add 5–10 annotations and respond to 3–5 posts, depending on the class level and article length. Before they begin, we discuss the kinds of annotation that would be most helpful in this context. I encourage definitions, links to research—including links to Wikipedia articles or YouTube videos—and questions. In a 100-level course, the groups are private so that only members of this course can see the annotations students compose. This provides a safe, protected space for lower level students to exercise their digital literacy habits. As the instructor, the private space allows me to monitor responses and enter the conversations when needed. If a disrespectful or inappropriate comment arises, I address it both online and during face-to-face class time. The ability to respond appropriately in online public spaces has become an essential digital literacy skill (think of the last YouTube comments thread or Reddit discussion you encountered). Therefore, building online conversations into the classroom context offers instructors the chance to teach students to engage in digital discourse in a thoughtful and respectful manner and hope they extend these lessons into their personal lives.

Figure 5.2 captures an exchange from a 100-level course using hypothes. is. You can see students highlight text frequently, adding comments that include videos, images, links, and replies. Ruminations formulated in their annotations are hashed out in greater depth in person, allowing conversations that are too big for the constraints of a comment section a place to evolve. This also provides students who are not comfortable articulating their opinions in class the space to share their readings. Commenting online gives students the chance to think through their contributions and use grammar and spelling checks when appropriate. Furthermore, I am often able to identify the areas where my students are struggling to understand a text by reading their comments—or in some cases by identifying sections in which no one commented. These omissions can signal a place where no one was brave enough to take on difficult language or advanced concepts. The way students engage with a text online informs the way lessons are structured. I am better able to use our limited class time strategically when provided with access to this new form of data.

In a viral YouTube video from October 2011 a one-year-old girl sweeps her fingers across an iPad's touchscreen, shuffling groups of icons. In the following scenes she appears to pinch, s..., they too were screens. When nothing happens, she pushes against her leg, confirming that her finger works just fine—or so a title card would have us believe.

The girl's father, Jean-Louis Constanza, presents "A Magazine Is an iPad That Does Not Work" as naturalistic observation—a Jane Goodall among the chimps moment—that reveals a gene he writes in the video's description. "Magazines are now useless and impossible to understand, for digital natives"—that is, for people who have been interacting with digital technologies fr

Perhaps his daughter really did expect the paper magazines to respond the same way an iPad would. Or maybe she had no expectations at all—maybe she just wanted to touch the magazin have never seen a tablet like the iPad or an e-reader like the Kindle will still reach out and run their fingers across the pages of a paper book; they will jab at an illustration they like; heck, tl so-called digital natives still interact with a mix of paper magazines and books, as well as tablets, smartphones and e-readers; using one kind of technology does not preclude them from un

Nevertheless, the video brings into focus an important question: How exactly does the technology we use to read change the way we read? How reading on screens differs from reading on [but to just about everyone who reads—to anyone who routinely switches between working long hours in front of a computer at the office and leisurely reading paper magazines and books a their convenience and portability, but admit that for some reason they still prefer reading on paper; and to those who have already vowed to forgo tree pulp entirely. As digital texts and tec more mobile ways of reading—but are we still reading as attentively and thoroughly onscreen text than to words on paper? Should we be worried or is the validity of such concerns paper-thin?

Since at least the 1980s researchers in many different fields—including psychology, computer engineering, and library and information science—have investigated such questions in more t no means settled. Before 1992 most studies concluded that people read slower, less accurately and less comprehensively on screens than on paper. Studies published since the early 199 slight majority has confirmed earlier conclusions, but almost as many have found few significant differences in reading speed or comprehension between paper and screens. And recent sur paper—especially when reading intensively—attitudes are changing as tablets and e-reading technology improve and reading digital books for facts and fun becomes more common. In the percent of all trade book sales.

Even so, evidence from laboratory experiments, polls and consumer reports indicates that modern screens and e-readers fail to adequately recreate certain tactile experiences of reading on importantly, prevent people from navigating long texts in an intuitive and satisfying way. In turn, such navigational difficulties may subtly inhibit reading comprehension. Compared with [resources while we are reading and make it a little harder to remember what we read when we are done. A parallel line of research focuses on people's attitudes toward different kinds of m approach computers and tablets with a state of mind less conducive to learning than the one they bring to paper.

"There is physicality in reading," says developmental psychologist and cognitive scientist Maryanne Wolf of Tufts University, "maybe even more than we want to think about as we lurch int too little reflection. I would like to preserve the absolute best of older forms, but know when to use the new."

Navigating textual landscapes

Understanding how reading on paper is different from reading on screens requires some explanation of how the brain interprets written language. We often think of reading as a cerebral a

Figure 5.2 A screenshot of an article annotated by first-year students at Stevenson University using the tool hypothes.is.

In comparison, the screenshot shown in Figure 5.3 was generated in an upper-level course in which students were unleashed to annotate in the public sphere. In this case, sites were selected based on my knowledge that the hosts openly encourage social commentary. *The Journal of Interactive Technology and Pedagogy* and *Hybrid Pedagogy* are both journals that have published pieces on the benefits of using social annotation tools, and having students read and annotate these articles provides support for adapting these tools on a number of levels. I often begin with a text that I know others have already commented on, so the students can engage with comments from the general public. In fact, in their comments many students specifically reflected on the fact that their annotations were public—and therefore susceptible to refute or even bullying. However, others commented that the public nature of this assignment lead to new discoveries about the text they wished would happen more often in all of their English courses. One particularly interesting moment is when sophomore student Lanett Bagley uses the annotation space to connect the work we were doing in an upper-level course on the history of publishing to the discussion her classmates were having in a critical theory course at Stevenson. These are the kinds of connections we cherish as instructors in higher education. By asking students to articulate their thoughts on a text to an audience of their peers, they often share these connections that may otherwise remain private. A collective wisdom grows from crowdsourcing the intellectual work of close reading.

Online social annotation tools can also be used to teach rhetorical analysis. Students select an article from an online journal and use hypothes.is to identify how the site addresses audience, context, genre, and purpose, along with critiquing design elements that shape the reading experience, such as the interface and information architecture. Students are instructed to reflect on design choices such as font, color, layout, and multimodal elements of the digital text. By analyzing these elements in professional publications, they are better positioned to experiment with these affordances when composing their own multimodal projects. Students develop a sense of how visual rhetoric relates to the alphabetic text present on their screens. As seen in Figure 5.4, my student Alaina Steg makes the astute connection between the use of hyperlinks in this article to Johanna Drucker's theories of hypertext presented in *Graphesis*, which we read earlier that semester. Again, these connections between texts within and across content demonstrate a high level of reading comprehension and analysis. Students can draw from their annotations when composing formal essays using these sources as evidence.

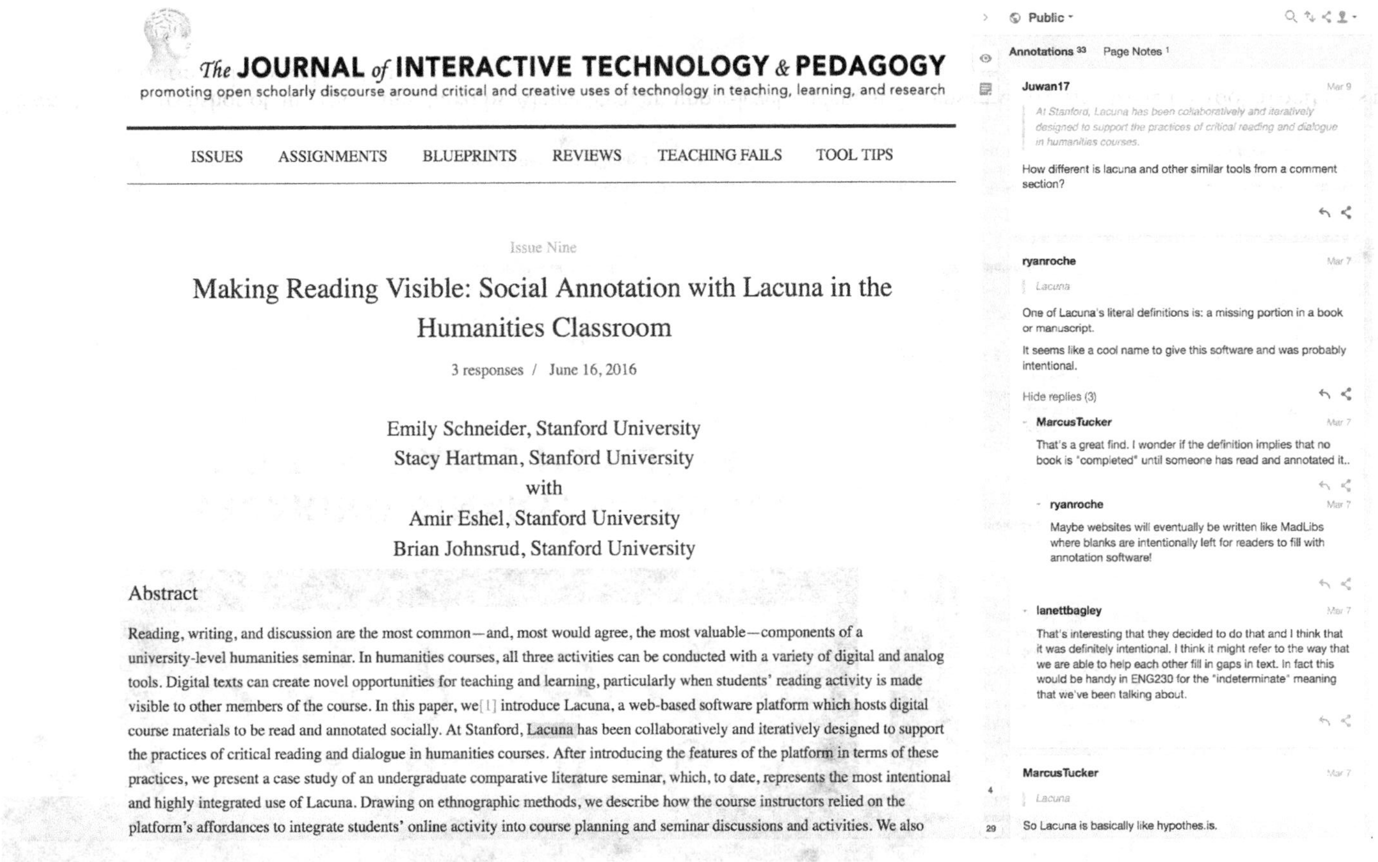

The JOURNAL of INTERACTIVE TECHNOLOGY & PEDAGOGY

promoting open scholarly discourse around critical and creative uses of technology in teaching, learning, and research

ISSUES ASSIGNMENTS BLUEPRINTS REVIEWS TEACHING FAILS TOOL TIPS

Issue Nine

Making Reading Visible: Social Annotation with Lacuna in the Humanities Classroom

3 responses / June 16, 2016

Emily Schneider, Stanford University
Stacy Hartman, Stanford University
with
Amir Eshel, Stanford University
Brian Johnsrud, Stanford University

Abstract

Reading, writing, and discussion are the most common—and, most would agree, the most valuable—components of a university-level humanities seminar. In humanities courses, all three activities can be conducted with a variety of digital and analog tools. Digital texts can create novel opportunities for teaching and learning, particularly when students' reading activity is made visible to other members of the course. In this paper, we[1] introduce Lacuna, a web-based software platform which hosts digital course materials to be read and annotated socially. At Stanford, Lacuna has been collaboratively and iteratively designed to support the practices of critical reading and dialogue in humanities courses. After introducing the features of the platform in terms of these practices, we present a case study of an undergraduate comparative literature seminar, which, to date, represents the most intentional and highly integrated use of Lacuna. Drawing on ethnographic methods, we describe how the course instructors relied on the platform's affordances to integrate students' online activity into course planning and seminar discussions and activities. We also

Public

Annotations 33 Page Notes 1

Juwan17 Mar 9

At Stanford, Lacuna has been collaboratively and iteratively designed to support the practices of critical reading and dialogue in humanities courses.

How different is lacuna and other similar tools from a comment section?

ryanroche Mar 7

Lacuna

One of Lacuna's literal definitions is: a missing portion in a book or manuscript.

It seems like a cool name to give this software and was probably intentional.

Hide replies (3)

MarcusTucker Mar 7

That's a great find. I wonder if the definition implies that no book is "completed" until someone has read and annotated it..

ryanroche Mar 7

Maybe websites will eventually be written like MadLibs where blanks are intentionally left for readers to fill with annotation software!

lanettbagley Mar 7

That's interesting that they decided to do that and I think that it was definitely intentional. I think it might refer to the way that we are able to help each other fill in gaps in text. In fact this would be handy in ENG230 for the "indeterminate" meaning that we've been talking about.

MarcusTucker Mar 7

Lacuna

So Lacuna is basically like hypothes.is.

Figure 5.3 A screenshot of an article from *The Journal of Interactive Technology and Pedagogy* annotated by upper-level students at Stevenson University using the tool hypothes.is.

NEWS

‖ Digital Pedagogy Lab

**25
MAR
2014**

BREAKING BINARY: FACEBOOK AND TEACHABLE MOMENTS

☞ Written by Sean Hackney / ☑ Reviewed by Sean Michael Morris and Valerie Robin /
☐ 4 Comments / 🖼 "trip to Seattle" by Liz Henry; CC BY-NC 2.0

PEDAGOGICAL ALTERITY

*This article is part of a series addressing the issue of difference and marginalization in
teaching. The goal is to intentionally make space for voices that are often silenced in
conversations about education. The discussion is ongoing — see all articles in this series or
the original call for papers that prompted them and consider adding your voice to the
conversation.*

I was in my car, pulling into the driveway after picking up some takeout. The radio was tuned to NPR,
but I wasn't paying that close of attention. I was exhausted after a long day of teaching and

---

🌐 Public ▾   🔍 ⤵ ⤴ ⚙▾

alainasteg   Mar 2, 2016

"try something new"

Hypertexts are found throughout the article. This particular
hyperlink takes the reader to the article *What is a Pedagogue?*
Which literally describes the title. Hyperlinks are crucial to a
scholarly article like this one because they serve as a form of
credibility, explanation, and the methodical process behind this
final result. As Johanna Drucker explains, "Each is designed to
allow multiple kinds of use and pathways, views into the data
and content, through analytic process as well as reading
experiences" (Graphesis, 160).

⤵ ⤴

LOOKING

alainasteg   Mar 2, 2016

*The truth is that we should jump at opportunities to connect
content to other contexts. In fact, Grant Wiggins, an educa... ...More*

2

Search D

Hackney says, "The truth is that we should jump at opportunities
to connect content to other contexts" (Breaking Binary:
Facebook). In other words, how are students supposed to be
well-rounded, open minded, and able to relate one educational
text to another if their teachers are unwilling to challenge their
minds to see more perspectives as well?

OPEN TO

VIEW RA

OUR EDI'

alainasteg   Mar 2, 2016

*I had fear narratives running laps in my head. What if a parent
calls? What if a student says something in class that offer- ...More*

14

These questions tie back into the audience. Hackney is placing
himself on the level of other teachers, giving them an
understanding not to worry about wondering these questions.

Figure 5.4 A screenshot of an article annotated by Alaina Steg, an upper-level student at Stevenson University, using the tool hypothes.is to perform a rhetorical analysis

Critiques and Considerations

However, as Drucker and others have argued, digital tools such as hypothes.is deserve careful critique from a humanities perspective. In its early days, Genius came under fire by the blogging community for failing to obtain permission from sites to "graffiti" unsolicited commentary over the work of the author (Dawson). As is the case with hypothes.is, you can use some social annotation tools on any URL—without consent. Genius and hypothes.is have publicly addressed this concern by moderating comments, allowing users to flag content, and by allowing sites to opt out or block the plugin. However, especially when annotating the work of marginalized or vulnerable voices, it is imperative that we talk about these concerns with our students and peers in order to model considerate and productive interactions in public spaces. Tools such as Annotation Studio and Google Docs eliminate these concerns by removing the text from the open web and safeguarding it in a private space, albeit still without consent from the content creator. The drawbacks are that the students lose the benefit from opening their conversation to the public, thereby engaging with an audience outside of the classroom, and it also eliminates the information architecture and multimodal aspects of a born-digital text. This act also falls into a gray area where copyright is concerned and diminishes the possibility that students will adopt the tool in the future, either for other classes or for personal use. Furthermore, Google is openly surveying and selling data collected from their tools—a practice heavily critiqued in academic circles, and Annotation Studio is no longer in development. These are concerns that should be considered when adopting any tool for educational purposes. Discussions of who has access to student data and how these platform-providers will use this data cannot be overlooked. As we increasingly require digital tools in the classroom, it is important to inform our students about the privacy issues at stake in their mandatory participation and to think through the intentions of a corporation before adopting their products.

Additionally, failures of technology inevitably foil even the best laid plans. In many cases implementing open educational resources means that we are eschewing the convenience of single sign-on university provided tools. So, sometimes students will forget their credentials. Or institutional email providers might block confirmation emails. And a few times my courses have overloaded the hypothes.is servers or tripped their spam blockers since our computer labs all run on the same IP address. However, I have never waited more than 10 minutes for a response—via email or tweet—from the dedicated team at hypothes.is. The response time of the development team is an important factor when choosing digital tools for classroom use. Even so, I cannot predict future complications. What if a nonprofit, open-source company is bought out by a larger corporation with questionable privacy policies? What if a tool loses funding? What if the development team abandons the tool? These possibilities loom ever present in the world of educational technology, but for me, they do not outweigh the benefits of exposing our students to the tools that will shape their engagement with technology.

Facilitating Transfer

In order to encourage the transfer of skills developed through analyzing texts using social annotation to their other coursework, students apply what they have learned when creating their final multimodal projects. Inspired by an assignment shared by Kari Kraus, I ask upper-level students engage in "design fiction" by imagining the future of the book. In a multi-stage process students combine their knowledge of the reading process gleaned from reading assigned texts with their own personal experience as consumers of content. Because they have learned the value of close read-ing, critical engagement with texts, and social annotation as a pathway to peer learning, these skills tend to be fore fronted in their final creations.

The first step always consists of a brainstorming session in which stu-dents are unleashed to imagine the future without limitations. Perhaps the most effective approach I have tried in my courses so far was led by a faculty member in the Stevenson School of Design, Inna Alesina. Alesina asked students to identify a problem with the way we currently consume, access, and store information, and devise solutions for a specific audience. They created an x/y axis to identify the needs of an audience, and then prototyped their solution using a variety of materials such as cardboard boxes, bubble wrap, egg crates, etc. This hands-on approach fostered incredible creativity and ingenuity in the students.

Next, students develop these products into full proposals directed at investors, which include an environmental scan, implementation plan, and marketing materials. For example, sophomore Ryan Roche envisioned an interactive bookmark that would allow the functionality of digital anno-tation tools to be applied to physical books. Users could capture words to look up, references to research, or quotes to save instantly without mov-ing from their book to a computer. Not only does this appeal to biblio-philes reticent to give up their physical copies, it also discourages the kind of multitasking that interferes with reading comprehension by relegating it to another space and time. In another example, a student designed an annotation tool that responds to eye movement in order to meet the needs of disabled users. Inspired by his aunt who suffers from ALS, junior Marcus Tucker conceived of a project that builds upon already available eye-tracking technology and online annotation tools, but combines these resources to address a population with a dearth of communication plat-forms. These are only two examples from dozens I simply do not have the space to showcase here. But I believe the evidence is clear. Each of the projects was supported by extensive research—incorporated in many forms—in these proposals, along with genuine passion and excitement that the students convey in their oral presentations.

Throughout this process students shift from being passive consumers to critical makers. They not only consider what a text says, but they also think about the role of the text in our society. Connecting online social annotation tools to the annotations being preserved in print editions by the Book Traces projects gives students a context for their work as well as a variety of models. Students see that historically annotations come in the form of pictures, questions, comments, and intertextual notes from research, and transferred those examples into their own marginalia. Students not only based their annotations on the marginalia they found in pre-1923 century texts, they also used Book Traces as inspiration for their final design fiction projects. Many students cited the research on Book Traces, as well as the articles on digital reading, as justification for the need for their inventions. My hope is that these students continue to use these digital literacy practices when tackling reading projects in other courses. Ideally, a longitudinal study examining the annotation habits of students over four years of coursework could determine this likelihood. In the meantime, offering faculty workshops on social annotation skills and sharing best practices in publications can proliferate the use of these tools across the curriculum.

Works Cited

Bush, Vannevar. "As We May Think." *The Atlantic*, July 1945, www.theatlantic. com/magazine/archive/1945/07/as-we-may-think/303881/. Accessed 9 Oct. 2017.

Carr, Nicholas. "Is Google Making Us Stupid?" *The Atlantic*, Aug. 2008, www. theatlantic.com/magazine/archive/2008/07/is-google-making-us-stupid/ 306868/. Accessed 9 Oct. 2017.

Davidson, Cathy N. "Collaboration by Difference, Yet Again." *HASTAC*, 23 Nov. 2008, www.hastac.org/blogs/cathy-davidson/2008/11/23/collaboration-difference-yet-again. Accessed 9 Oct. 2017.

———. *Now You See It: How Technology and Brain Science Will Transform Schools and Business for the 21st Century*. Reprint ed., New York, NY/Toronto/London/Dublin/Camberwell/New Delhi/Auckland/Johannesburg, Penguin Books, 2012. Print.

Dawson, Ella. "How News Genius Silences Writers." *My Business Is Generally Pleasurable*, N.p., 25 Mar. 2016. Web. 25 May 2017, https://ellacydawson. wordpress.com/2016/03/25/how-news-genius-silences-writers/.

Drucker, Johanna. "Humanistic Theory and Digital Scholarship." *Debates in the Digital Humanities*, edited by Matthew K. Gold, N.p., 2012. Web. 14 Sep. 2017.

Engelbart, Douglas C. "Augmenting Human Intellect: A Conceptual Framework." *SRI Summary Report AFOSR-3223*, Oct. 1962, www.dougengelbart. org/pubs/augment-3906.html. Accessed 9 Oct. 2017.

Gao, Fei, "Case Study of Using a Social Annotation Tool to Support Collaboratively Learning." *Visual Communication and Technology Education Faculty Publications*. Paper 21, 2013, http://scholarworks.bgsu.edu/vcte_pub/21. Accessed Feb. 2018.

Johnson, T.E., T.N. Archibald, and G. Tenenbaum. "Individual and Team Annotation Effects on Students' Reading Comprehension, Critical Thinking, and Meta: Cognitive Skills." *Computers in Human Behavior*, vol. 26, 2010, pp. 1496–1507.

Jones, Jason B. "There Are No New Directions in Annotations." *Web Writing*, 15 Aug. 2014, http://epress.trincoll.edu/webwriting/chapter/jones/. Accessed Nov. 2017.

La Farge, Paul. "The Deep Space of Digital Reading." *Nautilus*, 7 Jan. 2016. http://nautil.us/issue/32/space/the-deep-space-of-digital-reading. Accessed 9 Oct. 2017.

Logan, William. "Mrs. Custer's Tennyson." *The New Criterion*, Apr. 2017, www.newcriterion.com/issues/2017/4/mrs-custers-tennyson. Accessed Nov. 2017.

Paradis, Jim, Kurt Fendt, Wyn Kelley, Jamie Folsom, Julia Pankow, Elyse Graham, and Lakshmi Subbaraj. "Whitepaper: 'Annotation Studio: Bringing a Time-Honored Learning Practice into the Digital Age'." *MIT Comparative Media Studies/Writing*, 27 July 2013, http://cmsw.mit.edu/annotation-studio-whitepaper/. Accessed 9 Oct. 2017.

Reid, A.J. "A Case Study in Social Annotation of Digital Text." *Journal of Applied Learning Technology*, vol. 4, no. 2, 2014, pp. 15–25.

Schacht, Paul. "Annotation." *Digital Pedagogy in the Humanities, MLA Commons*, 2017, https://digitalpedagogy.mla.hcommons.org/keywords/annotation/. Accessed 9 Oct. 2017.

Su, A.Y.S., S.J.H. Yang, W.-Y. Hwang, and J. Zhang. "A Web 2.0-Based Collaborative Annotation System for Enhancing Knowledge Sharing in Collaborative Learning Environments." *Computers and Education*, vol. 55, no. 2, 2010, pp. 752–66.

van der Pol, Jakko., W. Admirall, and P.R.J. Simons. "The Affordance of Anchored Discussion for the Collaborative Process of Academic Texts." *Computer-Supported Collaborative Learning*, 2006, pp. 339–57.

6 Teaching Writing and Reading in Digital Spaces Through the Rhetoric of Social Commentary

Suzanne Cope

Introduction

"What do you read on a regular basis?" I asked my first-year writing class on the first day. They looked at me blankly, many clutching their cell phones like a lifeline—I would introduce my policy on technology in the classroom later in the class period. When no one raised their hand, I smiled to let them know the next question wasn't a trick.

"OK, how many of you didn't look at your phone or computer yet today?" Their class had started a few minutes after noon. One student raised her hand.

I raised my eyebrows and she explained, "I woke up right before this class."

They all laughed. The ice was broken, and I initiated a conversation about what they read, write, and otherwise compose on social media and in individual messages to their friends. They do read. However, for many of them, this reading is confined to bite-sized memes, digital-only articles, multimedia narratives, or tweets via social or "new" media. And as I introduced the concept of "social commentary"—which we collectively defined as any work that uses a rhetorical approach to bring awareness to, comment on, or critique any issue in society across genres as diverse as music, visual art, journalism, creative work, and more—they realized that much of what they were both consuming and authoring was just that. It was this connection between what media they do consume and the critical thinking, analysis, and writing outcomes of the course, that had inspired my approach to this class.

Thus, I organized my first-year writing course around the exploration of works of social commentary connected to various social movements over the last century, titled, "From Billie Holiday to Beyoncé: The Rhetoric of Social Commentary." While I have been teaching a similar course for more than five years, it was only in the previous few semesters that I added my own outcomes that focus on students creating and engaging in discourse on social commentary via digital spaces. I now require that students create a public digital home for their research and group classroom facilitation, which had already taken on a multimedia and digital storytelling aspect, including asking them to create original works that actively engage with a public audience, in addition to analysis and research-related outcomes that are endemic to the course and discipline. They are also required to engage with a class Twitter and Instagram page and create an original work of social commentary alongside a plan considering how this work would engage an intended audience in discourse on current social issues, with a focus on digital means. My intention here is to apply and practice rhetorical analysis on works of social commentary over the past century, through the lens of authorial craft and meaning-making. This happens alongside students analyzing the means (i.e., performative, technological) of communication of these works and how the craft, rhetoric, and technology have evolved in that time. Yet in addition to greater facility, understanding, and skills of analysis, my goal was also to give students the tools, confidence, support, and space to see themselves as authors, creators of knowledge, and agents of change, in part by giving them opportunities to see models of authors and means of communication that they use, recognize, and can relate to.

This chapter will discuss the conversation around engagement with publically facing digital sources for analyzing and creating social commentary, alongside the broader theoretical context for this pedagogy, the course's learning goals, the process, and end with a final analysis and recommendation moving forward. I will also include a brief case study for how I integrated these ideas in my first-year writing class and a final analysis and recommendation for moving forward.

Conversations

My particular interest is in the conversation about teaching first-year composition courses in digital spaces that advocate engagement in issues of social justice. My approach for this course, which has continued to evolve, was certainly was inspired by the understanding that if I were going to ask my students to engage in the analysis of social commentary, I needed to teach, model, and provide a framework for identification and assessment of the work being created today, in various media, while giving them the tools and agency to see themselves as part of the same conversations themselves. And I wanted to emphasize that much of the reading, writing, and interacting that they were already engaged in can be seen as social commentary.

I follow James Berlin's notion that that writing and other forms of rhetoric are "a political act involving a dialectical interaction engaging the material, the social, and the individual writer, with language as the agency of mediation" (488). Thus, all that my students read and write can all be viewed through a social-epistemic lens—or rather one that requires discourse in order for it to exist. Having students recognize that what they are already doing *is* engaging in social commentary, and providing them with the tools to assess and craft their own work, and assess the work of others, creates agency and supports feelings of competencies in a population who believes, because they are often told as much within certain institutions, that they "don't read" or "can't write." That is far from the truth—they are constantly reading, consuming, assessing, and composing—and on topics in which they are politically and/or socially aware—but using digital spaces and tools that are not often sanctioned in the academic spaces in which they reside. This perspective also implies that students-as-composers are already creating and engaged in the rhetoric that we identify and study within the composition classroom, and in fact are collaborators and authors of the larger discourse.

I believe that by asking students to only engage in traditional textual forms that they may rarely encounter, and to write to a similar limited and hypothetical audience in a similar format, we are limiting their view on how they might utilize their knowledge and agency as co-creators of modern rhetoric. Without this broader understanding of acceptable rhetorical spaces as well, they lose perspective on how relevant this discourse and these forms of communication may be in their lives as well as their ability to have a voice within these spaces pushing for positive social change that so direly need the engagement of the next generation of thinkers. For, as Kristin Prins says in "Composing (Media) = Composing (Embodiment)" her goal for students—and one that I share—is for them "to understand themselves and their writing as working in complexes of social, historical, and material conditions that all people are embedded in—and that they can work to change" (146). Thus, the integration of digital spaces, and in particular social media and the use of democratically accessible sites like free website-making or group wiki tools to organize and present scholarship and ideas—is aligned with both a social justice mission and the manner in which students are most apt to engage in and utilize the skills that they are honing in their first-year composition courses.

Yet while this issue of writing in "new" technological spaces seems like an issue we have only had to address since the "digital age" emerged, as the *English Journal* article "Same As It Ever Was: Enacting the Promise of Teaching, Writing, and New Media" discussed in 2012, instructors in this discipline been having these discussions for the past century: whether and how to integrate the newest technology into the writing classroom. Former writing scholars have asked: Will it still be "writing" if the essay is spoken, or "submitted on tape" or "celluloid"? The answer, the authors have found from those participating in this century-long discourse, has always been "yes." We have a charge to "embrace the playground of words and texts and ideas and the tools available to create and share them as our domain as language artists. . . . To build learning experiences that don't always do according to plan, but . . . striv[e] for innovation. . . . Embrace the technologies that our students use [and]. . . . Invite students to collaborate using technology that will be helpful in their lives." (73). And, the existence and sociopolitical implications of "writing" beyond printed text has been discussed as technology has continued to advance over the past century and will, inevitably continue to be in conversation, with scholars including Janelle Adsit, Adam Koehler, Katherine Haake, and Jeff Rice, among others. Thus, I argue, we must expand our thinking of what a first-year writing class engages in, analyzes, and, yes, even creates.

One way to move forward, as generations of writing instructors and scholars have done in the past, is to accept and recognize these new technologies as media in which to compose, and that this media comes with its own understanding of rhetorical approaches that may feel, for some, uncomfortably different than what has been typically employed in the composition classroom. This is particularly important to consider as move toward multimodal composition and analysis, and focus on the rhetorical choices the author made to create meaning. This "craft" approach to teaching composition is defined by scholar Kristin Prins as "a particular set of actions and relationships between people and between people and things," which causes, in her words, the value of writing to shift from "being located in a writer's ability to reproduce ideal discourses to the roles textual production plays in shaping writers and the uses a made object such as writing has in social circulation" (145). In other words, we must not only allow but encourage students to author in a voice that is appropriate for the medium and the audience with which they are engaging, rather than promote and expect their universal use of the, admittedly biased, rhetoric of the academy. And by doing so, we will be further democratize our classroom spaces, allowing for greater access to the role of authorship for our students, while also supporting their efforts taking part in public discourse where it is taking place and with whom the constituents are.

One way to do this, I argue, is to approach the analysis of rhetoric, and in my classroom there is a focus on the rhetoric of social commentary, from the craft perspective. In previous scholarship published in *Writing & Pedagogy*, I shared my findings from a study where I approached literary analysis "from the inside out," as I explained it, basically teaching literature in a non-major course through craft analysis (Cope). The question I asked of the students was how the author created meaning using various elements of craft. Students then practiced and honed using the same elements of craft in their own creative works, experientially trying out the same tools that they analyzed "real" writers using. Their reported learning included not only a greater understanding of literary devices, but also greater confidence in writing, more creative thinking, and even more empathy. This study inspired me to integrate a similar approach to teaching in my Composition course, where students analyze the rhetoric of social commentary throughout the past century from the reader's perspective, and then experientially utilize the same tools to create works in various modalities that engage in similar conversations—furthering the exploration of the rhetoric of social commentary from the inside out.

I have come to assert that within the context of writing, experiential learning occurs when we support students in writing within a specific style or genre and explicitly for a specific audience and purpose. Or, as defined by Jennings and Wargnier in the article "Experiential Learning—A Way to Develop Agile Minds in the Knowledge Economy?": "Learning combines four basic elements: the experiences we have, the opportunity to practise [sic] and embed those experiences in our long-term memory, the conversations and interaction we have with others, and reflection" (para 3). Thus, one learns best not just by writing into a void, but through discourse and reflection upon these learning experiences. The experiential interaction can occur via feedback from classmates or instructor, but I believe—as do experiential learning and adult learning scholars—that learning truly becomes experiential when the writing takes the form of the way students might actually interact in discourse beyond the physical and digital walls of the classroom. And this, increasingly, is in the form of social media and digital "new media" spaces.

Thus, as I was exploring how to best bring experiential learning into my composition classroom, while I viewed my integration of a high-stakes creative writing assignment in my previous study as experiential learning—for the students were using the tools we discussed to create a work for an audience of their peers—I have continued to expand the audience much more broadly. By integrating digital media—modalities that include written, visual, and audio compositions, the creation, consumption, and public engagement of which are familiar to almost every student—as acceptable approaches to compose and converse, students are exploring the idea of public discourse in deeper ways. Due to the nature of collaborative digital spaces and social media, they are able to compose, revise, interact, and reflect in real time, allowing learning to be immediate. This of-the-moment discourse, empowered in 280 characters at a time via Twitter, and expanded upon via the students' digital research projects, asks the students to compose experientially—for an actual and not imaginary or hypothetical audience, while also receiving potential feedback that cannot be necessarily anticipated. And while they are allowed to practice this experiential discourse under the guise of our class Twitter page and within the comfort of a group, the final project asks them to take ownership of their individual works or social commentary and make an effort to connect to an identified audience, preferably as themselves or at least as a version of themselves created as an avatar.

Further, while digital humanities and digital writing are increasingly an endemic part of the curriculum for many humanities courses, my course is among the first for many of my students to forefront them as public authors and ask them to engage in discourse with others outside of the classroom, using "modes of meaning making that extend beyond the textual, beyond the print technologies, and beyond a single English" (Fleckenstein 251) including multi and diverse media endemic to these native digital formats. Thus, the simple act of composing a tweet, when considered as thoughtful rhetoric, may look and sound like tweets that "go viral"—but are composed, interacted with, revised, and reflected upon in the same manner that we might approach an analytic essay or research project.

Finally, allowing, and in fact encouraging writing in commonly used digital applications including social media posts like Twitter, Instagram, Tumblr, and blogging democratizes knowledge, decentralized from the "ivory tower" and legitimizing the composition that is happening in these younger, more diverse, and more accessible spaces. One need not have a degree, a review of "experts" who may or may not be one's peers, nor familiarity with dense scholarly vocabulary to contribute to the current discourse. One can use their lived experience, unique perspective, or critical reasoning to add new, and often overshadowed voices to the discourse. This is especially important when teaching writing as a means of social commentary or change where inclusivity is even more necessary. And as we strive to give students agency in their voices and ideas, we must also embrace their identity as writers perhaps outside of the accepted definition of "scholarly" and using language or, increasingly, a symbol system endemic to the technology or spaces in which they are composing. As Composition and New Media scholar Kristie Fleckenstein asserts, integrating new media and writing for or about social change "requires that we teach with technologies in ways that increase our students' options for identity making and social justice by increasing their engagement with (rather than disengagement from) material realities" (241). In other words, we must encourage new media writing, not discourage nor merely accept it, as this is where many of the pertinent conversations on these issues are taking place—as engaging in the important discourse of the day is a goal shared among analog and digitally minded compositionists alike.

Mini Case Study

In its revised version my first-year writing course themed "From Billie Holiday to Beyoncé: The Rhetoric of Social Commentary" is structured to scaffold thinking about individual bias to looking outward to analyze works of social commentary from the last 80 years through both a historic and modern lens, to the engagement with modern issues of social justice through both critical analysis and the creation and experiential employment of an original work of social commentary.

The first major writing assignment is the "narrative bias paper," the goal of which is to move students from thinking about their own authorial perspectives and "lenses" through which they see the world to help them become strong critical thinkers about the multimodal works in the world around them. In this paper they are asked to tell a story of how they came to identify their own bias on any topic and reflected on how they came to see this topic—and their larger understanding of the world—in a new light. This is useful both in teaching narrative conventions as well as exploring the idea of bias—within ourselves, and in assessing the work and motivations of others, which is an idea we continue to come back to in our research and discussions.

I next introduce concepts of rhetorical analysis and model the analysis of multimodal works of social commentary, providing them with the language and skills to move toward doing the same on their own. Through scaffolded in-class activities that are intended to build skills and confidence through sequenced lower stakes assignments we move toward an individual paper that analyzes a work of social commentary of their choice with a focus on how the decisions the artist or author made helped create meaning. We identify both the perspective of the author as well as that of the viewer/ reader, as well as discuss how a work might connect with audiences of its time period versus today. The use of digital humanities resources is particularly valuable here as we can experience works from previous time periods, get a sense of the historical and social contexts of previous time through multimedia, and otherwise experience a work together that we can use as a classroom exercise for modeling and practicing assessment.

The recently available, and increasing number, of digital resources, as diverse as growing online art and media archives at universities to publically populated sites like YouTube that include both historic and modern videos, make our analysis richer and help students better understand the context of the rhetoric of the day. From videos of Billie Holiday singing "Strange Fruit" to digital copies of the 1930s magazine *The New Masses*, to new online libraries of propaganda artwork and print and digital zines, we learn from an ever-evolving treasure trove of digital resources from our first class periods. This also helps us better assess the work from the perspective of the period in which it was originally created. For example, we see images of the way in which *The New Masses* magazine was distributed and read Meridel Le Sueur's essay on images from the actual magazine, alongside other works and ads that may not still be read in classrooms but provide a broader context otherwise inaccessible if not read in its original format (Le Sueur 16). This practice is supporting the work of a group project that will later be shared with the class through student-led presentations and discussion.

As we read or watch these initial works, I then modeled the scope of each group's facilitation with my own discussion of these two works of social commentary, including pertinent historical context, activities that facilitated analysis of the rhetorical decisions made by the artists, and a discussion around chosen medium and intended audience. My goal was to assess each work within both its original context during the 1930s—Le Sueur's essay published in a left-leaning worker's rights magazine with national readership, and "Strange Fruit," which was initially a poem printed in a teacher's union publication and then later popularized when sung by one of the preeminent jazz vocalists of the day—as well as through our modern perspective on how these works resonate with individuals today. We practice textual analysis of the lyrics or essay, for example, alongside the performative and aural analysis of the song. This is also an opportunity to put today's ever present multimedia texts into context, as we assess multimodal rhetorics as working side by side, looking at them separately and in harmony, and showing how they, in fact, can elevate and support each other. We further discuss the intended audience of each work, why artistic choices were made during each time period, and the impact of the various works on a modern listener. Is it possible to include the texts in an appendix?

I then put the students into four groups who are responsible for creating an online, resource that is published on the internet that discusses works of social commentary from a specified period (of approximately 15 years), develops a specific argument drawn from their research, and then using their research and collaborative resource to teach the class the pertinent background information and lead them in a critical discussion or activity on what they are arguing. The work they create must be collaborative, nonlinear (i.e., interactive—not a static slide show), and public. And they are required to use Twitter and other social media to engage a broader public audience in similar ways through a class account. With these skills modeled for them as they move toward the group research and class facilitation project, they then practice research, critical analysis, and public writing through the creation of a public facing nonlinear resource, which introduces the classmates and any general public member who might encounter this, a multimodal exploration and analysis of social issues during their assigned time periods, that might extend from racial justice issues to the role of technology in society. While we discuss that most of our implicit bias keeps us focused on the United States, students are more than welcome and encouraged to bring international perspective and issues. The goal among the students in each group is to see how these conversations engage with each other, and how each time period's conversations engage with the decades before and after them as well. Students are given the freedom to choose their own technology with which to collect and share their work, and have used free website making technologies and collaborative wiki programs.

The student groups are in charge of leading two class periods where they share their information and engage the class in discussion questions or other activities. The final two assignments ask students to then engage their practiced research an analytic skills for an individual argumentative research project on any issue related to social commentary, that can use the student-made resources as a guide and must include an analysis of the modern discourse on their chosen topic, and then to create a unique work of social commentary and devise a plan for sharing their work with others already in discourse with that topic. The individual research assignment helps them further hone their research and writing skills, although they are given the option to create a multimodal project with certain required written and evidentiary aspects. Through the group and individual work, students are asked to continually reflect upon their learning, which keeps assessment of individual bias forefront in their mind and is also shown to deepen learning and critical thinking skills.

Throughout the class the students are asked, at various times, to use Twitter to comment about the class or compose tweets that engage in public discourse around their research and discussion topics. I also created a class Instagram page to explore the sharing of images and ideas, as well as connect with students about pertinent class information via a communication medium they most often use. What I have found, as I move the course more public facing as technology and my own reflective teaching evolve, is that the quality of student work increases the more broad the audience is, and that there is, unsurprisingly, stronger discourse with these works the more I require that the students look to an audience beyond the physical or digital borders of our classroom.

This practice of engaging in public discourse via social media and public-facing websites is particularly important as we move toward the final assignment, where students are tasked with creating an original work of social commentary and a plan for connecting with the pertinent audience. Through this cumulative activity they are given agency to utilize the same tools they have been seeing other authors of works use, and to various effects, analyzing their effectiveness. This, in essence, is experiential learning as they use the tools they have been discussing others use, rather than merely writing about something, and they themselves create an end product with meaning. However, the culminating project is meant as the ultimate experiential assignment, meant to create a feeling of authorship and agency after a semester of collaborative and analytical work. Here they can employ whatever creative multimodal craft approaches they feel most comfortable with—not just to compose a work of social commentary, but to engage in modern discourse with this. This final project, as well as the public-facing social media and new media works from tweets to webpages that the students are creating from the start of the semester, reinforce analytic and critical thinking skills necessary for the modes in which they are already composing outside of class. Through our scaffolded activities and assignments, students practice analytic assessment of works across time periods and contexts, which, I believe, gives them the skills to better assess and create modern works while acknowledging their bias. Because they have the language, confidence, and agency, learned from in-class activities and assignments, when tasked to create an original work at the end of class and present a plan to share it with an intended audience, they are even better equipped to thoughtfully join—or start—a relevant conversation about social justice issues beyond our classroom borders—or strengthen the work they are already doing on their own.

Conclusion

This approach to teaching first-year writing was based upon two premises: the first is the need to integrate digital sources and modes of authorship into the classroom to support student reading and composing in relevant formats and for real-life and relevant audiences; and the second is that it is my charge to understand that writing is, by definition, a political act and that I should support my students in exploring their critical thinking and authorship in ways that support social justice for all. The way that I have best found to do this is to use a variety of digital sources to practice the analysis of works of social commentary—many of which are preserved for modern audiences thanks to technological advances. We practice analysis of historic works, with students leading discussions after my initial modeling, creating public-facing resources that explore nearly a century of works of social commentary, connecting the past to the present via social media to the modern discourse. This provides a foundation for the students in the creation of their own work of social commentary and their plan for taking part in the modern discourse with that work.

Further, what this project does, by requiring a posted, public (or at least broadly accessible) nonlinear publication, is help students see themselves as knowledge creators—as a contributor to the digital humanities, and not simply a consumer. They have agency from the reframing of publication and knowledge as work that may look like a version of the media they most consume, and begin to embrace the identity of author as the creator of a work in their own voice and in a medium in which they are fluent. And this is, in fact, the "utopian" goal of the digital humanities: "to at least posit, if not fully enable, a future in which participation is possible for everyone, everywhere, anytime" (Burdick 94). I would add to this, and say that participation is not just possible, but agency is modeled and space is created—where there is not just the digital platform and system that allows for this space, but that the authors themselves feel as if their knowledge is valued, and part of the larger conversation.

As I continue to refine this approach, what I have found is that the more outward facing the audience, the stronger works the students create. And it is through digital media that students can primarily reach this audience. But yet integrating this kind of composition requires a flexibility in thought for traditional composition assignments and "voice." We must acknowledge that digital composition is often multi-model—and both teach and allow this kind of work. And we must also think beyond the academic voice or tone, allowing students to engage in discourse via these new mediums in a voice that is both endemic to the medium and authentic to them. This further democratizes authorship, decentralizing knowledge from traditionally print sources—which are often traditionally non-diverse in age, background, education level, and experience. This should be our charge as modern instructors of first-year writing—and it will also be our reward.

Works Cited

Berlin, James. "Rhetoric and Ideology in the Writing Class." *College English*, vol. 50, no. 5, 1988, p. 477. *Education Database; ProQuest Central Essentials; Research Library; Social Science Premium Collection*, http://jerome.stjohns.edu:81/login?url=https://search-proquest-com.jerome.stjohns.edu/docview/236914003?accountid=14068.

Burdick, Anne, et al. *Digital Humanities*, MIT Press, 2012.

Fleckenstein, Kristie S., et al. "A Pedagogy of Rhetorical Looking: Atrocity Images at the Intersection of Vision and Violence." *College English*, vol. 80, no. 1, 2017, pp. 11–34.

Cope, Suzanne. "Outside the Box: Incorporating High Stakes Creative Writing Assignments into Non-Major Literature Courses, a Case Study." *Writing & Pedagogy*, vol. 9, no. 2, 2017, pp. 353–67.

Hicks, Troy, et al. "Same as It Ever Was: Enacting the Promise of Teaching, Writing, and New Media." *English Journal, High School Edition; Urbana*, vol. 101, no. 3, Jan. 2012, pp. 68–74, https://search.proquest.com/docview/1314752833/abstract/F3E752A9AB764718PQ/1.

Jennings, Charles, and Jé Wargnier. "Experiential Learning: A Way to Develop Agile Minds in the Knowledge Economy?" *Development and Learning in Organizations*, vol. 24, no. 3, 2010, pp. 14–16. *ABI/INFORM Collection*, http://jerome.stjohns.edu:81/login?url=https://search-proquest-com.jerome.stjohns.edu/docview/218816817?accountid=14068, http://dx.doi.org.jerome.stjohns.edu:81/10.1108/14777281011037245.

Le Sueur, Meridel. "I Was Marching." *New Masses*, 19 Sep. 1934, pp. 16–18, www.unz.org/Pub/NewMasses-1934sep18-00016.

Prins, Kristin. "Crafting New Approaches to Composition." *Composing(Media) = Composing(Embodiment): Bodies, Technologies, Writing, the Teaching of Writing*, Utah State University Press, 2012.

7 Annotating with Google Docs

Bridging Collaborative Reading and Writing in the Composition Classroom

Janine Morris

Classroom

This chapter explores what happens when students annotate collaboratively using Google Drive to bridge reading-writing connections in the first-year composition classroom. As students read together in a number of ways throughout a semester, I am constantly asking them to make connections between what they read, the moves the sample writers make, and their own writing. In this chapter, I argue that using Google Docs for collaborative reading and annotating can help students (a) make reading-writing connections visible while modeling effective strategies; (b) integrate annotation into multiple moments of reading and writing, thus highlighting its usefulness for working through a text; and (c) decentralize my authority over the classroom, making collaboration and student voices central to the course.

Student Reading-Writing Problems

To help students become more effective readers, and thus stronger writers, students can benefit from strategies to enhance reading/writing interconnections. As a way of highlighting the connections between reading and writing, I argue that collaborative annotations can help students become more successful at both tasks. When reading processes are made visible to students through collaborative annotations, they not only start to see different ways of interpreting and responding to a text, but they can also gain awareness of the different moves writers make in their writing. In Chris Anson's review of *Write to Read*,[1] he emphasizes the importance of a reciprocal relationship between reading and writing in classrooms where the two practices are intertwined—not one where reading comes first and then writing comes after. In these classes, Anson provides students with instructions for what they should pay attention to as they read and then offers creative and interactive prompts that push them to move beyond merely summarizing a text and require writing throughout the process.

Students in my classes, like Anson's, use writing alongside different reading strategies (summarizing, questioning, rethinking assumptions) that necessitate their engagement with what they read in order to complete the task. Because the goal of writing-to-read is to think more fully about the text as students make meaning of it, these assignments are low-stakes and call for new ways of interacting with texts. By using these low-stakes activities throughout a semester, students have multiple opportunities to practice reading and writing connections. As Anson argues, low-stakes assignments do not "weaken the intellectual effort students must put in to respond to it" (31), but rather encourage more engagement than would a more formal, stylized task.

To successfully complete such write-to-read activities, readers must employ active reading strategies like annotation—an activity that has long been seen as a best practice for reading within composition scholarship. As Alice Horning explains, "Because [reading] is an active process, reading assignments need to be set up so that students must do the reading and engage with the material in some overt way" (7). Annotation is one such "overt way" that students can talk back to what they read. However, like other reading practices, annotation is something that should be modeled and made visible to students. According to Mariolina Salvatori and Patricia Donahue, "when carefully guided rather than left to chance, annotation can work as a record of reading and a site of reflexivity" (82). Annotation illustrates for a reader what they uncover within a text and can be used to prompt reflection as a bridge to writing. Along with making their own reading practices visible, seeing others' annotations can help students learn critical reading conventions and display the socially situated nature of academic writing As Horning explains, "[g]etting students to read mindfully is not easy, but it can be facilitated by making the invisible process of meaning-making more visible to students, so they can 'see' and reflect on those processes" (5). Giving students a better understanding of our expectations and what different reading practices look like, coupled with student reflection and application, can help to demystify academic expectations. Students can become more aware of what works best for them in different situations and can feel that they are equipped with a number of reading tools to employ in various contexts. As one potential strategy, I further detail the advantages of collaborative group annotations. When annotations are shared, students who are unfamiliar with annotation as a practice might learn new strategies from instructors or other students to apply to future readings. Students could then reflect on the differences between their reading processes and those of their classmates and be encouraged to try out new strategies going forward.

As is argued throughout this collection, one of the biggest challenges students face as readers and writers is that these activities are often presumed to be done alone, and students lack the vocabulary to precisely name reading/writing challenges they might be facing. As has always been, reading and writing are not solitary activities, despite the dominant cultural narratives that make them appear that way (Cornis-Pope and Woodlief; Gere). Even without explicit connection to reading/writing in the composition classroom, these activities are often socially situated. Students, when assigned readings to complete on their own, are asked to come to class prepared to discuss their responses. Students are asked to engage in scholarly conversations as they write and revise texts. Peer review, collaboration, and discussion are all means that instructors bridge reading and writing and socialize these processes in the writing classroom, even if the connection between these activities is left implicit. As students enter the workforce, they will be further expected to collaborate with others as reading/writing happens in response to situations within broader professional communities (see Ede and Lunsford, for example).

Collaborative reading and writing practices, then, can begin to create a bridge for students between what they do in their classes and later professional practices. The composition classroom is a place where collaborative relationships can be especially fruitful (Bruffee). As Donna Evans and Ben J. Bunting write, "[i]n an academic regime where single-author writing is often prized over comparatively ambiguous group work, FYC is one of the few classes that lends itself by default to the cooperative/collaborative ethos of group writing" (111). The benefits of collaborative learning lead students to "question the balance of power in the classroom, to put more stock in feedback given by their peers and not defer only to the 'sage-on-the-stage'" (112). Students in collaborative situations can gain more authority over their work and become more engaged in the process of learning. Thus, bringing collaboration together with reading and writing can help reinforce the scholarly practices we want students to utilize in our classes and beyond.

Google as a Collaborative Annotation Platform

In the last few years, smartphone and mobile technology use has greatly increased in the larger US population (Pew Research Center). In years to come, it's foreseeable that the number of smartphone users will increase even more as older versions of cell phones (and larger pieces of technology, like stationary desktop PCs) get phased out. As Casey R. McArdle writes, "it is important to note that as classrooms begin to move into the Post-PC era, mobile technologies are affording students the chance to compose, collaborate, and redefine the spaces of the writing classroom" (117–18). Per McArdle, ease of access to technology and increased mobility are two reasons for instructors to reimagine the traditional space of the writing classroom. As mobile technologies continue improving, and students use their technologies in higher education settings, compositionists will need to pay more attention to the role they play in student writing (Lutkewitte).

The Google suite is just one of many applications that instructors and students can use for reading and writing on mobile devices and in digital spaces. One of the advantages of using Google as a collaborative reading and writing platform is its compatibility with both stationary computers and smartphones, as well as ability to be integrated on the move. Furthermore, since Google Drive is accessible via the cloud, students are able to "access all of their writing and research for every assignment at all times" (McArdle 119). Because the Google platform is free and easily downloaded onto one's smartphone, users aren't necessarily required to read, write, and comment on documents from a computer, or utilize software tied to a particular device.

Along with Google Drive's interactivity and mobility, technological advances in general have made reading and writing on digital devices easier to accomplish on a large scale. This engagement helps facilitate what we are able to do with texts both as solitary readers/composers and as collaborators. As a singular digital reader, I can easily open a PDF, highlight, comment, and mark it up either with a mouse and keyboard or stylus. Using a program like Adobe Acrobat Reader, I can see my comments appear alongside the text and use a number of tools to annotate (like pens, sticky notes, or strike-through, underlines for editing). Besides Adobe Acrobat, there are multiple apps available that can facilitate annotating PDFs. Using internet plug-ins like Genius or Hypothesis,[2] students can annotate websites in a similar fashion to how they would mark up a PDF. Both of these plug-ins link to a sidebar on the page that can minimize while not in use. Furthermore, these web-based digital annotation plug-ins can easily lead to collaborative social commentary as readers share their annotations with others or annotate the same web page. The ability to annotate and interact with webtexts more seamlessly can promote student engagement with what they are reading and provide them with tools that will make interacting with materials online happen more easily.

One of the benefits of using digital technologies for reading and writing is that they can allow these practices to become public and collaborative. In *Mobile Technologies in the Writing Classroom*, Claire Lutkewitte explains how her students "enjoyed working with their mobile devices and found that in doing so, they were more engaged in the class" (vii). The engagement Lutkewitte's students experienced when she integrated mobile devices as part of her writing courses was in part due to student familiarity with using mobile and digital technologies outside of academic settings. Student familiarity with technologies enhances not only engagement, but also student collaboration within those spaces (Tekobbe, Lazcano-Pry, and Roen). An advantage of the collaborative nature of these platforms is that they can make the reading/writing process visible in ways that relying on print-based solitary reading do not. People can view comments/changes/and see the outcomes of others' engagement with texts.

As I discuss in the sections to follow, the Google Drive applications are one such social space that instructors can use to enhance student reading and writing. Known mainly for its writing capabilities, Google Docs (as I write in 2018) allows writers to compose online or offline; on computers, tablets, or smartphones; and automatically saves changes as you type ("About"). Along with these features, the current iteration of Google Docs allows users to share and collaborate with others; edit documents together in real time; chat and comment with others on the document itself; and keeps a record of edits and changes, allowing you to return to previous versions of a document ("About"). In their exploration of using Google Docs to assign students collaborative group writing assignments, Peter Kittle and Troy Hicks argue that "Google Docs possesses one distinct advantage as a writing tool: students can work on the same document, at the same time, and see the changes manifest themselves almost simultaneously in the text" (529). Students in my class often marvel the first time we write collaboratively on Google Docs as they watch others type at the same time they are. While many scholars have explored Google Drive's potential as a collaborative writing tool (Cotugno; Edwards & Baker; Evans & Bunting; Newsom & Kennedy), what I wish to arguer further in this section is how the collaborative elements of Google Drive can make visible the reading students perform in their first-year writing classes.

There are a number of benefits of having students read and write collaboratively within the Google platform itself. First, Google allows students to complete collaborative work asynchronously. As Tekobbe, Lazcano-Pry, and Roen note, "Unlike physical space that students inhabit together simultaneously, virtual space permits, even encourages, students to collaborate across time and space" (87). Students can read and comment on different kinds of texts anywhere, on their own time. Users can also add extensions like Kami,[3] a PDF, document, and image annotation tool that works within Google Drive. With Kami, users can collaboratively draw, comment, and add video or voice annotations to texts apart from the Google Docs. In addition, as an instructor, it's also helpful for me to be able to check in on student peer review sessions or on student group readings ahead of meeting in class. Being able to read and comment on their own time can allow readers to be more careful with their responses (Tekobbe, Lazcano-Pry, and Roen), though I would argue that the same kind of annotation and feedback modeling needs to be implemented via Google as it does with other classroom reading and writing. Finally, the fact that there is a shared record of these annotations and comments automatically saved to Google (as well as a history function to review past comments/records) might make students more attuned to the kinds of feedback they post.

In almost all the classes I teach, my students use the Google Drive platform in some capacity. In first-year writing, especially, I use Google

Docs in a variety of ways throughout the semester, first for collaborative low-stakes reading and annotating, and then for peer reviewing and revising student drafts. All of these activities involve using shared Google folders that the entire class can access. The record of these Docs can serve as resources for students later in the semester, and students have expressed that they return to the Docs as they work on writing tasks. There are three main ways I use Google Docs in my composition class that I will explore further:

1. To read and annotate texts collaboratively, particularly sample assignments;
2. To develop collaboratively written responses to readings;
3. To read and write as part of the peer review process.

Each of these activities makes reading/writing connections visible while modeling effective strategies, integrates annotation into multiple moments of reading and writing, and decentralizes my authority over the classroom, making collaboration and student voices central to the course.

The first manner of using Google Docs in my class is for students to read and collaboratively annotate sample assignments, often strong student texts from previous iterations of the course. On days when I introduce new assignments, I'll separate students into groups to read the sample text together and assign each group a focal point in their reading—such as analysis, or source use, or transitions. Students are informed that while the sample reading is an effective take on the assignment, there are strengths and limitations to the draft that are important to note. In their discussion of using former student drafts as models, Anson, Mathew Davis, and Domenica Vilhotti address how using sample drafts can help students become more aware of how to appropriately respond to different writing situations. As the authors write, "When students are asked to read and discuss each others' drafts in progress or review and revise their own drafts, they often work in a rhetorical vacuum, not really knowing what makes a successful response and guessing at whatever (often implicit or unexplained) criteria the instructor will use to judge their papers" (35). Providing students sample essays and then giving them different criteria to focus on can help them gather a better understanding of the assignment as well as learn more about the components that I wish for them to include in their own work. Anson, Davis, and Vilhotti provide students with what they term "interestingly problematic" former drafts that they then use to analyze the features individually and then collectively as a group (37). This kind of reading of past student work can "help students articulate and internalize readers' expectations for their assigned writing" (35). This collaborative kind of response is one way instructors have made the writing process increasingly visible for their students and is a useful way to bridge reading and writing. Especially early in an assignment, this kind of modeling of former student work can help demystify the writing prompt and give students a greater understanding of what my expectations as an instructor look like.

Michael Bunn employs a similar strategy of using sample texts to help students gain a greater understanding of assignments in his textbook chapter, "Read Like a Writer," when he asks students to "identify some of the choices the author made so that you can better understand how such choices might arise in your own writing" (72). Likewise, students in my class are asked to read along with the assignment prompt and then apply their understanding of what they read to the writing they will later produce. When I ask student groups to focus on different elements of a sample essay, I am encouraging them to search for rhetorical moves that cause particular reactions—be it ones they wish to emulate, or ones they wish to avoid. This "Says/Does"[4] approach "shifts attention away from content, which is often easier to figure out, and toward how a text or section of a text functions" (Carillo 15). Sure, students can easily read and understand the meaning of a sample text, but looking more closely at the specific moves a writer makes can give them ideas for their own essays. This process also encourages students to see writing as a series of choices a writer makes (and something they have agency over). Along with tracking their own readerly reactions, student groups in my classes are also responsible for teaching one another about their assigned move within the text, further strengthening their understanding of how a text works. For example, group 1 might read to find moments of analysis throughout the essay; group 2 might read to identify use of quotes and sources; and group 3 might read for organization, transitions, or style. Any of these elements can be modified along with the requirements of the assignment. After the groups read and annotate the sample text on Google Docs, we then come back as a class and discuss how the sample text was developed as well as how those specific pieces function for students reading them.

The kind of reading/writing I'm asking students to do on a sample essay can help move students beyond passively consuming the texts they read and instead engage with the text more actively. While students in my classrooms are looking specifically at a former student's work, this assignment could easily apply to analyzing an image using Kami or a website or webtext with Genius or Hypothesis and students could employ a focused says/does approach as they explore how visual or web-based texts function. This method of reading/writing gives students something to look for in the reading and note their reactions in writing while allowing everyone to see all of the responses. Even with online peer review on Google Docs, giving students something to "read for" can help them become more engaged in the reading process and can help them move beyond neutral "good job"-type responses.

The second way my classes use Google Docs collaboratively is to respond to readings and compile best practices to complete assignments.

For example, in a first-year writing class focused on research writing, I assign students articles about research methods and data analysis for homework, such as Dana Lynn Driscoll's open access chapter "Introduction to Primary Research." Driscoll's chapter acts as an overview of primary research and she describes several different methods, along with when and how researchers use them. In class, students are divided into groups focusing on different sections of the reading and are given a prompt on the Google Doc like the following:

> With your group, (a) explain how the research method described in your section works and when a researcher would use that method to collect data; (b) define key or unfamiliar terms; (c) come up with an example that would require you to use that method of data collection; (d) search for another credible source (using CRAAP[5] criteria) that offers more information about your assigned research method.
>
> Then discuss what kind of data collection methods from the chapter would be most useful for your own research questions. Additionally, consider how changing your question change the kinds of research methods you employ?

In groups, the students then answer questions on a Google Doc and report back on their findings to the rest of the class. This kind of activity asks students to return to a reading and think through how that reading applies to broader research contexts, connects with other scholarship, and assists with the research they conduct themselves. Students are working together on the Google Doc in class and then the record of their activity becomes a resource they can use later as they begin researching and writing. Students in this context become more knowledgeable on their specific chapter focus and can offer guidance to other students in the class. While this is a low-stakes example of reading/writing together in class, I believe that such an approach could easily apply to larger or more complex works.

A third way I bring in Google Docs to bridge reading and writing in my classroom focuses on peer response. The kinds of feedback that I ask of students in the peer reviews mirrors the kind of collaborative reading they perform earlier in the semester with the sample texts. What's valuable about using sample texts—or in this case, other students' work—is that, according to Bunn, is that they "emphasize reading as a means to learn about writing, not as a means to better understand a topic, issue, or worldview" ("Motivation" 506). For the writing instructors that Bunn interviews, using texts as samples helps students identify techniques that they can employ in their own writing. I share this same hope for students as they complete peer response—that they will recognize moves in their peers that they can emulate themselves.

In the peer responses sessions, I create a shared Google Folder for students and ask them to upload drafts as Google Docs to the folder. I either place students into peer response groups, or have the entire class provide feedback on drafts for a full-class peer review session. Students are provided guidelines for commenting on the drafts as well as asked to leave the writer with end comments that more fully develop a response to their writing. In these instances, students will pick up on one another's comments, respond, and build off of what each other has said as they provide feedback to the writers. The multiplicity of feedback on a piece of writing "parallels what writers outside of the classroom typically experience and expect," particularly in academic, peer-reviewed forums (Stramsa 154). Kip Strasma focuses on the benefits of "spotlighting" students once a semester in peer review sessions so that they can receive sustained feedback on their work. Even when students are not on the receiving end of comments, students can "benefit by reading drafts of their peers, writing comments to peer authors, and reading all comments by others posted in the class" (155). Like Strasma, I believe that by posting student drafts in a Google Folder for peer review, students have the benefit of getting and seeing multiple comments from their peers in one place. The feedback loop in these instances becomes collaborative and shared, not something between individual writers. I fully agree that the process of reading others' comments and providing feedback can strengthen all students' writing. Further building on the sociality of reading and writing, making student drafts and the response process visible can allow students to act as models for one another's work. Using Google Docs to complete these peer reviews is just as useful for the writer as it is for the reader.

Over the course of the Winter and Fall 2017 semesters, I regularly brought Google Drive and Google applications into my first-year writing classes. For their final project in these classes, I asked students to reflect on significant or memorable experiences from the course as part of a larger reflective essay. Several students from the Fall 2017 first-year composition course wrote about their experiences using Google Docs as part of this reflection. I share several of these reflections to highlight student feedback of our use of Google Drive over the course of the semester. For these students, the collaborative elements of Google Drive stood out as some of the most beneficial components of the activities for their reading/writing. For instance, one student wrote in their reflection that,

> The Google Drive software we used in class was new to me. Google Drive can be used as a source of reading, working together on assignments, and peer revision. We used Google Drive as a source of peer revision for the majority of the class. . . . It was quite confusing at first; I didn't really see a purpose for it until we actually started peer review. During the peer revision we were assigned into groups and within our groups we each got feedback from one another. We used the peer review in ou[r] synthesis essay, precis writing, and much more. With Google drive we were able to learn how to give proper

feedback[.] I liked reading everyone's essays because you got to learn their points of view as a writer. We used Google Drive throughout the whole semester whether if it was for short paragraphs or five paged essays. This benefitted our essays as we got a second point of view.

Although this student experienced a bit of a learning curve, they reflected on the benefits of using Google Drive for peer review and the impact it had on their own writing. Getting multiple perspectives on their draft in one place seemed to be the key takeaway for this student. In addition to receiving feedback from other students, modeling effective feedback was something that several students wrote in their reflections as a significant component of the course. Just as first-year students can struggle with their reading and writing, knowing ways to give proper feedback can be equally challenging. Reading what other students write can become a useful guide for students who are unsure of how to respond to drafts themselves. This same strategy of making responses visible through collaborative annotations could help students see different ways other students respond to assigned texts. Of note is the student's comment that the purpose of using Google Drive wasn't immediately clear to them. This lack of understanding points to the importance of making the purpose of reading and writing activities clear for students (which, as per this student's comment, I could done more clearly early on in the term).

In a different first-year writing class focused specifically on research writing, students reflected on using the different readings and Google Drive peer reviews as models for their own research essays (not just for feedback on student drafts). Reviewing sample literature reviews or methods sections from published scholarship helped students better understand the purpose and conventions of these sections within the context of a larger essay. As one student noted,

> I liked reading through the [sample lit review] document online and having the ability to highlight and comment . . . I just went through read and said what I thought about the essay. Looking at structure, synthesis, and analysis and establishing a research gap all appeared in the lit review and served as a good example for me when writing my own. Usually I do annotations by hand with printed text in this class I didn't look at grammatical or syntactical issues like I do when I'm reading hard text. Instead I focused on the objectives of the lit review.

What's significant about this student's comment is that they started seeing differences between their reading and annotating practices in different situations. When asked to read a sample literature review on the Google Drive, this student paid attention to the rhetorical conventions—"the objectives"—of the literature review. This way of reading was different for the student from what they typically did with "annotations by hand with printed texts." The student could then mirror the moves the sample writer made in their own literature review. Although not many students made explicit reference to these different reading practices in their final reflections, I hope that other students, like this one, took away how different reading tasks call for different reading approaches.

Finally, a second student from the research based first-year composition class made note in their reflection of how they found the collaborative reading for peer review illustrated different models they could employ in their own writing. Instead of relying just on the previous student drafts or published scholarship I asked the class to read, this student started looking towards their peers as models of good writing:

> When people uploaded their complete drafts to Blackboard, I chose to read 3 of my classmates' posts. While reading their draft, I got many ideas of what to include in mine. I noticed that mine was missing details. I would not want the reader to have any questions on the results so I had to think for myself "if I was a random reader, what information or how much information would be enough for me to understand the study and its results?" This activity helped me make my draft better. I could compare my section to the others and see where they differed and where they were similar. If I noticed something that most of the others included that I was missing, I would put a comment on mine that would say to expand more in this particular area.

For this student, the collaborative peer review on Google Drive helped them become more aware of their agency as a writer and the fact that they have control over what goes into the writing they produce. In looking over classmates' drafts, the student would note places where they felt their own was lacking. Instead of me telling the student that they were missing something from the draft, the student was able to come to that conclusion themselves after reading others' work. The reading the students completed as part of the peer review process often strengthened their writing and ultimately the essays they produced.

While these three student reflections outlined strong reading-writing connections between reading sample texts or student drafts on Google Drive and specific writing assignments, I note that not all students discussed those connections explicitly when reflecting on their experiences in the course. In fact, if students mentioned Google Drive in their reflections, it was often to focus on how it functioned as a tool for the writing they accomplished. Because the readings in these two courses related directly to the writing students were completing, I wonder if the connections to reading were less visible as this type of reading-as-writing sample is different from the other ways that students are asked to read in their courses.

Along with helping their understanding and completion of writing assignments, what the students seemed to benefit the most from in our use of Google Drive was the interactivity and engagement that it brought to the course. One student commented in their reflection that "it was very beneficial to get input from the whole class while we work as a team." Another wrote that "I had never collaborated as a class on the same [Google] docs. It was an amazing experience to work with my classmates and interact with them. This is one of the only classes I was in this semester that I actually engaged with other students and actively participated in group work." As students work on a collaborative Google Doc, the responses are visible to everyone, which encourages collaboration, keeps everyone on task in class, and promotes more engaged feedback on drafts outside of class. As a collaborative tool, I believe that Google Docs can be used in many ways to help students with their reading and writing and make the classroom a more interactive and communal space.

While I found this experience of using Google Drive in my first-year composing classes to be positive as a bridge between reading and writing, I do think that there are still many opportunities to expand this kind of reading-writing outside of first-year composition. For instance, by taking advantage of apps like Kami, or web platforms like Genius or Hypothesis, students can see the benefits of collaborative and social reading taking place outside the context of a singular course. Additionally, while students in my classes reported success with using Google Drive for their writing assignments in our class, I fear that students might not apply these lessons to other learning situations unless given opportunities to do so. Although I think that students in other courses could easily respond to readings collaboratively using Google Docs, share essay drafts, and use their reading as models for the kinds of writing they want to produce, I think that reinforcing those connections with students throughout a semester needs to be consistent. An activity that might help students make those connections would be to ask them to keep a record of their reading in other classes or situations and challenge them to find other ways themselves to make that reading visible and collaborative.

I believe that instructors wishing to promote collaborative classroom pedagogies that make reading-writing visible to students should consider bringing Google Drive into their classrooms. It remains necessary to make students aware of the importance of different reading-writing tasks and help students learn more about the practices that they find most useful. In opening up reading and writing by making it collaborative in the classroom, students can learn from one another, try out new strategies, and ultimately make connections between what they read and the writing they produce. I do think that there are important steps that instructors need to make as they introduce these tasks to students, yet the benefit of doing so can make the first-year writing classroom a less intimidating experience for first-year students.

Notes

1. The Carnegie Foundation's 2010 report *Write to Read: Evidence for How Writing Can Improve Reading* (Graham & Hebert) "is the first meta-analysis to examine the relationship between various writing practices' effects on student reading performance" (Anson 23).
2. More information on Genius (https://genius.com/web-annotator) and Hypothesis (https://web.hypothes.is/), including use in academic settings are available on their sites.
3. Kami (http://kamihq.com/) has a free, basic version, along with paid individual and educational licenses.
4. In her open access textbook, *A Writer's Guide to Mindful Reading*, Carillo has a chapter devoted to different reading strategies, including the Says/Does approach, which "asks you to notice what a text *says*—its content—and what a text *does*—how it functions" (14).
5. Many academic libraries introduce students to the CRAAP (Currency, Reliability, Accuracy, Authority, Purpose) Criteria as a way to evaluate sources. For example, see Nova Southeastern University's library guide for evaluating sources for more details: http://nova.campusguides.com/evaluate

Works Cited

"About." *Google Docs About*. Web, www.google.com/docs/about/.

Anson, Chris. "Writing to Read, Revisited." *Horning, Gollnitz, and Haller*, pp. 21–39. Web, https://wac.colostate.edu/books/collegereading/anson.pdf.

Anson, Chris, Matthew Davis, and Domenica Vilhotti. "'What Do We Want in This Paper?' Generating Criteria Collectively." *Teaching with Student Texts: Essays toward an Informed Practice*, edited by Joseph Harris, John D. Miles, and Charles Paine, Utah State University Press, 2010, pp. 35–45.

Bruffee, Kenneth. "Collaborative Learning and the 'Conversation of Mankind'." *College English*, vol. 46, no. 7, 1984, pp. 635–52.

Bunn, Michael. "How to Read Like a Writer." *Writing Spaces: Readings on Writing*, vol. 2, edited by Charles Lowe and Pavel Zemliansky, WAC Clearinghouse/Parlor P, 2011. Web, http://writingspaces.org/bunn-how-to-read-like-a-writer.

———. "Motivation and Connection: Teaching Reading and Writing in the Composition Classroom." *CCC*, vol. 64, no. 3, Feb. 2013, pp. 496–516.

Carillo, Ellen. *A Writer's Guide to Mindful Reading*, WAC Clearinghouse, 2017. Web, https://wac.colostate.edu/books/mindful/.

Cornis-Pope, Marcel, and Ann Woodlief. "The Rereading/Rewriting Process: Theory and Collaborative, Online Pedagogy." *Intertexts: Reading Pedagogy in College Writing Classrooms*, edited by Marguerite Helmers, Lawrence Erlbaum Associates, 2010, pp. 146–64.

Cotugno, Marianne. "Using Google Drive to Prepare Students for Workplace Writing and to Encourage Responsibility, Collaboration, and Revision." *TETYC*, Sep. 2014, pp. 65–76.

Driscoll, Dana Lynn. "Introduction to Primary Research: Observations, Surveys, and Interviews." *Lowe and Zemilansky*. Web, http://writingspaces.org/driscoll-introduction-to-primary-research.

Ede, Lisa, and Andrea Lunsford. *Singular Texts/Plural Authors: Perspectives on Collaborative Writing*, Southern Illinois University Press, 1990.

Edwards, Jennifer, and Credence Baker. "A Case Study: Google Collaboration Applications as Online Course Teaching Tools." *Journal of Online Learning and Teaching*, vol. 6, no. 4, 2010, pp. 828–38.

Evans, Donna J., and Ben S. Bunting, Jr. "Cooperative and Collaborative Writing with Google Docs." *Collaborative Learning and Writing*, edited by Kathleen M. Hunzer, McFarland & Company Inc, 2012, pp. 109–29.

Gere, Anne Ruggles. *Writing Groups: History, Theory, and Implications*, Southern Illinois University Press, 1987.

Horning, Alice. "Introduction." *What Is College Reading?*, edited by Alice Horning, Deborah-Lee Gollnitz, and Cynthia R. Haller, The WAC Clearinghouse, 2017. Web, https://wac.colostate.edu/books/collegereading/.

Kittle, Peter, and Troy Hicks. "Transforming the Group Paper with Collaborative Online Writing." *Pedagogy*, vol. 9, no. 3, 2009, pp. 525–38.

Lutkewitte, Claire, ed. "Introduction." *Mobile Technologies and the Writing Classroom: Resources for Teachers*, NCTE, 2016, pp. vii–xiv.

McArdle, Casey R. "Mobile Learning Just Keeps on Running: Renegotiating Online Collaborative Spaces for Writing Students." Lutkewitte, pp. 117–32.

Newsom, Carrie, and Kathryn Kennedy. "Google and Collaboration." *Journal of Library Administration*, vol. 46, no. 3, pp. 87–97.

Pew Research Center. "Mobile Technology Fact Sheet." *Fact Sheet: Pew Research Center*, 12 Jan. 2017. Web, www.pewinternet.org/fact-sheet/mobile/.

Salvatori, Mariolina, and Patricia Donahue. "Tracing the Moves: How Students Read." *Reader: Essays in Reader-Oriented Theory, Criticism, and Pedagogy*, 2012, pp. 80–8.

Strasma, Kip. "'Spotlighting': Peer-Response in Digitally Supported First-Year Writing Courses." *TETYC*, Dec. 2009, pp. 153–60.

Tekobbe, Cindy, Yazmin Lazcano-Pry, and Duane Roen. "Collaborative Learning and Writing in Digital Environments." Huzner, pp. 87–97.

8 Situating Design
Cultivating Digital Readers and Writers in the Composition Classroom

Molly E. Daniel

The nature of our technologies readily puts us and our students in the position of producer, so composing digital texts has the potential to directly inform and strengthen students' capacity for reading them, especially if we also begin to see ourselves and our students (and help them see themselves) as designers. Although it is true that reading and writing digitally necessarily include reading digitized versions of print texts and composing on a word processor, I am most interested in exploring the scope of digital reading and writing that pushes beyond our linear print practices. To that end, I agree with Jennifer Rowsell and Anne Burke's assertion that "to understand the complexities of reading online, teachers need to understand how the reading of linear print text forms differs from the reading of digital texts. Digital texts depend more readily on the design and representation of language and thus require a semiotic understanding on the part of the reader" (117). The complexities of reading (and producing) digital texts are situated within the multimodal layering that occurs; therefore, I suggest that students best hone their digital reading approaches while also composing digital texts with specific attention to design as a central activity. To better situate design within the practice of teaching digital reading and writing, I work to answer two questions:

1. How does design create a connection between digital reading and writing?
2. How can students use concepts of design to effectively approach digital reading and writing?

For the purpose of this chapter, I suggest it is not that students do not know how to read digital texts (websites, blogs, webtexts etc.); I contend that students do not identify navigating these texts as reading, potentially resulting in a loss of knowledge transfer. In other words, students are always already composing digitally and reading digitally but often, disconnect those practices from academic (digital) writing and reading analysis. So, students can use their preexisting knowledge not only to consume but also to produce and effectively design digital texts while being aware of the connections between both reading and writing them. By heightening this awareness, we can also use the tenets of design to develop a "pedagogy which will open up access to academia through making explicit how multimodal texts work" because "'academic literacies' in the twenty-first century entail being able to navigate multiplicity" (Archer 420). Students' attention is extended to design and arrangement of the text in addition to comprehension and articulation of content.

Insert design projects; these projects "require writers to look at successful models, to think deeply about audience, to design visual and verbal arguments together, and then actively construct new knowledge" (Hocks 652). Designing visual and verbal arguments together speaks to the multiplicity of modes that students interact with as they compose and read. Because of this, I will first discuss elements and theories of both digital reading and writing to create a foundation for the ways in which each influence and enhance the other in the composition classroom. Second this chapter will turn to unpacking the term *design* to highlight the intersections of these two practices, thus strengthening our understanding of the transferable elements of each. Ultimately, I argue that it is through the integration of design (and terms such as navigation, assemblage, and arrangement that support it) that students can identify elements within their digital reading and writing that show a critical awareness of digital spaces and how students function within them by both producing and consuming texts that circulate there. I situate my definition of navigation as the ways in which digital readers and writers make their way through a digital text, use it, and explore it. The term *assemblage*, stemming from media studies, refers to the ways in which elements—or modes—of a text come together. As Leander and Boldt remind us, "these things have no necessary relation to one another, and they lack organization, yet their happenstance coming together in the assemblage produces any number of possible effects on the elements," thus resulting in varied navigation and multimodal patterns (25). Finally, arrangement functions within design and supports the discussion in this chapter because it establishes the potential "blueprint" of the text spatially on screen as the writer produces the text as well as informs the spatial understanding for the reader. Design, although supported by other concepts as well, employs navigation, assemblage, and arrangement from both the perspective of the digital reader and the writer.

Digital Reading and Writing

As technology continues to advance, shift, and change, so must both our reading and writing practices and pedagogies. To some extent, this is of course already happening. One thing that has become evident is that both of these practices demand different approaches within the context of a digital environment, extending and shifting from a linear approach.

Those of us that cling to our print books know that we do not read the same digitally, even if we are just talking about a digitized print text (I am absolutely one of these people). For instance, I know that I still print texts out that contain the most important research elements in my own work, or I get the physical book, because my own reading practices are still making the shift into the digital from traditional print-based reading. My Advanced Composition students and I discuss this at length as we navigate through a range of texts that are print, digital, and networked. We each fluctuate in our reading comprehension depending on the complexity, how we plan to further use the text, and how we want to annotate it. This only becomes more complicated when we read webtexts, such as articles in *Kairos*. We cannot print those out; the digital design and arrangement of these articles lose something when they are printed—interactivity, layout, movement, sound, etc. We talk about how this both affords and constrains our reading practices, and we strategize about important differences in reading a print-based text and a digital one so that the newer experience is less frustrating and still valuable. Similarly, they do not only produce linear print texts, in fact those are in the vast minority in the course, but they compose via software and programs that ask them to write multimodally and digitally, which is becoming a more common practice—but it is starkly different than most of my current students' writing activities. These experiences with my Advanced Composition students suggest to me that, unsurprisingly, I must reconsider my pedagogical approaches to digital reading and writing. Digital reading and writing demands different ways of engaging with texts that arguably build upon more traditional print practices. In what follows here, I explore some of the existing scholarship that addresses both practices of reading and writing in print and digital forms, which informs the practices our composition students bring into our classrooms as well as how my situation of design compliments this conversation.

Reading

In addition to linear texts (perhaps the digitized book or article), students are increasingly reading more webtexts that garner interaction beyond the turn of a page. As is common with discussions of digital technology, affordances enter into the conversation regarding digital reading; "the implications of the dramatic shift from the affordances of print to the affordances of multimodal digital texts raise some important questions about how these texts are being transferred to a new space and if that transfer offers positive gains" (O'Brien and Voss 77). E-books and digital reading devices have become increasingly prevalent, and the functionality of these things have also shifted over a short period of time beyond the digitized version of a print text. E-books, for instance, create varied reading experiences based upon publisher, text, and content, and these varied experiences are only more complex when different platforms and pieces of technology are used to engage with the E-books. Therefore, the application used to read a book potentially displays differently depending upon the operating system and the kind of technology used to access it; variations are created in a multitude of ways before readers even open the e-book. Some e-books function as large PDF files that students navigate with varying success while others are interactive webtexts, so "the rapidly changing nature of e-books and digital reading devices depends upon a progressive research agenda that examines the use of new technologies in authentic school settings" (Larson 22). This demand cannot be specific to particular pieces of technology or formats. Instead, it needs to focus upon the transferable things readers do across these digital reading opportunities. The rapidly changing nature of e-books reminds us that it is more valuable to adjust our pedagogies to include tools rooted in rhetorical practices, and even troubleshooting, rather than honing in on a particular technology because that technology will update, change, or be replaced.

As we know, students often still need support with each program and piece of technology we integrate into our pedagogical practices. Sometimes we do need to teach basic navigation and troubleshooting in a program when students have never used it to read or write digitally. When I encounter this in my own classroom, I take time to acquaint students with the program, or technology, and I reinforce the value of troubleshooting—knowing where to look when an obstacle presents itself. This reality harkens back to Christina Haas's claim that "technology itself—rather than merely technology's consequence—must become an object of inquiry" (31). One way we are able to situate technology as an object of inquiry is through troubleshooting; this often leads us to better understand the technology and address its affordances and constraints. Therefore, we are not "simply" teaching students to use technology but to explore the purpose and audience (two key rhetorical elements in writing) of each piece or software as well. By addressing the rhetorical nature of digital technology, then, students can revisit and reinforce rhetorical concepts they employ in their writing as well as identify in their reading with, in, and through technology. Although we do often use digital technology as a tool, it is important to remember and interrogate the ways in which is it not neutral or transparent, so that students are better equipped to engage, consume, and produce in digital spaces. Considering the digital technology students use, such as applications or e-readers, through a rhetorical lens allows students to be critical of not only what they read and write digitally but also how they access it. Furthermore, students do not get caught up in learning a program or piece of technology without realizing that each update will change how they navigate or use it, which creates more time to attend to the rhetorical practices the digital technology supports.

For instance, webtexts ask students to click through and read a variety of elements—including words, images, and video—that potentially work together in more than one organizational schema. Drawing meaning from the assembled elements relies upon an understanding of rhetorical concepts such as purpose, audience, and context that also explicitly attends to multimodality. As we know, "for the reader of multimodal texts and settings, interpretation and meaning making can be quite complicated" (Karchmer-Klien and Shinas, 61). This complexity, in part, is tied to the potential interactivity of multimodal texts as well as the multiplicity of entry points. Readers of multimodal (and particularly digital) texts, then, explore content in a variety of reading paths supported by the interactive nature of the text itself. While linear, print texts are open to interpretation and the range of experience with which readers come to the text, the organization is more predictable. Karchmer-Klien and Shinas suggest further that "in digital environments, however, [the] reading path is largely determined by the reader; consequently, the reader may not follow the reading path the writer intended" in the way print texts depend on "culturally constructed rules" (62). While it is true that this provides readers with a greater sense of agency over how they consume a digital text, this agency can be overwhelming and lead to confusion. When readers engage with digital multimodal texts, they make rhetorical decisions that are socially and culturally rooted, but are less rigid than the lens that we have historically read print, linear texts: "multimodal texts allow for unique reading paths because the reader must choose the modes to follow, what mode holds the most meaning, and which mode will lead to the overall purpose" of the text (70). Although we cannot elide multimodal with digital (nor should we), we can see how this applies to digital texts that are always multimodal while multimodal texts are not always digital. The choice to follow a mode (or modes) is culturally and socially informed based upon preexisting knowledge that can be challenged by the overwhelming possibilities of paths in digital multimodal texts.

Writing

While it is unquestionably important to enable students' reading abilities within the context of digital texts, it is equally important to hone their digital writing as well. In fact, as students write digitally they gain a better understanding of the ways in which they can approach digital reading: the production of the text, and gaining that literacy, is equally as important as the consumption of it. Although it is not my intention to claim that word processed texts are not of value (because they are), I do suggest that we consider digital writing beyond the word processing our students engage in as they write essays because, "to write in today's classrooms is to generate or construct dynamic and multimodal texts as representations of learning or as an artefact of creative composition" (Edwards-Groves 51). In other words, "the view here is that multimodality does not replace important foundational writing skills but that the elements of the writing process are extended to account for the shift in textual practices that technology demands" (62). Many of us use the terms *writing* and *composing* interchangeably, depending on our audience; this allows us to discuss digital writing through the lens of digital multimodal composing. Although Cynthia Selfe's definition below defines new media, its elements are useful when we consider the scope of digital writing:

> Texts created primarily in digital environments, composed in multiple media (e.g., film. video, audio, among others) and designed for presentation and exchange in digital venues. These texts generally place a heavy emphasis on visual elements . . . and sound, and they often involve some level of interactivity.
>
> (Wysocki et al. 43)

The heightened emphasis on the visual elements, as well as other sensory engagement like sound in texts, composed in and for digital environments are important to consider when writing digitally. The audience, although also engaging other senses, first experience a digital text through sight, so the visual meaning must be clear and explicitly connected to the purpose articulated. Additionally, the interactivity of the digital texts must be addressed throughout the digital writing process because the writer has to attend to the way a reader will potentially experience it, how different interaction might result in different understanding, and how navigation can be organized for the most effective engagement. By connecting Selfe's definition of new media to digital writing, we can see how the digital environment of a text creates the possibility for interactivity at two levels: first how the modes interact with one another to achieve the overarching purpose of the text, and second the ways in which both the audience (readers) and the writer interact with the modes. The digital writer interacts with the modes as they layer them to create the overall experience as well as when revising a digital text. A digital writer's consistent interaction with the modes in production mirrors and establishes the foundation for the digital readers, or the audience. In other words, a digital writer uses visuals, sounds, and words as contributing elements to a digital text that invites the digital reader to interact with the elements.

Digital technology also shapes the social setting, or context of digital writing; these social settings set the foundation for interaction. Marilyn Cooper calls these social settings ecologies where the "fundamental tenet is that writing is an activity through which a person is continually engaged with a variety of socially constituted systems" (367). Social settings and systems function on multiple levels constantly with the addition of our varied digital spaces, thus extending the notion of a writing ecology into the digital realm as well. Information Communication Technologies (ICT) establish a set of such systems that support and extend the activity of writing with multiple modes and varied levels of interactivity. It is also important that digital writers interrogate approaches to multimodality and semiotics within Information Communication Technologies because writers "need to think about which media and modality best represent their ideas" (Doering, Beach, & O'Brien 43). In so doing, writers enact a variety of literacy activities throughout the production of digital multimodal composition while engaging varying ICTs. Jody Shipka reminds us that "just as new communication technologies have enlivened and provided a sense of urgency to discussions about where the discipline is headed and what our use of terms like authoring, writing, and composing include, or describe, recent changes to the communicative landscape have contributed to an interest in tracing the material dimensions of literacy" (35). Yes, technologies are changing, and we are using them at an increased rate when we and our students write; however, the effects of these new technologies do not only urge us to discuss their implications for the field itself but also urge us to discuss their implications for the material aspects of literacy and our own pedagogical approaches that include them.

Although digital reading and writing are separate activities, they work in tandem because the digital environment creates a space that requires a nuanced set of skills for readers and writers. It has been suggested that "the concept of multimodality entails interaction with text—digital affordances blur the lines between the processing of text (reading) and the production of text (writing); the two processes in interactive, multimodal spaces become virtually inseparable" (O'Brien and Voss 76). By developing digital reading and writing practices simultaneously, students develop a critical awareness of the potentiality of digital multimodal spaces, hone the ability to engage in and analyze the interactive processes, and attend to the layered elements within a digital multimodal space. While many factors can, and do, contribute to the connection between digital reading and writing, I suggest that the following explanation of design helps us situate readers and writers as designers.

Design

Before I establish how design is a central activity in both reading and writing digitally, it is important to understand how we, as a field, approach this term as well as the lens through which I approach it in this chapter. In the field of Rhetoric and Composition, design is "the organization of what is to be articulated into a blueprint for production" and "the task of the designer is 'architectural': the shaping of available resources into a framework which can act as the 'blueprint' for the production, of the object or entity or event" (Kress and Van Leeuwen 50). Put another way, design creates the foundation of texts while articulating the means and the modes that build it. It also has begun surfacing as a key term when discussing writing because of the integration of more modes, particularly digital ones. Therefore, the six design elements in the meaning-making process that are established by Bill Cope and Mary Kalantzis: "linguistic meaning, visual meaning, audio meaning, gestural meaning, spatial meaning, and the multimodal patterns that relate the first five modes of meaning to each other" inform the way our students are both reading and writing because of the layered modes and the range of technology they engage (7). The six design elements inform not only the production but also the consumption of texts; the blueprint functions to set a path of navigation as well as an approach to the development of the text. These six design elements are particularly useful when we consider how we approach teaching reading and writing within the context of digital space because they attend to the considerations the writer must make while a text is in production as well as how a reader comes to understand the text. Furthermore, Arlene Archer situates design as a notion that "suggests we consider both the material and visual nature of writing alongside its cognitive dimensions. Design is a useful analytical concept—it can be used as a verb (as in the notion of 'interested action') as well as a noun (as in the design of the text)" (412). This approach to design pairs nicely with the six design elements because it reminds us of the scope of the term as well as the need to address these elements of a text; it also positions design as an analytical tool, so it can also function within the realm of consuming texts, or reading them within the context of a digital space.

Since design works as a blueprint to a text, it necessarily includes attention to the assemblage of the elements throughout the composing process. Within the composing process, there are often elements (that exhibit the six elements of design) that are not clearly related to one another in the early stages, so assemblage comes into play because it combines "the collection of things that happen to be present in any given context" (Leander and Boldt 25). Based upon the blueprint of the design, the elements can be assembled into a variety of combinations that shape and organize the content while also fostering the design decisions that contribute to the created text. However, in writing, this does not just focus upon the ideas presented, as Jacqueline Preston reminds us, because "to regard writing as an assemblage is to insist that what is important about writing is not its capacity to represent ideas but, rather, what writing does, from whence it comes, and how it reproduces" (40). Considering writing as assemblage, then, is only more important when considering the added elements of digital writing and reading because they highlight the "doing," which relates to action and interactivity in digital spaces in both reading and writing.

When we consider design, it also is impossible to separate it from a conversation of navigation because part of the design, particularly of digital texts, attends to how a reader (or user) actively engages with it. Due to the relationship between reader and text, navigation is becoming an important term within Rhetoric and Composition because digital multimodal composition often creates a need for considerations of the reader or what David Chapman calls the navigator because "navigating a hypertext often produces disorientation and cognitive overload for a reader who must determine what to read and what order to read it in" (252). This shift from more traditional, linear texts results in the majority of current considerations of navigation within the field being audience centered—how readers navigate the text. Revisiting notions of audience that student writers already consider when they write for audiences in a linear text helps students consider navigational organization of a digital text. They build upon that preexisting knowledge to explore the range of possibilities that invite audience members into their digital texts; instead of one set path through the text, students must understand the entry points their audience may find when the audience has more control over how they navigate a digital text. While our students, as digital writers, still articulate a clear purpose, the pathways to understanding that purpose are in the audiences' control. Therefore, readers navigate digital texts in a multiplicity of approaches, which creates disorientation for students as they experience it as digital readers; choosing your own pathway through a text is often an uncomfortable experience because it differs from the majority of traditional reading practices and pedagogies. Not only is it important for students to encounter digital texts as readers, but it is also important for them to produce these texts with intention by focusing on the needs and experiences of their audiences. Students as digital writers, then, consider to whom they are writing as well as how and where their projected audience will interact with their texts. Unlike the previous approaches to reading and writing, navigation reminds both readers and writers to consider a text beyond the conceptual and directly attend to the spatial needs of the digital reader and writer. For example, reading a website relies upon the way a designer situates the elements. We look to the top or sidebar to find buttons that help us shift from page to page within the site, and these buttons are generally simple in structure and use familiar terms to direct readers through the content. The spatial organization of pages on a website often use similar placement of text and image, as well as other modes, to create consistency and comprehension for the reader. Design within both reading and writing extends our approaches because, as elements are combined, spatial positioning—or arranging—becomes more inherently tied to comprehension and production; therefore, the act of design occurs when conceptual action—the envisioning of a text as a whole—is supported by attention to the spatial, thus realizing it fully. In other words, reader as designer builds upon Chapman's reader as navigator by adding the analytical element that design provides to the approach for a reader.

Design, then, has three purposes that all rely upon the constraints and affordances of the contributing elements: (a) it spatially arranges the assembled parts (including words, images, video, and sound), (b) it constitutes the writer's aesthetic vision (and reader's reaction to it) through the arrangement of the components, and (c) it implements a theme that ties everything together, which often is established through the navigational paths available to the audience. These purposes directly inform our pedagogical approaches to reading and writing digitally because the cultivation of one informs the other, thus finding a balance between the conceptual and the spatial design of a digital text. Therefore, situating readers and writers as designers creates a foundation for approaches to reading and writing digitally because digital texts house a multiplicity of modes that work together to articulate their purpose to their audience who relies upon the spatial and visual organization to interact with the text.

Digital Reader and Writer as Designer

Although a digital writer/designer initially designs a digital text, a digital reader/designer designs their own path through it. Design creates a bridge between digital reading and writing because it is a central activity in the production and consumption of a digital text. Digital writers as designers use concepts of design to articulate meaning instead of only focusing upon content or delivery; these elements are intertwined to work together. The very same concepts digital writers contend with as designers are employed by digital readers as well, given the way design functions as both a verb and a noun. Digital readers have more freedom in the selection of their reading paths in a digital text because of the multiplicity of modes and the fact that they are not only following the design a writer set forth but also designing their own reading path through the text based upon the way they interact with it. Therefore, readers as designers use design to analyze the meaning-making elements—linguistic, visual, spatial, audio (when applicable), gestural (when applicable) and multimodal patterns. Multimodal patterns as the sixth element of design, speak to the ways in which the first five elements each establish individual pathways through a text as well as combine with one another to support navigation. Because readers often have more agency over the way they engage with a digital text, the writer, or designer, must systematically account for the multiplicity of entry points that rely upon navigation and arrangement on screen.

Digital writing requires attention to design and layout because if a reader cannot navigate the text, then it has not achieved its purpose for its audience. As Archer establishes, "the tasks set for students' assignments often require competence in using and integrating modes and even written assignments take design and layout into consideration" (412). This competency cannot be presumed when we facilitate digital writing with our students, meaning that our pedagogical approaches need to include teaching it. Therefore, digital writing needs to have design as a central activity so that a digital writer can address and integrate spatial arrangement to support and create meaning. Not only do digital writers make rhetorical decisions about content they produce, digital writers also rhetorically consider the blueprint of the text as it happens on the screen, which employs design because they have to set a foundation that allows digital readers to interact with the text. Design allows us to revise our pedagogical approaches so that students develop critical awareness of the practices that have already been engaging in as well as ways to further cultivate rhetorical decisions they make as they consider how verbal and visual design coalesce in the work they produce. Similarly, a digital writer designs the aesthetic vision on screen. This aesthetic vision both situates the appearance of the text and communicates meaning. For example, the visuals and textual elements on a website create an aesthetic experience for the reader that uses both form and content to achieve a purpose. The aesthetic appeal and usability matter when choosing to find information or read content on a website. Similarly digital writer as designer, then, cultivates multimodal patterns during the drafting process to articulate the aesthetic vision that compliments the content, thus furthering the visual meaning for the digital reader and creating opportunity for the reading paths the reader takes. Closely related to aesthetics is the theme a digital writer designs so that readers can navigate the text as effectively and efficiently as possible.

Just as the design elements (linguistic meaning, visual meaning, audio meaning, gestural meaning, spatial meaning, and the multimodal pattern) support digital writing, they inform reading paths students establish as they navigate digital texts based upon the design they are presented within it. Readers as designers use the analytical approach of design to select and navigate their chosen reading path because a reader uses the design (as noun) to decide how to move through a digital text while the digital writer as designer engaged in the initial designing (as a verb) of the text; based upon the original arrangement of the text, a reader designs their reading path. In order engage design as an analytical tool, a digital reader/designer relies upon the interpretation and identification of the six design elements. For example, spatial meaning impacts the way a student navigates a text because of the arrangement on screen.

When a student reads through the lens of design, I contend that they can make stronger connections between arrangement (or perhaps form) and meaning-making, and this, in turn, allows them to more effectively move through a digital text. Often, spatial meaning-making is less complicated in linear print reading, so the reader as designer chooses the reading path based upon the spatial design they detect as they interact with the digital text. Spatial meaning-making sets the foundation for the way a digital reader/designer understands and uses a digital text. Additionally, they take cues from visual meaning that pairs with linguistic meaning as the multimodal patterns provide a starting point for them to read. For example, one digital reader may be drawn to the linguistic meaning, so they navigate the text based upon the language used to choose their next step while another student may connect more readily with the visual elements that suggest a slightly different path based upon layout or integration of images. The combination of the multimodal patterns that digital readers identify contributes to their chosen reading pathway that depends on the meaning articulated by the modes as they work together as well as how they function on their own within the text. Because of the multimodal patterns, the digital reader/designer also, often, interprets audio meaning and gestural meaning because of the multiplicity of opportunities for the assemblage of modes in a digital text. Additionally a digital reader/designer uses cues from the layout or arrangement of the digital text to create the reading path so they do not miss an element that contributes to the whole of the text. While a digital writer/designer considers the six design elements as they develop a usable and navigable text, the digital reader/designer employs this same set of meaning-making elements to understand both how the digital text works and what it contributes to their knowledge base. Therefore, the analytical element of design also works to position digital reader as designer, thus strengthening design analysis as a central activity to include in pedagogical approaches to reading.

It is not new to position writer as designer, as I have established; yet, transferring the tenets of design to digital reading is a new approach that relies upon such a position. Pedagogically, we know that the visual design of a text contributes meaning in tandem with, and provides space for, the linguistic elements that students write and read. Using design in our digital reading and writing pedagogy positions us, as teachers, to facilitate deeper understanding of both the production and consumption of digital texts and help us give students a critical and analytical eye that supports their navigation of a digital text as well. Digital reading and writing are complex activities, due to some extent, to the multiplicity of possibility: possibility of navigation (or reading path), possibility of modes, possibility of assemblage, possibility of interaction, and possibility of interpretation. By simultaneously teaching digital reading and writing through design, students develop a foundational knowledge of the six design elements that enables them to think like a designer when they read and write digitally by using and identifying the six elements as well terminology that supports design. Being able to identify the usage of these six elements of design positions students to think like a designer as they read digital content and use their understanding of the elements to create their navigational path through the content, and they can analyze the way digital writers considered the design elements as designers. Approaching digital readers as designers also responds to the participatory nature of our culture that necessarily surfaces within educational settings as well. Not only, then, do the six design elements (linguistic meaning, visual meaning, audio meaning, gestural meaning, spatial meaning, and the multimodal patterns) apply to writers as designers, but they also support the reader as designer. Readers are making meaning from the digital texts they engage based upon their own interaction with the modes that are assembled and arranged within a digital text. Articulating the six elements and concepts of design to students as we teach them to write and read digitally as designers fosters greater understanding of texts based upon their own rhetorically effective decision-making in the digital writing process. Digital reading requires an understanding of digital writing design because that knowledge informs how a reader navigates a digital text. Therefore, gaining skills as a designer of digital texts transfers to the reading approaches in digital spaces. When students begin navigating readings that are webtexts, such as articles published in *Kairos*, they tend to miss the depth on their first read until they realize the layers of meaning that are woven, or designed, into the fabric of the text. However, approaching reading through the concepts of design makes the text more accessible because reading relies upon the arrangement of information as well as the chosen path of navigation the reader takes. In other words, students who are designing digital texts as well as reading them through the lens of design are learning to use the elements of design so that they experience a text in its entirety while also knowing, or becoming secure in their agency that they are able to create their own reading path. Approaching both digital reading and writing as designing redistributes agency for the designer in each role because they have control over how they encounter information within the text; digital readers and writers as designers are active and interactive meaning-makers because they not only comprehend content, but they also understand how design contributes to and establishes a basis for the content. A digital writer/designer and a digital reader/designer engage a digital text actively because a digital reader/designer is not simply consuming a text that was designed by a digital writer/designer; instead, they too enact design as they choose their own reading paths as they experience the ecology of the digital space within which they are functioning. Approaching digital reading and writing as design in our pedagogy invites students to push beyond both software and technological skill and to build connections between the rhetorical practices that inform the content they design and the rhetorical value of the programs and technology they use to read and write. Students increase their agency as digital readers and writers through design because it asks them to actively interact regardless of the position they are in (writer or reader); they are designers.

Works Cited

Archer, Arlene. "Writing as Design: Enabling Access to Academic Discourse in a Multimodal Environment." *SAJHE*, vol. 26, no. 3, 2012, pp. 411–21.

Chapman, David. "Brave New (Cyber) World: From Reader to Navigator." *Teaching Writing: Landmarks and Horizons*, edited by Christina Russell McDonald and Robert L. McDonald, Southern Illinois University Press, 2002, pp. 249–58.

Cooper, Marilyn. "The Ecology of Writing." *College English*, vol. 48, no. 4, 1986, pp. 364–75.

Cope, Bill, and Mary Kalantzis. "From Literacy to 'Multiliteracies': Learning to Mean in the New Communications Environment." *English Studies in Africa*, vol. 49, no. 1, 2006, pp. 23–45.

Doering, Aaron, et al. "Infusing Multimodal Tools and Digital Literacies into an English Education Program." *English Education*, vol. 40, no. 1, 2007, pp. 41–60.

Edwards-Groves, Christine Joy. "The Multimodal Writing Process: Changing Practices in Contemporary Classrooms." *Language and Education*, vol. 25, no. 1, 2011, pp. 49–64.

Haas, Christina. *Writing Technology: Studies in the Materiality of Literacy*, Mahwah, NJ, Lawrence Erlbaum Associates, 1996.

Hocks, Mary. "Understanding Visual Rhetoric in Digital Writing Environments." *College Composition and Communication*, vol. 54, no. 4, 2003, pp. 629–56.

Karchmer-Klein, Rachel, and Valerie Harlow Shinas. "21st Century Literacies in Teacher Education: Investigating Multimodal Texts in the Context of an Online Graduate-Level Literacy and Technology Course." *Research in the Schools*, vol. 19, no. 1, pp. 60–74.

Kress, Gunther, and Theo Van Leeuwen. *Multimodal Discourse: The Modes and Media of Contemporary Communication*, New York, Oxford University Press, 2001.

Larson, Lotta C. "Digital Readers: The Next Chapter in E-Book Reading and Response." *The Reading Teacher*, vol. 64, no. 1, 2010, pp. 15–22.

Leander, Kevin, and Gail Boldt. "Rereading 'A Pedagogy of Multiliteracies': Bodies, Texts, and Emergence." *Journal of Literacy Research*, vol. 45, no. 1, 2012, pp. 22–46.

O'Brien, David, and Scott Voss. "Reading Multimodally: What Is Afforded?" *Journal of Adolescent & Adult Literacy*, vol. 55, no. 1, 2011, pp. 75–8, doi:10.1598/JAAL.55.1.9.

Preston, Jacqueline. "Project(ing) Literacy: Writing to Assemble in a Postcomposition FYW Classroom." *College Composition and Communication*, vol. 67, no. 1, 2015, pp. 35–63.

Rowsell, Jennifer, and Anne Burke. "Reading by Design: Two Case Studies of Digital Reading Practices." *Journal of Adolescent & Adult Literacy*, vol. 53, no. 2, 2009, pp. 106–18, doi:10.1598/JAAL.53.2.2.

Shipka, Jody. *Toward a Composition Made Whole*, Pittsburgh, University of Pittsburgh P, 2011.

Wysocki, Anne Francis, Johndan Johnson-Eiola, et al. *Writing New Media: Theory and Applications for Expanding the Teaching of Composition*, Logan, Utah State University Press, 2004.

9 Reading, Writing, Produsing

Fostering Student Authors in the Public Space

Catherine Gabor with Riley Nelson

> *I ended up showing my Uncle my Wikipedia project on Thanksgiving and his reaction actually surprised me. He's not at all a technology geek, so when he seemed so interested as to how it started and the ending result, I was a bit shocked but happy that he wanted to hear more about it. He said to me, "You and your group should feel very proud! I think that this project was an awesome idea. It really gets the brain working and to see how well you can work collectively with others."*
>
> *For the Wikipedia project, we were developing research questions and composing substantial arguments in response to those questions, incorporating extensive independent library research and demonstrating mastery of standard academic documentation modes. I felt that I was going into the library with a solid set of criteria for my research, rather than letting the articles I found define my process. This was a new and much more "confidence boosting" way to research.*

One question this book addresses is "How has digital reading affected researched writing in terms of authorship and student investment in writing?" The two student quotations above bring up issues central to the theme of this collection: collaborative writing and rhetorical awareness of one's engagement in a research process. When we embarked on this study, we were curious about how our students' digital reading and writing practices would impact their emerging definitions of "authorship" and whether these digitally mediated practices would help students move from being primarily *digital readers* to become(ing) *digital writers* with enhanced rhetorical sensitivity.[1] Specifically, we challenged students to situate themselves within the following questions from the course syllabus:

> Do you change how you write when you switch from the pencil to the pixel, from the page to the screen? Do you feel like an "author" when you post on Facebook? When you retweet? Are you reader or a writer on Tumblr, Reddit, or Snapchat? What is your role in social media: are you a producer or a consumer of text? Or are you a "produser"?

Our hypothesis was that students would develop increasingly capacious definitions of authorship as they reflected on their digital reading and writing practices, many of which were collaborative. We supposed that these new definitions would lead students to a level of engagement and awareness that would transfer with them to other rhetorical situations. In other words, we hoped to foster student investment and rhetorical self-awareness, which, according to Elizabeth Wardle, is the most feasible transferable knowledge arising from required Rhetoric and Composition classes (82). Most interesting to us is that students did forge *theoretical* definitions of authorship that include collaboration with others to compose nontraditional products (digital texts); however, when pressed to discuss their own writing, they often relied upon traditional "individual genius" authorship paradigms. We take students' adherence to these two contradictory epistemologies as a sign of their intellectual engagement with the concepts of the class and with implications of the world of digital texts that they inhabit. If their simultaneous belief in two "authorship" definitions is the most interesting result of our study, the most unexpected is the students' focus on responsibility. The networked nature of the texts they read and wrote drew their attention to authorial ethos in a way that "school writing" had not. Although it was not an explicit focus of the class (maybe it should be), students returned to definitions of authorship that made them careful about their own research, wording, and purpose.

1. Background of the Course

The course, a seminar for transfer students, Rhetoric 295: NewMedia/YouMedia: Writing in Electronic Environments, provides students with a structured opportunity to look at the digital reading and writing spaces that are ubiquitous in their lives and to form definitions of authorship—of themselves as authors—in digitally mediated environments. Students begin the semester by participating in and reviewing a new "online writing space of their choosing." Per the assignment, they are prompted to find places to insert themselves as writers and craft definitions of these spaces in which they consume and produce multiple rhetorics (graphic, aural, written, etc.). Following this assignment, they engage in a more traditional technological literacy autobiography, in which they revert to "twentieth century" notions of authorship and literacy sponsors (Brandt). Complementing these assignments is the large research project for the class, in which students substantially edit Wikipedia entries. For virtually every student, this is the first academic assignment in which they encounter a public writing community (i.e., the Wikipedia contributors) researching, drafting, discussing, and editing the entries alongside them (see Appendix 9A for Assignment Sheet).

The first time the course was offered (Spring 2015), each student wrote a traditional 12–15-page research paper submitted to an audience of one:

the professor (Cathy). I feared that "students did not understand the exigency for their writing beyond the need to fulfill instructor expectations" (Blythe and Gonzales 628). Therefore, I modified that assignment with the desire to gain a larger—and more authentic—audience for their research: in groups, students would significantly edit a Wikipedia entry, based on academic research. In addition to audience concerns, the shift from "research paper" to Wikipedia entry allowed me to structure the assignment as one that required collaborative research and writing, further expanding students' conceptions of (co)authorship. In Courtney Werner's brief history of new media in Composition Studies, she claims that "audience participation or interaction is a defining mode or characteristic of new media and the new media rhetorical situation" (727). The Wikipedia editing project is interactive in two keys ways: the students work in groups and must interact with each other at every stage of the process in order to write cohesive passages for the Wikipedia entry. And, after posting their suggested edits to the "Talk Page" for the Wikipedia entry they are working on, the students then interact with any other "Wikipedians" who are actively editing the same entry.

After three semesters of experience with the Wikipedia project, we hypothesized, based on anecdotal evidence, that the students had expanded their conceptions of "who" an author is and "what" an author writes. In order to test our hunch, we administered a survey to the 64 students who took the course between 2015 and 2017; 26 students completed the survey. We asked students about their online and off line reading and writing habits to see if they had changed after taking the seminar. Additionally, we asked them about perceptions of authorship before and after taking the class (see Appendix 9B for survey questions). We followed the survey with focus groups of five students (see Appendix 9C for focus group questions).

2.   Produsage

Students' readerly identities can serve as a springboard for not only their writerly identities but also knowledge transfer when taught in the context of *produsage*,[2] which inevitably bridges passive consumption and active production. Most scholars and students alike would agree that print and digital writing spaces are also already reading spaces. Reading, however, often happens without writing; many of the students cited numerous online and off line examples of reading without writing a word. For example, students did not name "book" when asked them to generate a list of "writing spaces." On the whole, students entered the class separating reading and writing in their minds but grew to see them as intertwined in Web 2.0 writing spaces.

In the early days of the web—Communications scholar Axel Bruns points out—most people consumed or "used" text, as opposed to producing online content themselves. He explains that when the World Wide

Web first came into public use, people were strictly users who read text on webpages and clicked on links to buy things. A few early adopters became producers of content on the web; those very early personal homepages that look ridiculously simple now required a substantial amount of programming knowledge and free time. There were essentially two groups: on the one hand, "users" (most people), and, on the other hand, "producers" (including early adopters and corporations who paid professional web developers to make their content).

With interface advancements, most notably the Web 2.0 turn, much online content is created or produced by the users/readers/audience members themselves. Thus, Bruns argues, a new category has emerged:

> What emerges is that in the online, networked, information economy, participants are not simply passive consumers, but active users, with some of them participating more strongly with a focus on their own personal use, some of them participating more strongly in ways which are inherently constructive and productive of social networks and communal content. These latter users occupy a hybrid position of being both users and what in traditional terms would have to be described loosely as producers: they are productive users, or produsers, engaged in the act of produsage.
>
> (21)

Like the Burkean parlor, sites of produsage are "ongoing, perpetually unfinished, iterative, and evolutionary" (Bruns 20). Rather than a traditional method of authorship, in which the author or producer of the content is writing to a receiving audience, produsage involves the audience themselves participating in the creation of the content. The important difference that produsage creates—in comparison to more traditional forms of authorship—is the exceedingly blurred lines between production and consumption.

One of the first formal reading assignments students tackle in Rhetoric 295 is Bruns' chapter-long definition of "produsage." We introduce this concept early in the semester as an anchor of the first major project: the Writing Space Review (see Appendix 9D for assignment sheet). As part of this assignment, students must craft a short definition of "writing space" and use this definition to evaluate an app or website that they have not used previously. For example, one student reviewed Steller, "a mobile app where you can create visual stories through photos, videos, or text," by saying,

> Steller is a perfect example of produsage, where the users create the content on the app. Without users of the app, there would be no app, no stories, and no creativity. Who made the story is also who uses the app. Given the writing space, consumers can not only read

others creations on Steller but create stories of their own for other consumers to see.

Students' understanding of produsage started with analyses of how they typically interact with text and other users in Web 2.0 spaces, as seen in the example above, and continued through class discussions and into the Wikipedia project which inherently required them to toggle between consumption and production of texts.

In 2008, Bruns dedicated an entire chapter to illustrating how Wikipedia is the quintessential produsage environment. He also highlighted blogs and Second Life, both of which have been eclipsed by other social media platforms such as Twitter, Tumblr, and Instagram. However, Wikipedia has held up as an enduring site for produsage. Near the same time, in 2009, Composition Studies scholar Robert Cummings observed the shift from reading (only) to produsing and named Wikipedia as a prime example of this shift:

> Networked consciousness has thus far been shaped as a download model, envisioning student writers as consuming information found on the Internet. The upload model, or "Web 2.0" concept, reverses the flow of information and transforms networking reality from consuming to contributing, a potential made most visible by Wikipedia.
> (28)

Like Bruns and Cummings our students embraced the concept of produsage in their analyses of what a writing space is, as well as what an author is, and how Wikipedia works.

Additionally, the participants in the focus groups built upon their previous knowledge of produsage when they extrapolated this concept to describe productive off line learning environments. Both of the focus groups brought up the Rhetoric 295 classroom environment as a site of produsage. In other words, the environment and structure of the classroom aided in their ability to simultaneously produce and use. Camille noted, "Just the way that we were prompted in class, I learned so much from everyone else in the class just through our discussions and what everyone brought to the class,"[3] to which her classmate Lexi added, "You wanted us to engage with one another by reading part of our homework aloud, by real-time commenting on each other's tumblrs, and by participating in peer workshops." The focus group conversation led Lexi to link produsage to other "in real life" situations such as team work at her internship where she "offered ideas and used someone else's idea to produce something better." The focus group students began to see that produsage was not a term limited to digital spaces but could be used to explain versions of authorship in other areas of their lives.

3. Authorship

As they deepened their understanding of produsage, students recrafted their definitions of authorship to include themselves as digital authors. In large part, their new definitions of authorship sprung from their expanded conceptions of what an author can write. Formerly, they had considered books and articles as the only things that "authors" wrote, noting, in many cases, that these publications were "owned" by the author (Survey answer). For example, one student wrote, "I figured that an author needed to have professionally published a book or article. I never really realized that I myself am an author" (Survey answer). Likewise, several survey respondents described themselves using their expanded definitions of authorship; for instance, one student wrote: "Now, I view authorship as a role that takes part in producing and consuming content." Although three of the twenty-six respondents said they had not changed their definition of authorship at all, the vast majority had, represented by definitions such as "Since taking Rhet 295, I still think authorship is someone who has published a written work but the work can either be published traditionally, like a book or be a digital work, like a blog entry or social media post" or "My current definition of authorship is anyone who contributes to the page, website, and article."

In the first focus group, participants stated that "likes, captions, and emojis [on social media] count as authorship" when asked about their *general* definition of authorship, whereas they retreated to much more traditional definitions of *themselves* as authors. For instance, when asked about authorship at the general or theoretical level, Micaela referred to the Wikipedia project as a writing space where her group edited each other's words. In addition, Micaela described her internship with a health and beauty blog and noted that on any given blog post she may be listed as the author but that she coauthors the content with those she interviews and with "her team" who fact checks and organizes the blog. Sophia's answers push the envelope of authorship even further: she names sharing an article on Facebook with a comment as an instance of co-authorship. However, neither of them adhere to a shared sense of authorship when asked specifically about themselves as authors, for both emphasize the originality of their school papers as evidence that they are real authors. When asked, "Do you consider yourself an author?", Sophia said, "I think I'm an author. I've written a bunch of critical analysis papers that no one else has written. I am an author because of those papers, even if only a small circle reads them, even if they are not A papers." Similarly, Micaela referred to herself as an author only in extrinsically sanctioned situations. Specifically, she identified as an author of her school papers and of the blog she works on for her internship. When pressed to explain why school papers are the first thing they think of when asked about their own authorship, Micaela and Sophia acknowledged that they still subscribe to an author "stereotype" as "someone who has written a formal thing." This definition aligns with the kinds of artifacts students named in the survey in response to the question about their impressions of authorship before taking Rhet 295. For instance, several students listed "books" and "published articles" as evidence of authorship, items that are surely "formal things."

These focus group answers presented us with curious conundrums. While we worried about students depending too much on the myth of the individual genius author, we certainly acknowledge that they need to feel confident in order to persist as authors. In a similar vein, we were concerned that students were too sure of their own "originality" that might be flawed or underexamined. Were they exhibiting traits of iGen (the term coined by Jean Twenge to describe the generation of people born between 1995 and 2014)? Twenge claims that "iGen takes the individualistic mindset for granted" (275). Their subscription to the "original genius" notion of authorship seems to undermine their previous answers about collaboration in online writing spaces. Or does it? Does one cancel out the other? Do we need to be able to see them holding both definitions aloft while still considering the question of authorship, writ large?

While the survey does confirm our hunch that students are broadening their general definitions of authorship to include digital spaces and the collaborative processes therein, we did not expect students to emphasize "responsibility" in the ways that they did. One student states, "Authorship seems to include more than professional authors and includes everyone who does any form of writing, with an added dimension of responsibility." Another student noted,

> Since taking Rhet 295, I realized authorship is more than just owning a piece of work, but entails a huge reputation and responsibility behind one's name. . . . We are responsible for what is written or created to be shared or seen by others. It's extremely important to take pride in one's own work, because it does reveal itself through those creations.

Although we do not know which student made this comment on the anonymous survey, we both wonder if the response comes from a student who edited one of the more controversial Wikipedia entries, such as "Fake News" or "Alternative Facts."

The question of digital authorship and responsibility is so provocative that we made it one key element of our focus groups. When asked if the notion of responsibility figured into their ideas about authorship, Natalie stated, "Morally, I feel an obligation to make sure everything I post is super credible and have all of my evidence to back up what I wrote. So definitely I feel more responsible." Camille followed up, "I need to know that anyone can access it and just being able to know what you want to

say and why you are saying it . . . now I do feel a greater responsibility."
Both women expressed the need to feel sure of their own role as authors
and the attached obligation to correctly inform or cater to their online
audiences. Natalie focused on gathering credible evidence and ethically
representing the ideas of others while Camille emphasized the responsibility of word choice ("what you want to say") and clear purpose ("why you
are saying it"). Composition Scholar Robert Cummings refers to Wikipedia writing assignments as "Commons-based Peer Production (CBPP)."
In other words, he explores the particular nature of research assignments
that require students to write with peers in a public commons, such as the
Wikipedia community. He claims: "Perhaps least understood, and least
examined, is the shift in ethos that accompanies incorporation of CBPP
into the traditional composition classroom. Ultimately CBPP emphasizes
the individual; by placing so many of the production decisions into the
hands of individual students, CBPP fosters greater maturity and self-
awareness" (24). In Natalie and Camille's answers, we see a burgeon-
ing awareness of their own ethos that stems from the responsibility they
feel when writing for a public audience, both as "solo" authors and in
co-authorship.

4.   Transfer of Knowledge

We can ask the same question of digitally mediated education that we
ask about all of our classes: is the knowledge transferable? Can and do
the students retain what they learn and successfully apply that knowledge
in a new semester, a new educational situation. Maura A. Smale and
Mariana Regalado, both librarians at the City University of New York,
conducted a large study of public college students in New York City.
Although their focus is on the affordances and barriers of digital technologies, their work is relevant to discussions of digital authorship and
transfer of knowledge. While expanding upon Tim Ingold's concept of
"taskspace," they write that a student's "experience with technology . . . is
dynamically constructed by the student within her environments and with
different purposes over time" (14). Smale and Regalado's findings could
be described by John Dewey's claim that an experience is "educative" *only*
if it is brought to bear in a future setting, which assumes that any bit of
knowledge has the potential to transfer to another setting.

Survey respondents offered information about how they have transferred the knowledge they gained in Rhetoric 295 to other reading and
writing situations, even though we did not ask directly about that. For
example, one student reflected,

> In regards to reading, Rhet 295 has made me into a more analytical
> reader. Because of the class projects, namely the Wikipedia project,
> I am more likely to question texts that I encounter and look into the

authors, collaborators, and other contributors. In regards to writing I don't think much has changed in my style both online and off line.

This student's comment provides a direct link between the Wikipedia assignment processes and the student's newfound critical curiosity as a reader. Although this student does not note a change in writing style, others did. Another student claimed, "After studying and researching online content, I view what I read and how I write online differently. I've come to see myself as a produser now and I closely monitor the online content I produce and consume." Not only has the concept of produsage become part of this student's working vocabulary, they have also refined how they interact with online text. This student brings the reading and writing habits practiced and explicitly studied—by reading texts like Bruns'—into daily practice.

Elizabeth Wardle tempers Dewey's aforementioned claim about educative experiences by stating that "meta-awareness about writing" may be the only transferable knowledge springing from first-year writing classes—and is certainly the most important. Digital rhetoric scholar Crystal VanKooten rightly points out that "meta-awareness," "metacognition," "metacognitive awareness," and "rhetorical awareness" have been used interchangeably and sloppily in that "researchers who use [these terms] do not define or specify what aspects of thought are most relevant" to them (58). We start with the broad definition posed by Howard Tinberg, in which he points out the difference between cognition and metacognition:

> "Do you know your knowledge?" asks Samuel Taylor Coleridge, trying to point out the difference between knowing *what* we know and knowing *that* we know (emphasis added). The first calls upon cognition while the second requires metacognition. . . . For those of us who teach writing, the objective is not just to have our students produce effective writing—that is, to respond in logical and thoughtful ways to the question posed. We also want our students to demonstrate consciousness of process that will enable them to reproduce success. Metacognition is not cognition. Performance, however thoughtful, is not the same as awareness of how the performance came to be.
>
> (75)

To answer VanKooten's call to "define or specify" what we mean by meta-awareness or metacognition, we focus on students' awareness of themselves as authors and the spaces and tools they can choose to use.

Our students may not have remembered the gist of every assigned reading and may have forgotten all of the rules of the citation systems they used in our seminar, but they do "demonstrate consciousness of process" (Tinberg 75). They articulate their progressively expansive definitions of authorship which they deploy "for different purposes over time" (Smale and Regalado 14). For example, one survey respondent wrote about multiple intersections of "authorship" and "produsage": "I never thought about the concepts of writing space before [taking Rhet 295]. I can use [writing spaces] to influence or be influenced. Everything I write makes me an author. And that has never occurred to me." Equally significantly, this student casts their role as an author more deeply than just "producing" and "using" by bringing up the notion of influence. This student's consciousness of authorship recalls our previous discussion of responsibility and points at the power dynamics embedded in rhetorical acts.

Additionally, this survey response brings up the broadest possible definition of authorship: "everything I write makes me an author." This firm declaration of authorship recalls for us the competing definitions of authorship that Sophia and Micaela offered in the focus groups: an all-encompassing general definition and a quite narrow personal definition. We have come to see this tension as a step along the path to transfer and rhetorical self-awareness. In our view, they are creating a hierarchy of authorship and placing themselves in an inferior position. They are not yet able to see themselves as representative of their most generous definitions.

After analyzing students' class texts, survey responses, and focus group answers, we have come to see a deeper level of learning and metacognition with each iteration. The Wikipedia project reinforced and deepened the students' understanding of produsage and digital authorship, which was introduced with the Writing Space Review assignment. The survey asked students, sometimes two years later, to name the ways in which their writing and reading habits have been influenced by the subject and practice of Rhetoric 295. And, the focus groups "conducted after the course concluded may have facilitated students' most profound learning insights" (Gabor 181) because the student-to-student interaction reassured them that their definitions of authorship apply to one another, and, by extension, to themselves.

Appendix 9A
Wikipedia Entry Assignment Sheet

Working in groups of four, you will choose a Wikipedia Entry to improve and/or expand. This project will require extensive research, careful editing, attention to Wikipedia's "neutral" style, and collaboration with your group members. To support this project, we will have access to editing tools and spaces provided by Wikiedu. Your final drafts should end up being published on Wikipedia. There will also be a group presentation associated with this project.

Your Group Will Work on One of the Following Topics

Concepts We Studied in Class

- Alternative Facts
- Cyberbullying
- Discourse community
- *Eloquentia Perfecta*
- Fake News
- Produsage
- Remediation & Remix
- Writing Across the Curriculum

Biographies

- Danah Boyd
- Sherry Turkle
- Jean Twenge

Class Learning Outcomes

1. Incorporate multiple texts of length and complexity within a unified argumentative essay, addressing connections and differences among

them. *The main function of your Wikipedia entry will be to incorporate multiple sources, showing the connections and differences among them.*

2. Develop sophisticated research questions and compose substantial arguments in response to those questions, incorporating extensive independent library research and demonstrating mastery of standard academic documentation modes. *You will come up with questions that drive your research, which will be extensive and independent; proper documentation is vital.*

3. **Style:** Students edit their own prose to achieve a clear and mature writing style in keeping with the conventions of academic and/or professional discourse. *Wikipedia requires a specific kind of nonpersonal, neutral tone, which we will learn for this project and you will employ in your entries.*

4. **Revision:** Students develop their own revision strategies for extending and enriching early drafts and for producing polished advanced academic writing. *You will spend twelve weeks working slowly though the steps of composing and revising your Wikipedia entry.*

5. Compose texts in a range of electronic environments *You will compose in Wikiedu and Wikipedia electronic spaces.*

6. Demonstrate the ability to reflect upon their own visual and verbal rhetorical strategies and choices *You will informally reflect upon your own rhetorical strategies and choices throughout this project, and you will formally share those reflections in your final presentation.*

Appendix 9B
Survey Questions

1. When you signed up for Rhetoric 295 (NewMedia/YouMedia: Writing in Electronic Environments), did you expect to do:
   - more writing than reading
   - more reading than writing
   - an equal amount of reading and writing

2. When you enter a new online space, do you generally expect to engage as
   - a reader
   - a writer
   - other, please explain: _____

3. I read differently **online** after taking Rhet 295
   - Yes
   - No

4. I read differently **off line** after taking Rhet 295
   - Yes
   - No

5. I write differently **online** after taking Rhet 295
   - Yes
   - No

6. I write differently **off line** after taking Rhet 295
   - Yes
   - No

7. Please explain your answers to Questions 3–6

8. What was your definition of *authorship* before you took Rhet 295?

9. What is your current definition of *authorship* (since taking Rhet 295)?

10. Would you be willing to participate in

   - a focus group with other Rhet 295 students
   - an individual interview with the Primary Investigator (Catherine Gabor) and/or co-researcher Riley Nelson?
   - neither
   - both

If you are willing to participate in a focus group and/or interview, please fill out the following information:

   - Name: _____
   - Best email address: _____
   - Best number for calling/texting: _____

Appendix 9C
Former RHET295 Student Focus Group

If any, please discuss what types of Rhetoric courses you have taken prior to RHET295?

What other Rhetoric courses have you completed since RHET295?

Was RHET295 the first college course you have taken with an emphasis on writing in the digital age? If not, please explain the course.

How did this course (RHET295) differ from a standard Rhetoric course?

Based off of survey results, 65% of former RHET295 students said they read differently after taking the class. If this was your experience, can you elaborate?

How does your approach to text differ? Can you provide any specific examples?

Did this shift or change occur in mostly online text or offline? Both?

Did you notice a change in your writing or approach to writing after RHET295? Was there a specific assignment that had an impact on this change?

Was this a change that occurred only offline or online? Or both?

One survey respondent notes that s/he feels a much greater "responsibility" when writing in online spaces (as opposed to off line). Do you? Why or why not? Discuss.

Talk about yourself as a digital reader and a digital writer. Do you see those as separate or do you feel like you are always a *produser*? Explain.

Most former students felt their definition of "authorship" changed during the class. There is a recurring pattern in responses from students that their definition became more casual, more broad, and/or more collaborative meaning students no longer felt authorship had to be contained to a formal, traditional, or educational place.

Canyou elaborate based on your own experience

How do you view yourself as an author?

What was your number one takeaway from the class? Why? Have you used it in other settings?

Appendix 9D

Pick a writing space or writing tool that you have never used before. Spend ten days using it and writing a review of it. Your review will be in the form of multiple posts on the tumblr account you create for this class.

Writing Space Review Assignment Sheet

Important Intellectual Tasks for This Project

- Definition of "writing space" and/or "writing tool"
- Description of your writing space/tool
- Criteria of what you value in a writing space/tool
- Judgment: how does this space/tool measure up to your criteria?

Class Learning Outcomes

1. Analyze writing tools, genres, and textual delivery methods: *The main purpose of this assignment is to analyze writing tools, the genres they support/encourage/prevent, and their textual delivery methods.*
2. Compose texts in a range of electronic environments: *You will compose in at least two different electronic environments for this assignment, your tumblr and the writing space you choose to review.*
3. Demonstrate the ability to reflect upon their own visual and verbal rhetorical strategies and choices: *Part of your review and analysis will be a reflection on the kinds of visual and verbal composing you did in your target writing space.*
4. Engage in critical discussions of the nature of writing in the twenty-first century: *The assignment itself is a critical discussion of writing in the twenty-first century.*
5. Intelligently distinguish among the production and reception of text: *As part of your description and analysis, you will distinguish between the production tools and reception spaces of the writing site you analyze.*

Acknowledgements

We would like to thank all of the students who took the Rhetoric 295 seminar between 2015 and 2017. We would especially like to thank the five students who participated in the focus groups; their insights made this article much richer. Finally, we would like to thank Tina Kazan of Elmhurst College, who read an earlier version, and editor Mary R. Lamb.

Notes

1. The authors, Cathy and Riley, are professor and undergraduate teaching assistant, respectively. Riley's participation in the class started when she was a student and continued for two semesters through her role as an undergraduate teaching assistant. Throughout the chapter, we use the plural personal pronoun to represent our collective thinking. In parts, we refer to one of us specifically, using the singular personal pronoun and first name.
2. The word "produsage" is a portmanteau combining "production" and "usage" in the context of how people interact with online text (Bruns).
3. All student names are pseudonyms.

Works Cited

Blythe, Stuart, and Laura Gonzales. "Coordination and Transfer across the Meta-genre of Secondary Research." *College Composition and Communication*, vol. 67, no. 4, 2016, pp. 607–33.

Brandt, Deborah. "The Sponsors of Literacy." *College Composition and Communication*, vol. 49, no. 2, 1998, pp. 165–85.

Bruns, Axel. *Blogs, Wikipedia, Second Life, and beyond: From Production to Produsage*, Peter Lang, 2008.

Cummings, Robert E. *Lazy Virtues: Teaching Writing in the Age of Wikipedia*, Vanderbilt University Press, 2009, *EBSCO eBook Subscription Academic Collection*, web.b.ebscohost.com/ehost/ebookviewer/ebook?sid=8444785a-11db-4841-8f2c-e0539920baaa%40sessionmgr103&vid=0&format=EB.

Dewey, John. *Experience and Education*, Touchstone, 1997, 1938.

Smale, Maura A., and Mariana Regalado. *Digital Technology as Affordance and Barrier in Higher Education*, Palgrave MacMillan, 2017.

Tinberg, Howard. "Metacognition Is Not Cognition." *Naming What We Know: Threshold Concepts of Writing Studies*, edited by Linda Adler-Kassner and Elizabeth Wardle, Utah State University Press, 2015, pp. 75–6.

Twenge, Jean M. *iGen: Why Today's Super-Connected Kids Are Growing Up Less Rebellious, More Tolerant, Less Happy: And Completely Unprepared for Adulthood*, Atria Books, 2017.

VanKooten, Crystal. "'The Video Was What Did It for Me': Developing Meta-Awareness about Composition across Media." *College English*, vol. 79, no. 1, 2016, pp. 57–80.

Wardle, Elizabeth. "'Understanding Transfer' from FYC: Preliminary Results of a Longitudinal Study." *WPA: Writing Program Administration*, vol. 31, no. 1–2, 2007, pp. 64–85.

Werner, Courtney L. "How Rhetoric and Composition Described and Defined New Media at the Start of the Twenty-First Century." *College Composition and Communication*, vol. 68, no. 4, 2017, pp. 713–41.

10 Reorienting Relationships to Reading by Dwelling in Our Discomfort

Julie A. Myatt

We've all been there: the teacher stands behind the podium, turns to the class, and issues the directive, "Let's discuss the homework reading." The students, several of whom do not even have their books out on their desks, aren't sure how to respond or have little to say. The teacher, growing increasingly uncomfortable, interrupts the awkward silence by sharing her own thoughts on the reading. Relieved not to be called upon, the students allow the teacher to talk *at* them rather than *with* them. They listen, but this exchange likely leaves students questioning the point of completing assigned readings.

I'm sorry to say I have seen this scenario play out more than once during my career, and, reluctant though I am to admit it, I'm certain I played the role of that struggling teacher at some point. When our attempts to provide students with meaningful reading assignments fall short, we must consider why. Uncertainty about the role reading should play in the first-year composition classroom can leave instructors wondering, *"How can I motivate students to read?"* That's a question I hear often in my role as writing program administrator, and it may be one you have asked yourself.

Perhaps you, like many others, possess concerns about how reading practices in the digital age are changing our relationship to the written word. Perhaps like Nicholas Carr, author of *The Shallows: What the Internet Is Doing to Our Brains*, you worry about how our online reading habits, often characterized by distraction, interruption, and incomplete or partial reading, are influencing how we read. You may worry that students are no longer reading as deeply as they once did. If so, you are not alone; the work of scholars such as Rebecca Moore Howard, Tanya K. Rodrigue, and Tricia C. Serviss should prompt concern among writing faculty about how closely students are reading and how well they are comprehending the sources they cite. You also may have been one of many who in the aftermath of the 2016 Presidential election, amid evidence that many voters were easily manipulated by inaccurate information, questioned the efficacy of writing instruction, wondering whether our collective efforts are actually helping to produce a literate citizenry.

Perhaps our situation is not without hope. Rather than bemoan the challenges associated with teaching research and writing in the digital age, we should recognize the possibilities digital texts afford us, for our ability to access digital texts *can* be harnessed in productive ways in the writing classroom. Of course, doing so demands that we make students active participants in the process, inviting them to explore along with us the challenges we all face as readers and writers of digital texts. As author and educator Kelly Gallagher reminds us, "Learning begins when we encounter confusion." Worth noting is that, rather than merely be aware of it, Gallagher invites us to "welcome and embrace" this confusion (63). For our bewilderment to be generative, we must dwell in the uncomfortable space brought on by our lack of understanding; we must use it to learn something about ourselves as readers and what in the text—or ourselves—led to our frustration. All too often, however, and despite the work of scholars who advocate for attention to difficulty (see Salvatori and Donahue), the classroom is a space in which reading-related confusion is dismissed as the student's problem instead of something for students and teachers to acknowledge and grapple with as part of the learning process. Or, in a more generous interpretation, teachers are unaware of students' confusion because students aren't forthcoming about it. As educators, we must consider why this is: we have to ask why students may not feel comfortable seeking our help upon encountering obstacles to their reading comprehension.

Much in the way that students who are fearful of being labeled poor writers may hesitate to take risks in their writing, those reluctant to be considered weak readers may not readily articulate their reading difficulties. As I have argued elsewhere, we must create spaces for these formative negotiations in our pedagogies—yes, even at the university level, and especially in writing classes, because teaching students how to read is central to teaching students how to write (Barger). Perhaps a more troublesome question than why students won't share with us their reading challenges is *why don't we as members of the academy accept our responsibility to teach reading?* In *Securing a Place for Reading in Composition*, Ellen Carillo explains that our inattention to reading is due partly to the belief that students should have mastered reading by the time they arrive at the university: "For *professors* to teach reading would be to 'lower' themselves to do work that should have been done by K-12 *teachers*" (9). In tracing the fading influence of reader-response theory, Patricia Harkin similarly contends that we as a field lost interest in reading because it was too egalitarian, and the professoriate benefits from exclusionary practices: "There is much to be gained by keeping reading mysterious—by refusing to reveal the processes through which readers decipher 'hidden meanings'" (417). Certainly, it is easier to blame students for failing to complete reading assignments or to call their intelligence into question because of their poorly supported interpretations than it is to teach the kinds of sustained, recursive readings that fuel our own lengthy and cerebral conversations with texts. And yet, perhaps now more than ever, eliding reading from writing instruction possesses grave implications for student learning and civic engagement. In this chapter, I draw from my experience revising a research-writing course (see Appendix 10A for an overview of the major projects) to offer strategies that can promote productive reading practices in the digital age. Some of these strategies may foster discomfort on the part of both students and teachers, as they require us to interrogate long-held assumptions about how and what we should read in the writing classroom.

Recognize that Collaboration Is Key to Promoting Productive Relationships to Reading

In the introduction to her 2003 *Intertexts: Reading Pedagogy in the College Writing Classroom*, Marguerite Helmers reminds us that as writing teachers, we are uniquely equipped to consider the role of the social in our teaching. My orientation to the revised research-writing course is indebted to Helmers's assertion that "to teach reading is to teach the relationships between readers and texts and between readers and the spaces where they encounter texts and other readers" (23). Indeed, prompting students to consider how they respond to others' texts is not enough; we must also allow students to explore their reading practices in the context of others' experiences as readers. Students should spend time not only identifying their reading preferences; they must also learn how to anticipate other readers' expectations for texts based on genre, location, etc. On a related note, Michael Bunn explains that "the process of reading is a *negotiation* between the knowledge and purposes of the writer and the knowledge and purposes of the reader" ("Motivation" 501). Similarly, Linda Adler Kassner and Heidi Estrem write, "When instructors expect magic, they sometimes take for granted that reading is a complex interaction between reader, text, and context" (45). My hope is that students will recognize that though reading and writing are indeed complex acts, they are acts that can be approached thoughtfully and purposefully by pausing to consider these relationships.

Because students enrolled in FYC classes may consider themselves poor readers when in reality they are people who have not been taught how to read deeply, I begin the semester with a discussion about the struggles we all, myself included, have with reading. We brainstorm strategies we use when reading, and I make sure to convey my belief that reading is difficult for all of us at times. Borrowing from Gallagher, I present students with a mantra of sorts, "Learning begins when we embrace confusion." I want students to understand that it is okay—productive, even—to ask questions of texts. Students, especially those at my university, many of whom commute and work off campus, have many demands on their time, and I value selecting texts students want to spend time reading. On the recommendation of a colleague, I consulted *The Best American Magazine Writing of 2014* to locate examples of the kind of researched yet accessible and engaging writing I thought students would get excited about. The readings I assigned included pieces from *The New Yorker*, *Runner's World*, *The Washington Post*, *ProPublica*, and a *This American Life* podcast. These aren't traditional scholarly sources; they aren't peer-reviewed journal articles or excerpts from monographs. Those certainly have a place in introducing students to the concept of research, but because students' investigative research projects require them to contribute to an ongoing cultural conversation important to them, we primarily read popular, yet well-researched publications indicative of how writers approach potentially divisive debates in compelling ways.

How teachers introduce assigned readings is key. I don't just list these titles on the syllabus; I preview them in class, offering teasers by asking students to predict what a given article might be about based on its title or a brief quote. The act of previewing texts in this way captures students' attention, and, when combined with prompts asking them to respond to the reading—whether a letter to the author, questions about passages that confuse them, or a list of strategies the writer used that they want to steal for their own writing—it gets them thinking critically about assigned readings, thus cultivating productive relationships between student readers and assigned texts.

Establish Connections between What Students Read and What They Write

FYC instructors may find students reluctant readers resistant to engaging with course material or possessing misconceptions about writing and the work required of them in writing classes. We cannot assume that if we assign it, students will read it. We can make reading more likely by highlighting the connections between the reading and writing students do in FYC. Indeed, students may be surprised to enter a writing class and find a heavy emphasis on reading, as was the case for one of my Fall 2015 students, who wrote in an end-of-semester course evaluation:

> Although at first I did not like the reading aspect considering it was a writing class, once I was able to conceptualize your overall goal I began to really enjoy the readings for this class. Discussing them in class is what really helped me to put all of the pieces together because it helped to really understand what it's like to be a published writer and the methods they apply to strengthen their writings, which I then can apply in my own writings.

To promote the kinds of rhetorical and analytical readings necessary for success in research writing, instructors must choose well-written, thought-provoking texts, explaining to students that assigned readings can serve as models for their own writing. Bunn's study of how writing instructors perceive reading reveals that though instructors acknowledge the associations between reading and writing, they do not always convey this to students ("Motivation," 501–3), potentially to students' detriment because "the degree to which students are motivated to read assigned texts is influenced by whether or not they perceive connections between that reading and other aspects of the course, especially their writing assignments" (505). In keeping with Bunn's call for foregrounding reading-writing connections for students, I strive to present readings as inspiration for students' own writing because that orientation offers students a purpose for reading beyond merely completing a homework assignment.

Foreground Rhetorical Reading Over Reading for Content

To support students in recognizing the choices they can make in their own writing, I emphasize the process of reading rhetorically—determining how a text was constructed—and why. Similarly, we attend to writers' exigencies, both those of published authors and of students completing research projects. By analyzing the larger context surrounding a publication, students come to understand writing as a response to a particular need; this knowledge helps students adopt a problem-oriented approach to their own research and writing as they learn to identify ongoing social debates they want to enter.

To shift students' orientation to reading from one that is content driven to one that is rhetorical, I assign Malcolm Gladwell's "Offensive Play," an article that compares professional football to dogfighting. For homework, students write their questions and reactions in the margins. At the beginning of the next class, students are instructed to look back over their marginalia, then use the following sentence starters (Gallagher 70) to record their thoughts on Gladwell's "Offensive Play."

> I noticed . . .
> I don't understand . . .
> I'd like to know . . .

Students then discuss their responses in trios with the charge: *Work together to clear up any lingering confusion about the text before reporting back to the class about what you discussed.* During the group reports, students have the opportunity to hear how others in the class outside of their group reacted to the text. We then analyze the Gladwell article using the rhetorical triangle, identifying the article's purpose, audience, and exigence, which, following Lloyd Bitzer's definition (cited in "Rhetorical

Situation") we define as "The problem motivating the writer to act in hopes that, through writing, the problem can be addressed." This activity not only helps students analyze Gladwell's article rhetorically by attempting to identify his purpose and audience, it invites them to consider what existing social problems motivated him as a researcher and writer—a question they have to ask themselves when developing topic proposals for their own research.

Next, I assign Bunn's "How to Read Like a Writer" chapter from *Writing Spaces*. Students are instructed to read it and then re-read the Gladwell "Offensive Play" article, applying the five questions Bunn provides on pages 79–81 to Gladwell's article:

1. How effective is the language the author uses? Is it too formal? Too informal? Perfectly appropriate?
2. What kinds of evidence does the author use to support his/her claims? Does he/she use statistics? Quotes from famous people? Personal anecdotes or personal stories? Does he/she cite books or articles?
3. How appropriate or effective is this evidence? Would a different type of evidence, or some combination of evidence, be more effective?
4. Are there places in the writing that you find confusing? What about the writing in those places makes it unclear or confusing?
5. How does the author move from one idea to another in the writing? Are the transitions between the ideas effective? How else might he/she have transitioned between ideas instead?

This kind of rhetorical analysis helps students recognize that the choices successful writers make are intentional and are informed by the writer's assessment of the rhetorical situation. Though contemplating the rhetorical aspects of composing may be second nature to us as writing instructors, many students, even those with healthy extracurricular writing lives, come to FYC believing that all academic writing is generic; they seek the formula that will allow them to address any future academic writing situation with ease. Too many FYC students enter university with extensive (and yet limiting) experience writing in acontextual, standardized test-based situations. A student from Spring 2016 explained that prior to this class, "I never envisioned an exact audience or what my true purpose was in writing other than to receive a grade." As a result, students may not feel authorized to critique another author's choices. By inviting students to do just that, Bunn's questions actively engage students in *thinking like writers*, the very work Kathleen Blake Yancey, Kara Taczak, and Liane Robertson say *is* the work of first-year composition.

Devote Ample Class Time to Exploring Readers' Reactions

The next model text students read is Steve Friedman's "Bret, Unbroken," originally published in *Runner's World*. As usual, I preview the text by introducing the title in class and asking students to characterize its tone as well as to predict what it might be about. For homework students are instructed:

1. Write a double-entry journal in your writer's notebook.
   1. Draw a line down the page, about 1/3 of the way from the left margin.
   2. To the left of the line, record a passage you find compelling, word-for-word, including the page number.
   3. To the right of the line, write a response to the passage.
2. Write a letter to Steve Friedman explaining your reactions to "Bret Unbroken." Be sure to discuss what in the text inspires your reactions, and include direct quotes and page numbers.

The next class meeting, students collaborate in small groups, discussing their letters to Friedman, deciding as a group on a passage/technique they want us to discuss as a class, and explaining to the class what technique the writer uses and for what effect. Classmates then have the chance to respond. After that, the entire class considers Friedman's purpose in telling Bret's story, as well as how his piece is different from examples of the profile genre we often encounter. Clearly, a significant amount of class time is devoted to analyzing this text and our responses to it, but it is a worthy investment of time.

I once overheard two classmates talking about how they simply could not understand why anyone should care about the titular character Bret, but as class went on and more students shared their reactions to the text, it became clear that many students were genuinely inspired by Bret's story, and their observations no doubt gave the two students who were initially dismissive of the text more to consider. We could write these two students off as being shallow or as not having attended closely to the text, but perhaps they simply needed to see it through someone else's eyes. As one student from Fall 2015 observed, "I really enjoyed the open discussion. Though sometimes I didn't want to listen to my fellow students' comments, most of them ended up opening my perspective for writing in general. They are part of what helped me realize how important the audience is when considering how to write an article or essay." To once again invoke Helmers, students benefit from seeing how others relate to texts. And as Bunn, Adler-Kassner and Estrem, and others have observed, students also need to understand that what they read can inspire their own writing. To that end, I have students write in response to the following prompts:

1. How does this article—or your classmates' reactions to it—introduce you to new ways of thinking about writing? What technique(s) from this article would you want to use in your own writing?
2. Who is someone you know who has a story worth telling? Bret's story not only speaks to those for whom running is an important part of life, it reminds us that people are more than what they appear to be on the surface, that we need to learn not to judge others based on our initial impressions. How is the story of the person you just identified part of an ongoing cultural conversation? What could it teach us? And to tell the story effectively, whose perspectives would you have to include?

Attend to How Writers Use Sources

Additionally, because both "Offensive Play" and "Bret, Unbroken" are available online, we analyze not only the articles themselves but their context; we talk about how the location of a text can help us learn about its readers' expectations for the publication. Considering how each work functions in its larger context adds yet another dimension to students' rhetorical analyses. This was also the case with the *This American Life* podcast "The Problem We All Live With." Informed by Nikole Hannah-Jones's research into the Normandy, Missouri school district, this podcast offers yet another example of how a writer uses research to address an ongoing social problem, in this case, education inequality and how it disproportionately affects students of color. In addition to assigning the podcast because I consider it a good example of how a writer approaches a divisive social issue in productive ways, the podcast allows me to introduce students to the concept that the writer is responsible for selecting information from sources and interpreting it in ways that support listeners in understanding its significance. To promote this idea, I provide students with guided listening questions to answer during the podcast, including:

1. Use the column headings below to: (a) list the sources Hannah-Jones uses and (b) identify how they help Hannah-Jones answer her research question/tell the story of the challenges facing Normandy students/make claims about integration.

   Source Name or Title / Purpose

2. Identify an instance when Hannah-Jones's commentary helps you understand the significance of a source she chooses to use. What

was being discussed at the time, and how did her voiceover help clarify the meaning for you?

Then, in groups, students share their responses and also identify techniques Hannah-Jones use that their group would want to use in their writing.

Model texts such as the podcast and the companion article, "School Segregation, The Continuing Tragedy of Ferguson," are particularly helpful in exposing students to various ways writers draw from and credit sources, an important skill in research writing, though a process students may find mystifying, particularly if their past experiences with sources lead them to view source integration as a mere assignment requirement rather than as a method of enhancing their position on a given topic. As teachers, we must help students develop productive attitudes toward source material, and inviting them to attend to other authors' use of sources is one strategy.

Rather than write a research paper for a general audience, students in the revised research-writing course must locate an existing popular publication appropriate for their chosen topic or purpose. In practically every case, the target publications for students' investigative research articles do not use MLA citation or even a bibliography. Instead, the published authors after whom students model their work use clear signal phrases, hyperlinks, or, albeit less often, footnotes. Students tend to be surprised (and even pleased) to learn about the many and varied ways they can integrate source material into their writing. Tailoring source use to the chosen publication venue requires students to consider the options available to them rather than simply follow a formulaic citation style dictated to them by the teacher—which opens their eyes to the various options for source integration and attribution. This practice may elicit discomfort in students accustomed to formulaic writing tasks or to those familiar with MLA citation style (and with teachers committed to teaching MLA), but it fosters in students a valuable awareness of how citation practices differ widely from one context to the next. I also hope that by attending to how published authors introduce and follow up on sources, students will recognize the importance of integrating sources in thoughtful ways into their own writing.

Promote Information Literacy by Reading Digital Texts Laterally, Not Just Vertically

Close reading and critical thinking have long been the touchstones of teaching research writing, but issues surrounding production and access in the digital age challenge close reading as the sole and direct route to critical thinking. Gone are the days of reading a text in isolation, certain we can trust its authenticity; to help students become literate citizens, we must encourage them to question their sources of information. Sam Wineburg and Sarah McGrew, researchers at the Stanford History Education Group, ask a compelling question: "what if the problem is not that we're failing to teach media literacy, but that we're teaching the wrong kind?" (44).

To explore this question, Wineburg and McGrew attempt to identify what sets "expert" internet readers apart from those unable to identify credible, relevant sources. To determine what counts as "expert" reading practices, they survey PhD historians, fact checkers, and Stanford undergraduates. One practice the authors associate with expert readers is "lateral reading" (going outside of a source to learn more about it rather than just reading vertically by conducting a close reading of the single source). They write, "Paradoxically, a key feature of lateral reading is *not* reading" (Wineburg and McGrew 38). Before you grow too concerned, know that Wineburg and McGrew aren't calling for a curriculum that elides reading. They concede, citing Shanahan's blog and Wolf's book, that "Close reading, the careful, analytic search for pattern, detail, and nuance, is essential to any thoughtful curriculum (Shanahan, 2012; Wolf, 2007). But when the goal is to quickly get up to speed, the close reading of a digital source, when one doesn't yet know if the source can be trusted (or is what it says it is)—proves to be a colossal waste of time" (Wineburg and McGrew 43).

Wineburg and McGrew explain that "In evaluating digital information, we distinguish between widely used but flawed *weak heuristics*, such as using a domain designation as a proxy for trustworthiness, and *strong heuristics*, like lateral reading which not only save time but often lead to more accurate judgments than more complex methods" (41). They caution against checklists (like the widely used CRAAP Test) that rely on websites' "most easily manipulated features" (44) because

> when the Internet is characterized by polished web design, search engine optimization, and organizations vying to appear trustworthy, such guidelines create a false sense of security. In fact, relying on checklists could make students more vulnerable to scams, not less. Fact checkers succeeded on our tasks not because they followed the advice we give to students. They succeeded because they didn't.
>
> (Wineburg and McGrew 44–5)

Wineburg and McGrew continue by explaining that

> The checklist approach cuts searchers off from the most efficient route to learning more about a site: finding out what the rest of the web has to say. This was the biggest lesson we learned from watching these experts: They evaluated unfamiliar websites by leaving them. For fact checkers, the direct route to credibility was indirect.
>
> (45)

These findings run counter to what we have historically valued in the teaching of reading, and they reinforce that reading texts in isolation, as we are inclined to do with print texts, is not good practice in the digital age. Instead, we also need to encourage students to read *outside* the text, particularly when teaching students how to evaluate sources.

Before reading "School Segregation: The Continuing Tragedy of Ferguson," I follow my usual practice of previewing the text with students, asking them to predict what the text discusses based on key terms and an excerpted sentence or two. Then I also instruct students to do some research on Nikole Hannah-Jones, the author of the piece, and on *ProPublica*, the site housing her article. This activity models for students what they should do when attempting to determine the credibility of a new source—look outside the source for answers *before* reading it in its entirety. Then in class after students have read the article, we use the embedded hyperlinks to explore Nikole Hannah-Jones's sources, seeking to determine their credibility. Students should be encouraged to conduct similar readings of potential sources they encounter during their research—but they shouldn't stop there; following Wineburg and McGrew's recommendations, students should see what other sources on the Internet are saying about the topic, with the understanding that the "web [is] a maze filled with trap doors and blind alleys, where things are not always what they seem" (Wineburg and McGrew 15). To that end, students are also encouraged to use some of the key terms in Hannah-Jones's article to locate other sources discussing school segregation, white flight, and apartheid schools, etc., sharing what they discover with the class. Teaching students to read closely and carefully is of great value, but reading texts in isolation prevents students from considering the bigger picture, which is of equal importance when fostering a rhetorical awareness and information literacy.

Learn to Do More with Fewer Texts

Perhaps of all of the misconceptions hindering our success teaching students to read in the digital age, the most detrimental is the notion that for a course to be rigorous, it must involve a heavy reading load that requires little more of the teacher than assigning the texts and facilitating subsequent class discussions. Dan Keller's "A Framework for Rereading in First-Year Composition" offers a helpful challenge to this "more is better" mentality. Keller observes that

> Assigning more readings probably leads to scaffolding each of them less. We assign fewer pieces of writing because we want students to work through and experience how a piece of writing can develop. This pedagogy should be mirrored in how we teach reading, providing the

curricular space to slow down, focus, and achieve a sense of expertise with a few texts.

(Keller 46)

Pared-down, recursive reading practices such as those Keller advocates and I have described throughout this chapter illustrate that our quest for rigor need not result in the reading equivalent of abandoning students in the wilderness without a compass; it can find us leading students on an edifying revision journey by guiding them in retracing their steps through a given text by looking for something different each time or even by cutting them loose and allowing them to chart their own course as they seek answers to their questions about potential sources. If instructors can recognize that limiting the number of assigned readings can actually result in more intentional and involved readings, then students are more likely to take with them strategies for navigating texts actively and critically—and they may even enjoy themselves along the way, potentially resulting in more engaged readers and better-informed citizens. The paths to that point may be rocky and winding, but the destination is worth any potential discomfort.

Works Cited

Adler-Kassner, Linda, and Heidi Estrem. "Reading Practices in the Writing Classroom." *WPA: Writing Program Administration*, vol. 31, no. 1–2, 2007, pp. 35–47.

Barger, Julie Myatt. "Reading Is Not Essential to Writing Instruction." *Bad Ideas about Writing*, edited by Cheryl E. Ball and Drew M. Loewe, Digital Publishing Institute, 2017, pp. 44–50.

Bunn, Michael. "How to Read Like a Writer." *Writing Spaces: Readings on Writing.* vol. 2, edited by Charlie Lowe and Pavel Zemliansky, Parlor Press 2011, pp. 71–86.

———. "Motivation and Connection: Teaching Reading (and Writing) in the College Classroom." *College Composition and Communication*, vol. 64, no. 3, 2013, pp. 496–516.

Carillo, Ellen. *Securing a Place for Reading in Composition: The Importance of Teaching for Transfer*, Utah State University Press, 2015.

Gallagher, Kelly. *Deeper Reading: Comprehending Challenging Texts, 4–12*, Stenhouse, 2004.

Hannah-Jones, Nikole. "School Segregation: The Continuing Tragedy of Ferguson." *ProPublica*, 19 Dec. 2014, www.propublica.org/article/ferguson-school-segregation. Accessed 11 Aug. 2015.

Harkin, Patricia. "The Reception of Reader-Response Theory." *College Composition and Communication*, vol. 56, no. 3, 2005, pp. 410–25.

Helmers, Marguerite. *Intertexts: Reading Pedagogy in the Writing Classroom*, Lawrence Erlbaum Associates, 2003.

Howard, Rebecca Moore, Tanya K. Rodrigue, and Tricia C. Serviss. "Writing from Sources, Writing from Sentences." *Writing and Pedagogy*, vol. 2, no. 2, 2010, pp. 177–92.

Keller, Dan. "A Framework for Rereading in First Year Composition." *Teaching English in the Two-Year College*, vol. 41, no. 1, 2013, pp. 44–55.

"The Problem We All Live With." *This American Life from WBEZ Chicago*, 31 July 2015, www.thisamericanlife.org/562/the-problem-we-all-live-with-part-one.

"Rhetorical Situation." *CCC Poster Pages*, Conference on College Composition and Communication, 2010, www.ncte.org/library/NCTEFiles/Resources/Journals/CCC/0613-feb2010/CCC0613Poster.pdf.

Salvatori, Mariolina, and Patricia Donahue. *The Elements (and Pleasures) of Difficulty*, Pearson, 2005.

Shanahan, Tim. *What is Close Reading?* [Blog post]. 18, June 2012 http://shanahanonliteracy.com/blog/what-is-closereading#sthash.mxxi0paG.rtIrn0KW.dpbs.

Wineburg, Sam, and Sarah McGrew. "Lateral Reading: Reading Less and Learning More When Evaluating Digital Information." *Stanford History Education Group Working Paper No. 2017-A1*, 2017, www.ssrn.com/abstract=3048994

Wolf, Maryanne. *Proust and the Squid: The Story and Science of the Reading Brain*, HarperCollins, 2007.

Yancey, Kathleen Blake, Liane Robertson, and Kara Taczak. *Writing across Contexts: Transfer, Composition, and Sites of Writing*, Utah State University Press, 2014.

Appendix 10A
English 1020 Revised Course Design

Writing to Learn—20%

For these informal process writings, the emphasis is on *cognition*—this is where you can explore and develop your thoughts. You are encouraged to experiment with new ideas and new forms of expression. You need not be concerned with style and correctness at this stage in the process.

- Weekly Metacognitive Blog Posts (to be completed in class and submitted to D2L)
- Homework and in-class writings, annotations, informal presentations about projects and sources
- Drafts and conferences

Writing to Communicate—80%

For these developed projects, the emphasis is on *rhetoric*—this is where you must demonstrate your understanding of your chosen topic, genre conventions, and the audience's needs by presenting your ideas clearly and convincingly. You will need to attend carefully to the formal characteristics of the text prior to submitting these projects.

- **Project 1: Investigative Research Exploration—20%**

  Topic Proposal—10%

  > This project will find you working to convince your reader that the topic you are interested in pursuing is worthwhile. This will require you to conduct preliminary research. You will learn how to discuss your project's exigence (what's motivating you to research this topic, and how you hope to effect change) in ways that help others recognize its relevance to their lives.

  Rhetorical Annotated Bibliography—10%

  > This project will find you going more in depth with your research on your approved topic. You will develop information literacy

by learning how to locate, evaluate, and use source material effectively. You will also continue "reading like a writer" by analyzing sources rhetorically, introducing you to choices available to you in writing your own research article for Project 2.

- **Project 2: Investigative Research Article for a Real-World Publication—20%**

  This project allows you to share what you learned through your research with an audience of your choosing. Your article should persuade the audience to agree with your position or take action in some way. Please note that your article must include thoroughly developed content *and* design features (images, hyperlinks, etc.) appropriate for your target real-world publication. After receiving and addressing my feedback, I encourage you to upload your article to the D2L e-portfolio, as you may decide you want to share it with audiences outside of our class in the future. You are likewise encouraged to submit your work to your chosen real-world publication, and if it is accepted, please let me know!

- **Project 3: Presentation of Investigative Research—20%**

  This poster presentation will afford you the chance to share your semester-long research with a live audience outside of our class during the Celebration of Student Writing.

- **Project 4: End-of-Semester Reflection—20%**

  This project gives you the opportunity to reflect on the skills and habits of mind you have developed this semester as documented in your blog posts and other class writings before predicting how and in what contexts those skills could be of value to you in the future.

11 Clip, Tag, Annotate
Active Reading Practices for Digital Texts

Jason McIntosh

As a composition teacher, I approach reading instruction through writing. I want students in my classes to learn the practice of picking up a pen or pencil and annotating, through markup and marginal notes, the high-stakes texts they read in college. *High stakes* is a term that I borrow from Peter Elbow, who uses it in the context of writing assignments (5–6), to describe all of the reading tasks where we are required to *do* something (participate in class discussion) or *produce* something (a research essay) from texts that we read. Most of the reading that students do in college is high stakes, and active reading is crucial to the critical thinking and writing with sources that is required of them. However, active reading becomes a challenge as more and more of the texts that students read in college are digital.

Evidence of the rise of digital reading in school abounds. Sales of e-textbooks continue to increase each year (Straumsheim, "Highlights"), while publishers explore new business models for delivering digital course materials in a struggling textbook market (McKenzie). And while faculty are not adopting digital textbooks en masse, many see the learning and financial benefits of digital texts and are considering using them at some point in the future (Green). While the open education resources (OER) movement has seen slow growth with the awareness and adoption open textbooks (Seaman and Seaman), the United States Congress just funded a $5 million grant for open textbooks in universities, the first substantive recognition of the OER movement by Congress (Allen). Add to this digital landscape the rising costs of textbooks, a factor leading many students to acquire digital copies of texts, legally or otherwise (Cusker). Then there is the explosive growth of Google Scholar as the premier academic search engine (Ortega 138–42), providing access to nearly 100 million of the estimated 114 million scholarly English-language documents online (Khabsa and Giles).

Because students are reading more digital texts in school than ever before, it is important that educators explore digital tools that not only facilitate active reading with digital texts, but also allow students to organize or otherwise manipulate them in productive ways. PDF readers are one solution, but they are limited in the types of texts they support and how readers can interact with them. However, note-taking apps like Evernote and Microsoft OneNote make it easy to annotate and work dynamically with digital texts. Note-taking apps allow users to clip texts from the Internet (PDFs, websites, videos, et al.), tag them with searchable metadata, and annotate them with markup tools and marginal notes. The process of clipping, tagging, and digitally annotating isn't difficult to learn. I've found that students pick it up quite easily, teaching me many tricks in the process, and because the basic practices of annotation, especially markup and marginal notes, are fundamentally the same, we can use what we know about teaching active reading with print.

In the first part of this chapter, I describe note-taking apps and the process of clipping, tagging, and annotating. The best way to learn these apps is to make them a regular part of our everyday professional and personal reading. In this way, we learn the basic functions of an app and can better plan for how to teach it to students. Like any new literacy practice or technology, students benefit from a scaffolded approach that "help(s) [them] build the skills needed for [a] final assignment" (Bean 96). Therefore, I describe in the second half of this chapter how I scaffold my teaching of OneNote in a research-writing class. My hope is that my example provides ideas for how to teach other types of note-taking apps in classes other than first-year composition. Finally, one of the problems with writing about software applications is the speed at which they change. New features are added, and existing ones are dropped on a regular basis. For this reason, I chose to describe clipping, tagging, and annotating conceptually rather than provide a step-by-step "how to." I include an appendix that lists the "how to" resources I found useful for learning and teaching note-taking apps.

What Are Note-Taking Apps?

Note-taking apps range in complexity from simple to-do lists to complex and multifaceted digital notebooks. Their appearance and organizational structures are often analogous to real-world writing tools like sticky notes, legal pads, and three-ring binders. The uses of digital note-taking apps for writing are as endless as those real-world analogies—writing lists of all kinds, reminders, a place to just "jot things down." However, it is the more complex apps like Evernote and Microsoft OneNote that provide the most benefit to students reading and writing in the digital age. This is especially true as students accumulate multiple digital texts in a single course, many texts across courses in their fields of study, and when working on lengthy research projects.

On my Evernote bookshelf are notebooks for home and school. My home notebook includes shopping lists and vacation plans as well as

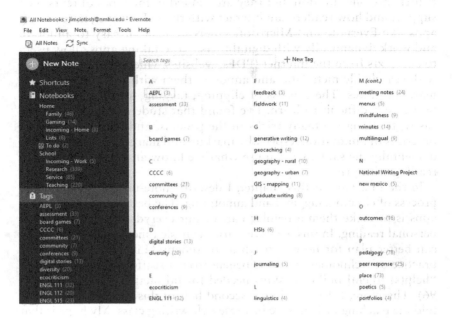

Figure 11.1 A page from my Evernote account, the virtual bookshelf that holds my digital notebooks

articles and videos that I share with my family. I have notebooks for work that are organized around the three areas of teaching, research, and service. This is where I save the articles I clip while researching a subject or just browsing the Web. Most note-taking apps support plug-ins that can be added to Web browsers, allowing users to clip and upload Web content to a digital notebook. For example, when I access an article in an online teaching journal, I can click the Evernote icon that I added to my browser, clip the article, and upload it to my teaching notebook. I can then use Evernote's markup tools to annotate while I read. I can also add my own tags (see Figure 11.1) to make it easier to find the article in my notebook. With clipping, tagging, and annotating, I have more control over how I read online journals. It makes my reading experience more active (and interactive) and brings it closer to the experience of actively reading a print journal.

Clipping

A Web clipper is a tool that allows readers to "clip" content from a website and add it to a digital notebook. If you've ever used Pinterest to save a recipe, do-it-yourself project, or craft idea, then you are familiar with the basics of Web clipping. Like Pinterest, most note-taking apps that support Web clipping include browser plug-ins that users can download and install. Plug-ins make it easy to clip text, images, video, and audio while reading online. Clipping options typically include full page (everything displayed in the browser), simplified versions of articles (with layout removed), and screenshot clipping defined by the user.

The benefits of Web clipping for active reading include changing how texts are delivered, clipping parts of texts rather than the whole, and cloud saving. Perhaps the most useful part of clipping is the ability to separate text from its original source location or delivery method. Students read, watch, and listen to many digital texts throughout college, and these texts are delivered in a variety of ways, including course management suites, blogs, websites, video sites, and research databases. Most of these delivery methods do not natively support markup and annotation; however, texts delivered in all of these formats can be clipped and uploaded to a digital notebook. Another benefit is that students can be selective about what they clip. Rather than uploading an entire PDF file or Web article, readers can excerpt longer texts or break them into parts. This is especially important when summarizing, paraphrasing, and quoting natively digital texts (i.e., many scholarly texts today) and when breaking them into parts for analysis. With the use of a smartphone, virtually anything in the "real world" can be photographed and uploaded to a digital notebook and then tagged and annotated later. This is useful for students conducting field-based and archival research, but also useful for students who want a photograph of whiteboard notes to accompany the notes that they took during class.

A third benefit of clipping is that clips are automatically saved to the cloud. This means that students can access their clips from any networked device, including smartphones and tablets. It also means that they can access clipped texts at any location, including the classroom, around campus, and at home. Finally, because they are digital, clips can be endlessly organized and reorganized in the different sections of the notebook as needed.

Tagging

A tag, sometimes called a label, is a user-defined word or short phrase that describes a clipped text or page in a digital notebook. Tags are similar to other types of metadata, such as hashtags on Twitter and Pinterest. The tags that I created for my teaching notebook include "assessment," "peer response," and "feedback." When I clip an article and send it to my teaching notebook, I select a tag from my existing list or create a new one. Multiple tags can be added to the same clip, so when I clip an article about writing groups, I add the "peer response" tag as well as the "feedback" tag.

Tags promote active reading because they are descriptive. Since only a few words are used, tagging requires readers to think holistically about the texts that they clip and how best to describe or summarize them. There are many ways that we can use tagging as part of reading assignments or that students can use as part of schoolwork. For example, tags might be categorically descriptive. A student working on a research project might tag clipped articles according to topics or segments of the essay she is writing. Tags can describe reading tasks, such as "to read," "print," and "sort." Tags can be rhetorically descriptive. For an analysis assignment, a teacher might require students to find, clip, and tag texts that demonstrate different rhetorical appeals or genres of writing.

A more general benefit of tagging is that it allows readers to quickly sort and search clips. When I click on the "place" tag in my Evernote (see Figure 11.1), I see all of the clips related to my research with place-based writing and teaching. By clicking additional tags, I can narrow those results (e.g., "place" and "New Mexico"). This is especially helpful with lengthy research projects, classes that include a significant amount of digital texts, and when students need to search texts across multiple classes.

Annotating

The biggest problem that digital texts pose to active reading is that there is no easy way to annotate them in their native digital form. This prevents readers from highlighting, underlining, drawing stars, and drawing other forms of markup. It also prevents marginal comments where students summarize their "takeaways" from the text, note questions that they have, and read "against the grain" of the text. Clipping with a note-taking app like Evernote opens these texts to all of the annotation tools provided by the app, including markup and marginal comments.

Annotating digital texts in a note-taking app works mostly like annotating print texts. Tools like highlighting, underlining, and arrows allow readers to mark up the text. Readers can also write marginal comments, and those comments are easily cut, copied, and moved as needed. Students can copy marginal comments and paste them into other documents for studying and assignments that require the use of sources. Of course, this introduces all of the problems we encounter with other digital writing tools, like moving or deleting a comment accidentally. We can often apply the same methods for teaching active reading with print texts to teaching active reading with digital texts and note-taking apps. I provide an example method in the following section.

Viewed from the perspective of literacy education, note-taking apps like Evernote are more than just a convenient way to "jot things down." They are one answer to the problem of how to actively read a wide range of digital texts in their native digital forms. Note-taking apps do not replace other types of writing that sponsor active reading, such as reading logs, double-entry journals, or reading responses. They are one solution to the technical gap that exists between the active reader and static, non-interactive digital texts and reading platforms.

OneNote in a Research-Writing Class

I began teaching Microsoft's OneNote, another popular digital note-taking app, in my Composition II classes as a way to introduce more active reading during the research process and to help students organize the digital sources they collect during sustained research projects. Composition II is a research-writing class at my university. The course teaches students some of the common conventions of academic discourse, rhetorical moves common in academic writing, how to use research databases, and how to write with peer-reviewed sources. Students spend the first half of the semester writing a series of short assignments that lead to a capstone research essay that they write during the second half of the semester. These short assignments include developing research questions about a topic, conducting an initial survey of the scholarly sources, a research proposal, and an annotated bibliography. While each short assignment has a start and finish date, students use their OneNote notebooks throughout the semester, much as they would a writer's journal.

My philosophy for teaching the Composition II research essay is informed by Ken Macrorie's *Searching Writing* and Bruce Ballenger's *The Curious Researcher*. Macrorie argues in *Searching Writing* that genuine research is driven by inquiry, by the need to answer important questions (i–iv). This is as true for the university professor researching magnetic anomalies on the seafloor as it is for the sophomore student researching acequia conservation in northern New Mexico, or at least it should be. Macrorie believes, and I agree, that we should teach the ethos of inquiry that is at the heart of research and avoid the "research report" whereby students begin with a thesis and then find sources that help them argue that thesis in a paper.

If genuine research is driven by inquiry, then it should include lots of writing. In *The Curious Researcher: A Guide to Writing Research Papers*, Bruce Ballenger echoes Macrorie's call for teaching research as inquiry:

> The college research paper, probably the most common writing assignment in the university, presents an ideal opportunity to encourage inquiry-based learning and the kinds of thinking it demands. When students wrestle with sources, listening in on the never-ending conversation among experts on a topic, the drama of inquiry can unfold for students with questions like these: *What questions does this raise that interest me? How do I decide what's true? What gives me the authority to speak?*
>
> (xxiii)

Ballenger emphasizes how important writing is to answering these and all of the other questions that emerge from the research process, and, as Ballenger states, "we need to teach students how to use writing not only to report the results of their research but also to think about what they're discovering *as* they do research" (xxiv). When we consider this from the perspective of actively reading digital texts, writing should not be something that students *just* do after they locate and print sources, but something that they do throughout the research process. Because so much research is done online, students need to be able to actively read online without having to print. Relying solely on printed text for active reading stifles the inquisitive researcher by limiting the written reflection that can support critical thinking throughout the research process—assessing and learning from sources, identifying key words to use for tags and searches, and discovering the emerging essay.

For the past three years, I have taught Composition II classes in a computer lab instead of a traditional classroom. Being in the lab means that I have more time than ever before to work one-on-one with students while they conduct research with online databases like ProQuest and Academic Search Complete. This was a significant change from my past experience teaching academic writing. Aside from occasional class meetings with our reference librarians and in our writing center's computer lab, students in my previous classes did most of their database research at home. Spending more time with students while they research showed me that many have trouble staying organized and save most of their active reading for after they find the minimum number of sources required by the assignment. Both practices inhibit inquiry. Being in the lab full-time helped me understand how important it is to teach students digital tools and active reading practices that support research as a process of inquiry and not a source-gathering task completed before writing the essay.

Before using OneNote, students relied on a combination of print and online methods including research database accounts, browser bookmarks, on and offline Word files, email, handwritten notes, folders on flash drives, and printing. Each of these methods has problems. Research databases require different accounts to save sources. Browsers must be synched across computers. Flash drives are lost or left at home. Perhaps most importantly, printing is expensive, and students do not always have reliable access to printers outside of class. As such, students tend to settle for sources found and printed quickly, regardless of whether those sources are the best for answering their research questions. These are more than inconveniences. They hinder the process of inquiry and discovery that is central to authentic research.

OneNote

After experimenting with several note-taking apps, including Evernote, Simplenote, and Google Keep, I decided to use Microsoft OneNote with my Composition II classes. OneNote was a good choice mainly because all of my students have access to it through their Office365 student accounts. It should be noted that as of the time of this writing, students and educators can use a school email account to download a free version of Office365. Evernote, my second choice, is currently available for $35 with a school email account. The free (basic) version of Evernote includes clipping and tagging but not annotating.

I scaffold the introduction of OneNote with three in-class activities that we complete during the first five weeks of class. I begin by engaging students' prior knowledge about the different uses of reading in their everyday lives, including in school. We then practice annotating a print text chosen by me followed by a digital text also chosen by me. Finally, students incorporate OneNote into their research process, actively reading and organizing sources, until the end of the semester when the final essay is due.

Activity 1: Engaging Prior Knowledge

As teachers and academics, we know that some reading tasks require more attention than others, and we have developed habits of picking up a pen and writing in those moments. I seldom pick up a pen when I'm reading a Stephen King novel. I read *It* because I want to experience a good story and get lost in the fictional world of Derry, Maine. However, I always pick up a pen when I read the latest issue of *College English*. I underline sentences, draw stars and checkmarks next to paragraphs, and scribble notes in the margins.

Our students also understand that some texts require more attention than others. They come to our classes having studied for tests, written book reports and experienced many other high-stakes reading tasks. Somewhere along the way, they put pen, pencil, or highlighter to printed page. They have also developed their own ways of writing on and alongside texts. Before introducing OneNote, I engage this prior knowledge by asking students to reflect on the different types of reading that they do in and out of school.

We begin with a quick-write, creating lists of the different types of reading that we do in a typical week during the semester. We share our lists and create clusters on the whiteboard, typically around the domains of our lives where reading happens—home, school, work, communities. We use these clusters to discuss the different rhetorical contexts of reading and why some texts require a closer, deeper reading than others. I make sure that we discuss if and how we write when we read. This discussion not only helps us collaboratively articulate a rationale for active reading, it also allows us to share the many ways we already annotate. This introduces the next activity, wherein we practice annotating a print text and further develop strategies for markup and marginal notes.

Activity 2: Practice with Print Texts

Students practice annotating a print copy of an article before they annotate digital texts with OneNote. Starting with paper allows us to focus on the practice of markup and marginal notes without also having to learn how to clip, tag, and annotate in OneNote. It also avoids the distractions that inevitably happen when a class of twenty-plus students turn on computers. To practice annotating a print text, I follow the activity Carol Porter-O'Donnell describes in her article "Beyond the Yellow Highlighter: Teaching Annotation Skills to Improve Active Reading."

In "Beyond the Yellow Highlighter," Carol Porter-O'Donnell describes how she teaches her ninth-grade students to draw on their own experiences as readers to learn how to annotate texts. Students begin by reading a story and writing a short narrative response. They take turns sharing sentences from their responses and placing them into categories that describe the type of response—opinions, questions, connections to personal experience, connections to other ideas in the text. The activity is an opportunity for students to hear the range of responses that readers have to a text as well as to collaboratively develop terminology for describing ways of responding. At the end of this activity, Porter-O'Donnell's students create a visual aid, a markup guide, using the categories and terms they created. She says that students typically come up with six or seven approaches to response. She shows them ways of marking a text and how they can use different marks to represent different ways of responding (e.g., a wavy line under difficult vocabulary words, underlining important information, question marks for things they don't understand).

Students annotate a second short story using their markup guides. At this point, Porter-O'Donnell teaches students how to also write marginal notes that help them "make connections, pose questions, and interpret ideas" (82). Porter-O'Donnell shows students how some markups identify "surface meaning ideas" while others identify "deep-meaning ideas," and how marginal notes can be used to probe the deep-meaning ideas (83–5).

After the first semester teaching annotations in this way, Porter-O'Donnell asked her students to write about how their reading changed as they developed their own approaches to annotating texts. She identifies three ways that annotating taught students to be more active readers. First, annotating taught students to see reading as a process. Comments from students revealed that marking texts with their markup guides and ways of responding made the normally "invisible" process of reading more "visible." With that visibility came a recognition that they can be flexible with the annotation strategies that they apply to texts (85–6). Second, annotating changed the way that students comprehended what they read. Students described how annotating, especially marginal notes, helped them move beyond surface-level questions and just making connections to personal experiences. They were more likely to probe the text and ask questions that weren't easily answered (86). Finally, Porter-O'Donnell learned that annotating promotes active reading because it slows the reading process. Students observed that while annotating made reading slower, it took less time than rereading passages multiple times (87).

Modeling markup and marginal notes, including how to create personal markup guides, practicing with multiple texts, and opening the annotation process up to class discussion are the key takeaways from Porter-O'Donnell's activity. I share my own markup guide with students (circles for key terms, checkmarks for important ideas, stars for even more important ideas) and give them time to create and share their own while annotating sample texts. We also practice and share our marginal notes, discussing how they help us "go deeper" into the texts. While our markup guides sometimes change when we move to OneNote, the extended practice with print provides a foundational understanding of the annotation.

Setting Up OneNote for Research

We begin by setting up our OneNote notebooks. While students develop their own styles of organizing OneNote and their clips, we start with a basic notebook format that includes a section titled "incoming" and another titled "research notes." The "incoming" folder is the default folder where clips are sent while researching. It is inspired by the "literature repository" feature on Docear, an open-source reference-management software based on mind mapping (Beel). The "incoming" section acts as a default location for storing clips before they are tagged and moved to other sections. The incoming folder typically gets used less and less as the scope of the research becomes more focused. The "research notes" section begins with a single page that includes several lists—search terms, research questions, rough-drafts of essay titles. We update the notes page at the start of every class meeting, and I encourage students to students to continue to update it on their own. The notes page also includes a very rough outline that students revise as they begin to answer their research questions and as the thesis and essay begin to emerge.

Activity 3: Practice with Digital Texts

With the notes page set up, I introduce the basic functions of clipping, tagging, and annotating with an in-class active reading assignment. As we are at the start of our research, I pick an essay related to one of the short assignments we are completing, such as L. Lennie Irvin's "What Is Academic Writing?" I also pick a PDF file because they can be tricky to upload to OneNote. This is an opportunity for me to make sure that we all know how it works.

Students are tasked with finding the article online, clipping it to their "incoming" folder and creating a tag that broadly describes the article. I typically provide one or two discussion questions to guide their reading.

Students use these questions, the markup guides they previously created, and the "textbox" feature (for marginal notes) to annotate the article in OneNote. While students are reading, I monitor their progress with the app, answering questions and assessing their understanding of both OneNote and annotation. This activity concludes with a discussion of both the article and their experience with actively reading a digital text.

After practicing OneNote as a class, students are ready to apply what they have learned to their own research projects. At this point, they have completed a brief proposal and are now working on an annotated bibliography. The annotated bibliography is a midterm goal and includes a sample of the peer-reviewed sources that they will likely use in the final paper. Before students write the annotated bibliography, they spend several weeks research and writing about their findings. This "diving in" moment is often overwhelming and sometimes disorienting (as they follow multiple tangents). Faithful use of OneNote is key, as is receiving regular instructor feedback. Students share their notebooks with me (a collaborative feature of OneNote), and I read and respond to them at least twice before the final essay is due.

Conclusion

The practice of active reading with note-taking apps is more important than learning all the ins-and-outs of an app or following prescriptive rules for markup and marginal notes. We should recognize that annotating, like all writing processes, is unique to each writer. How we assess our assignments should reflect both points. Assessment, especially for lengthy research projects, can seem overwhelming when we have multiple classes of twenty-plus students. The purpose of formative assessment with note-taking apps is to provide accountability and to reteach aspects of digital annotation if needed. For this reason, we can assess students' use of note-taking apps much as we do with journals, with a quick "skim and dip" reading combined with the occasional note that provides encouragement, answers questions, and offers suggestions. Similarly, summative assessment can be as simple as "passing" (clearly practiced digital annotation throughout the assignment) and "no passing" (clearly did not).

Learning how to use a digital note-taking app helps all of us, teachers and students, develop the literacies needed for reading and writing in the digital age. However, the idea of bringing a new literacy technology into the classroom can be daunting. The most important thing that teachers can do to learn and teach with note-taking apps is to make them a part of our own reading habits. We all do a significant amount of reading, whether for our own research, preparing for classes, participating in committees, not to mention all that we read outside of school. Most of this reading is digital, and like our students' reading in school, much of it is high stakes. Three types of online resources helped me learn note-taking apps and include them in my reading and teaching.

Technology magazines and blogs such as *TechRadar* and *Lifehacker* regularly review note-taking apps and are a valuable resource for quickly assessing which apps (especially free versions) currently support clipping, tagging, and annotation (Fulton, Klosowski). I recommend that readers look for apps that include browser plug-ins that make clipping easier. Next are the many YouTube videos that provide step-by-step instructions on topics such organizing digital notebooks for research, clipping texts from the Web, creating tags, and annotating ("Researching with OneNote," "Using Tags," "Microsoft OneNote," "Setting up Evernote"). Apps are frequently updated with new features, and existing features are dropped or changed. YouTube videos, whether from the developer or users, are an excellent way to stay current. Finally, there are a number of articles on developer and education blogs that provide tips for reading with note-taking apps and incorporating them into the classroom ("Evernote Blog," Holland, "Microsoft 365 Blog").

Works Cited

Allen, Nicole. "Congress Funds $5 Million Open Textbook Grant Program in 2018 Spending Bill." *Scholarly Publishing and Academic Resources Coalition*, 20 Mar. 2018, www.sparcopen.org/news/2018/open-textbooks-fy18/. Accessed 1 Apr. 2018.

Bean, John C. *Engaging Ideas: The Professor's Guide to Integrating Writing, Critical Thinking, and Active Learning in the Classroom*. 2nd ed., Jossey-Bass, 2011.

Beel, Joeran, Bela Gipp, Stefan Langer, and Marcel Genzmehr. "Docear: An Academic Literature Suite for Searching, Organizing and Creating Academic Literature." *Proceedings of the 11th ACM/IEEE Joint Conference on Digital Libraries*, ACM Digital Library, pp. 465–6, doi:10.1145/1998076.1998188. Accessed 21 Oct. 2017.

Cusker, Jeremy. "Online Textbook Piracy: A Literature Review." *Issues in Science and Technology Librarianship*, Spring 2016, doi:10.5062/F4154F2X. Accessed 1 Mar. 2018.

Elbow, Peter. "High Stakes and Low Stakes in Assigning and Responding to Writing." *New Directions for Teaching and Learning*, no. 69, Spring 1997, pp. 5–13.

"Evernote Blog: Remember Everything." *Evernote*, https://blog.evernote.com/. Accessed 21 Apr. 2018.

Evernote Corporation. *Evernote*, Computer Software. *Evernote*, Vers. 6.7. Evernote Corporation, 2017.

Fulton, Kane, and Steve McCaskill. "The Best Notetaking Apps in 2018." *TechRadar*, 26 Feb. 2018, www.techradar.com/news/the-best-note-taking-apps-in-2018. Accessed 20 Apr. 2018.

Green, Kenneth. "Going Digital: Faculty Perspectives on Digital and OER Course Materials." *Campus Computing Project*, 19 Feb. 2016, www.campuscomputing.net/content/2016/19/going-digital-2016. Accessed 20 Oct. 2017.

"Highlights from Student Watch Attitudes & Behaviors Toward Course Materials 2016–17 Report." *National Association of College Stores*, www.nacs.org/research/studentwatchfindings.aspx. Accessed 25 Oct. 2017.

Holland, Beth. "Note Taking with Technology." *Edutopia*, 4 Aug. 2017, www.edutopia.org/blog/the-4ss-of-note-taking-beth-holland. Accessed 21 Apr. 2018.

Khabsa, Madian., and C. Lee Giles. "The Number of Scholarly Documents on the Public Web." *PLoS One*, vol. 9, no. 5, 2014, doi.org/10.1371/journal.pone.0093949. Accessed 5 Nov. 2017.

Klosowski, Thorin. "The Best Note Taking Apps for Students." *Lifehacker*, 8 Aug. 2016, https://lifehacker.com/the-best-note-taking-apps-for-students-1784974783. Accessed 20 Apr. 2018.

McKenzie, Lindsay. "'Inclusive Access' Takes Off as Model for College Textbook Sales." *Inside Higher Ed*, 7 Nov. 2017, www.insidehighered.com/news/2017/11/07/inclusive-access-takes-model-college-textbook-sales. Accessed 27 Feb. 2018.

"Microsoft 365 Blog: OneNote." *Microsoft*, www.microsoft.com/en-us/microsoft365/blog/onenote/. Accessed 21 Apr. 2018.

Microsoft Corporation. *Microsoft OneNote 2016*, Computer Software. *Microsoft OneNote*, Microsoft Corporation, 2015.

"Microsoft OneNote: 2018 Detailed Tutorial." *YouTube*, uploaded by Teacher's Tech, 5 Mar. 2018, www.youtube.com/watch?v=zjfIMCRJUAo. Accessed 21 Apr. 2018.

Ortega, Jose Luis. *Academic Search Engines: A Quantitative Outlook*, Chandos, 2014.

Porter-O'Donnell, Carol. "Beyond the Yellow Highlighter: Teaching Annotation Skills to Improve Reading Comprehension." *English Journal*, vol. 93, no. 5, 2004, pp. 82–9.

"Researching with OneNote." *YouTube*, uploaded by Paul Smythe, 19 May 2014, www.youtube.com/watch?v=ToHS-YU539g.

Seaman, Julia E., and Jeff Seaman. "Opening the Textbook: Educational Resources in Higher Education, 2017." *Babson Survey Research Group*, 2017, www.onlinelearningsurvey.com/reports/openingthetextbook2017.pdf. Accessed 2 Nov. 2017.

"Setting Up Evernote for a Research Project." *YouTube*, uploaded by Ms. DeGroat, 27 Oct. 2015, www.youtube.com/watch?v=budjS8M20z8. Accessed 21 Apr. 2018.

Straumsheim, Carl. "Digital Overtakes Print." *Inside Higher Ed*, 30 Mar. 2016, www.insidehighered.com/news/2016/03/30/publishers-report-digital-sales-overtaking-print-sales. Accessed 20 Feb. 2018.

"Using Tags in OneNote." *YouTube*, uploaded by Intellezy Learning, 22 Jan. 2018, www.youtube.com/watch?v=eSs3uI7urMw. Accessed 21 Apr. 2018.

Part 3

Implications and Institutional Contexts

12 Reading and Writing Digital Contexts Across Campus

From FYC and FYE to ME to CE

Ed Nagelhout and Philip Rusche

As our worlds become immersed in the digital, as literacies become defined by the digital, as learning becomes appended to the digital, the relationships between reading and writing become more vital, more relevant, more necessary for all academic and intellectual pursuits. Researchers and teachers in composition studies have historically promoted multiple literacies in the classroom and across campus. In fact, many first-year composition programs across the country are models of advocacy (Finer and White-Farnham).

But researchers and teachers in composition studies must continue to reexamine and rearticulate what constitutes literate practices, especially in higher education. And we must continue to explore new pathways to literate action. This exploration should not be limited, however, to first-year composition courses or first-year experience courses; more importantly, literate practice should not be limited to a single course or single experience in a student's education, but should entail a consistent approach that embodies lifelong learning with digital writing and digital reading at the center of educational activities. We should aspire to offer more than limited content or content limited to a single course at a time.

This chapter explores a Domain of One's Own initiative at the University of Nevada, Las Vegas. This initiative is designed to be programmatic, built as a part of the general education core using domains as a tool to emphasize rhetorical practices for digital reading and writing in a networked learning environment. As we will explain, access to Domain of One's Own as a tool for all students to use from day one encourages a more collaborative approach, privileges informal and situated learning, and promotes decision-making, student self-monitoring, and lifelong learning. More importantly, access to Domain of One's Own offers more than a simple e-portfolio product; instead, access provides the keys to long-term content management, to a process for lifelong learning with digital reading and writing at its core, as well as the means for connecting first-year composition to first-year experience, milestone experience, and culminating experience general education requirements to help students construct more transparent relationships between projects, between courses, between programs, between disciplines, and across campus.

Digital Reading and Writing as Context

We begin this section by situating digital reading and writing in the context of the humanities and in the context of educational programs. We will conclude this section by establishing digital reading and writing as context for student learning activities and as context for lifelong learning practices.

As scholars in the humanities, our thinking and teaching are firmly entrenched in a belief in the value of the humanities: for understanding languages, histories, and cultures; for fostering social justice and equality; for teaching empathy and encouraging creativity; for demanding critical thinking, reading, and writing; in other words, for developing an informed citizenry. For us, digital reading and writing occur in this context, as a part of, more precisely, the digital humanities:

> a universe in which: (a) print is no longer the exclusive or the normative medium in which knowledge is produced and/or disseminated; instead, print finds itself absorbed into new, multimedia configurations; and (b) digital tools, techniques, and media have altered the production and dissemination of knowledge in the arts, human and social sciences.
>
> (The Digital Humanities Manifesto 2.0)

This definition expands the ways that we think and know, the ways that we do research and what counts as research, and the ways that we engage with each other.

Therefore, we argue that digital reading and writing are always contextual, that digital reading and writing are rhetorical activities, always the result of the complex interactions among writer(s), reader(s), text(s), and context(s). As a complex process, digital reading and writing allow learners to "explore thinking and create new knowledge" and "involves the hand, eye, and both sides of the brain as one makes connections and constructs meaning" (Bromley 296). For decades, research has studied reading and writing as complex, rhetorical, and recursive activities. When seen in these ways, effective readers and writers are those who know about and know how to choose and use a wide range of strategies that will aid in the expression of critical thought, the understanding of discourse conventions, the reasons for communicating graphically, and the production of an effective piece of writing.

When preparing students to read and write rhetorically, teachers and educators must recognize their role in instructing students to think of digital reading and writing as complex, rhetorical, and recursive activities, oftentimes interrelated and interconnected. In this sense, there exist a wide range of activities from which readers and writers can choose as they work through a rhetorical problem, including, but not limited to, the following array of activities:

- analytical heuristics to help readers and writers map rhetorical situations
- strategies for invention, discovery, and exploration
- strategies for planning, conducting, and using results of various kinds of research, including primary and secondary research
- multi-stage/multi-level revision and metacognitive strategies that would include questions and concerns on which readers and writers might focus throughout the rhetorical activity
- contextual, annotation, and reflective strategies for readers; drafting, editing, and proofreading strategies for writers;
- various methods of eliciting and using effectively feedback to work in progress, whether from others or as a critical reader and writer of one's own work
- strategies that help students understand the conventions of specific discourse communities, such as appropriate arrangements, appropriate evidence or support, and appropriate stylistic conventions

From a pedagogical perspective, teachers can best introduce and incorporate these activities by teaching digital reading and writing as rhetorical and by teaching digital reading and writing in and through a reflective process.

Teaching digital reading and writing as rhetorical means that students see reading and writing as purposeful and context-specific. This approach, for us, can be traced through the disciplinary and genre studies of scholars like Charles Bazerman, Christina Haas and Linda Flower, Richard Haswell, and James Warren. Readers read and writers write for reasons, to accomplish things, to DO something. We want students to understand who they are as readers and writers in any situation, most especially as the agent of their own learning and their own understanding. Too often, students, even college students, relinquish their agency to teachers who, with all the best intentions, "correct" their understanding, their insights, their writing, rather than helping them take control of their reading and writing in order to develop effective strategies for the future. We want students to understand the ways that both readers and writers bring certain expectations to any rhetorical situation based on a range of factors, from age to education to cultural to socio-economic status; more importantly, they also bring expectations about what a text should look like, how a text should be constructed, what content is acceptable for a particular genre, and the kinds of support appropriate when making an argument.

Thinking of digital reading and writing in this way clarifies that a primary learning goal is to guide students in developing the skills and habits of mind that will help them participate in a wide range of digital reading and writing situations that they will encounter, as students and as citizens. This may mean something as simple as understanding the conventions of an email to/from a friend or an email to/from a professor or an email to/from a potential employer: each has different rhetorical considerations, such as the purpose for each, the different potential readers, and the language expectations inherent in each situation. Treating digital reading and writing as rhetorical can also lead students to a more complex understanding of the epistemological and formal conventions that inform a range of academic and non-academic (electronic) texts. For only in this complex understanding can students see beyond the classroom to the reading and writing that they will perform for the rest of their lives as professionals and as citizens.

As we discussed previously, research shows that helping students know about and know how to choose and use a wide range of strategies for digital reading and writing can occur most effectively when teaching students in and through a process. Historically, composition theorists have emphasized the recursive nature of effective writing, and while teachers can introduce different strategies or heuristics for each stage of the writing process, they also need to emphasize that these don't have to occur in any set order. The effective writer can move back and forth in a recursive fashion in order to successfully complete a writing assignment, and different writers can follow different paths to success based on their own strengths and weaknesses as writers. Digital reading, in many respects, affords the same opportunities, especially as students read more materials that are online or presented hypertextually. This leads to another key point of emphasis: digital reading and writing are each a cognitive process in the sense that individuals never wholly "get it" or develop to a point where "reading" and "writing" can be automatic. In this respect, learning about reading and writing, as core literate practices, is always an ongoing process, and that a student's apparent competence may fluctuate from performance to performance. Teachers need to avoid focusing too much on a single assignment, on a single product; they need to avoid "correcting" student reading or "fixing" student writing; they need to avoid teaching a lock-step, linear process in order to get the reading or the writing completed so that students will "learn" it. Instead, teachers need to promote the growth of the digital reader and writer.

General Education at UNLV

At UNLV, we are thinking about Domain of One's Own (DoOO) as a platform for student learning, with digital reading and digital writing at its core, and especially as a platform that can offer pathways for both students and faculty to break down classroom and disciplinary walls and connect learning experiences in broader and more effective ways, to make connections between courses, and over time, from first year to culminating experience. Before discussing how we will incorporate the DoOO initiative, in this section we will describe the curriculum at the University of Nevada, Las Vegas. DoOO will be one tool among many that will allow universities to create relationships between first-year composition, general education, and disciplinary practices in a student's major.

At UNLV, our general education requirements include fairly typical offerings of first-year composition, a first-year experience, a milestone experience, and a culminating experience. Their goals are to promote both the University Undergraduate Learning Objectives and disciplinary practices. More specifically, first-year composition and the first-year experience courses introduce students to the rigors of university learning; the milestone experience, completed by a student's sophomore or junior year, introduces students to disciplinary critical thinking and communication practices; and the culminating experience provides a means to review, consolidate, and assess a student's college career. For us, making rhetorical practices for digital reading and writing explicit across courses is paramount to achieving these goals.

Since UNLV is primarily a commuter campus, with a high percentage of transfers, as well as a majority of students working 20–40 hours per week outside of their studies, we can't force students down a single, linear educational path, teachers down a single, prescribed curriculum, or programs through a top-down, standardized regimen. Instead we must enable a flexibility in developing program materials, course design, project design, student competencies, and program assessment plans that can account for different students with different skill sets and different experiences when they begin, and when they finish. We want students in a particular course to be successful and to feel confident in their learning when completing a particular project, no matter their digital experience or previous coursework.

Our goal in all these courses is to prioritize relationships through digital reading and writing, which means not limiting our thinking to the perspective of the scholar or the perspective of the student, but to make more transparent those relationships between projects, between courses, between programs, between disciplines, and across campus. Everyone should contribute to program development. To do this, we need to privilege the different ways that students learn in a program, in a learning environment, and the different ways their learning connects to the learning of other students. We want our students to chart their own paths, develop effective processes and habits of mind, create their own formulas, and put their learning in their own context. We expect students to take control of projects and develop them to fit their learning goals. We want to minimize program (teacher) dependency. In other words, we want to decenter the authority of the program for providing all the materials, and, since learning is messy, we want to emphasize that students must be given ample time to muddle, to struggle, to get frustrated, to make mistakes. The path to insight is rarely direct or singular.

Domain of One's Own: Digital Reading and Writing in Practice

A platform like a DoOO initiative, or common tool, or common assignment, introduced in a student's first year, developed over the course of their college career, and encouraged in various iterations through digital reading and writing practices in all of their courses, provides the means for a true culminating experience, a more valid preface to lifelong learning. More importantly, as we will show, these kinds of shared practices promote student agency and force teachers to build in the time necessary for students to work, to play, to make mistakes, to share, to collaborate, to reflect: to learn.

In this section, we will describe digital reading and writing in practice through three different levels of application: platform, tool, and assignment. Our goal is to examine digital reading and writing in the context of the application, as well as digital reading and writing as context for the application. In other words, using a specific example for each level of application, we hope to describe practices that are flexible for use in FYC, FYE, ME, and CE and that can offer developmental opportunities for improving digital reading and writing for students throughout their college experience.

Enhancing Digital Reading and Writing on Platforms

DoOO empowers faculty and students to manage and control their online digital identity through an integrated online domain, which allows them to create (and OWN) a professional hub for work (or coursework): research, portfolio, social media, film and video archives, civic engagement resources, etc. More importantly, for this chapter, DoOO provides a platform for enhancing digital reading and writing skills.

Through DoOO faculty and students have autonomous control over the tools and the information in their own domain, which includes a suite of over one hundred open-source tools:

- website development tools
- project management tools
- file management tools
- research tools
- databases
- wikis
- groupware, and
- a range of portals

Access to these apps, and the time and freedom to experiment with them, can allow students to create knowledge in their own way, in all of the messiness that knowledge-making entails, by encouraging marginal thinking and knowledge-making that occurs outside the boundaries of an assessment spreadsheet. Students are able to create their knowledge within the strictures of discipline and across disciplines, among alternative voices and alternative perspectives, so that they can build internally while always engaging externally.

One of the key advantages DoOO offers is in breaking and disrupting the standard pathways of information exchange within the classroom. Too often materials and assignments are restricted along a line of exchange from teacher to student and back to teacher. This compartmentalization does little to benefit other students in the class, not to mention other students in the university community or members of the wider public. DoOO allows for a much more open exchange of information, where the student can begin to connect learning experiences in a single course to those in other courses, to the program and discipline, and where the intellectual life of the university can be open to anyone.

Each student now becomes the curator or archivist of their own work, preserving it, adapting it, rethinking and rewriting it as they continue to develop their online identity. As Bill LeFurgy argues, "One of the still unfolding impacts of the computer age is that everyone now must be their own digital archivist. Without some focused attention, any personal collection is at high risk of loss—and quick loss at that" (3). A DoOO initiative puts that front and center: faculty and students can incorporate their domains and associated tools into their research and coursework for developing their digital identity. Chris Long (2016), Dean of the College of Arts and Letters at Michigan State University, echoes this sentiment: "[S]tudents and faculty need a domain of their own, an online space they control to curate and present their work in ways that are consistent with the values and commitments of their research" by highlighting the important ways that a Domain of One's Own initiative provides a necessary tool for the twenty-first century and, in the words of Jim Groom, allows universities to frame higher education as fundamental preparation for the shifting notions of identity and reality that will everywhere shape our connected future.

As a way to get students thinking about the issues revolving around the control and access to digital materials, as one of the first assignments we give in a first-year experience course, we ask students to explore what it means to be a digital archivist, how a domain helps them do this, what kinds of apps will be the most effective. Students begin to craft a digital identity over the course of a semester based on their goals.

Typically, our student body includes students who range from minimal experience beyond Facebook to running their own servers, so it's important for students to build from where they are starting and see that first-year experience course as an opportunity to prepare short-term and long-term plans for their domain and to take the time to do it. We recommend self-generated grading contracts at this level to help students articulate educational goals for their domain and strategies for incorporating it seamlessly into their daily activities. Likewise, a milestone experience can use domains to introduce students to a variety of digital tools for disciplinary research, for disciplinary communication, and for disciplinary identity. Students can learn when to use different tools in different contexts and for different purposes, why some tools are more effective than others, and how to evaluate new tools in the future.

These assignments can be extended in practice to the program, major, and even college level. For example, in a first-year experience course, after some initial guidance, students should be expected to contribute resources, readings, software, or apps relevant to their explorations of domains. These can be personalized, based on their particular goals, and students can then share their digital reading and writing experiences with the rest of the class. They should contextualize their use of the resource, summarize it, evaluate its strengths and weaknesses, and explain why they do or do not recommend its use. These resources can be assembled and archived for the class but can also be used as models for evaluating materials for specific purposes. Programs or majors can then create repositories by combining resources from milestone experience or culminating experience courses. DoOO offers potential tools for automating this process or developing a series of curation projects, especially at the milestone level, that can help students understand disciplinary practices in more depth and from their own perspectives.

Finally, a key feature of our model asks students to define and construct deliverables, including the criteria for evaluating those deliverables, in a way that builds their competencies for a particular situation: for that particular project, in that particular course, for that particular program, always with the idea that they will reflect on how this project connects with their larger learning context and learning goals. These conversations about evaluation and assessment not only provide transparency in our teaching, but also empower students to contribute to the larger goals of the course or program and explain how they understand the expectations for success in these learning environments. This practice improves their ability to understand the deliverable in more rhetorically astute ways and to understand its connection to digital reading and writing skills learned in other courses and across the program. And while this practice can be applied broadly, a domain perspective offers concrete opportunities to explore depth and nuance in delivering rhetorically effective deliverables in a particular discipline, whether that's a multimodal portfolio or an interactive database or a static infographic.

Enhancing Digital Reading and Writing Using Tools

As a centralized platform for a student's work, DoOO offers a place for students to curate a number of tools, both those offered by DoOO itself, such as blogging and wikis to database and file management, and others available elsewhere on the web. By giving students their own space and the time in which they can explore these tools, DoOO fosters the ability for students to make connections between their assignments and courses and to experiment with the use they make of these tools in different learning environments. The desired goal is that as they proceed through their program they will have access to and the knowledge of how to use a series of apps that will reflect their own learning goals and projects they have worked on throughout their college career, with their domain as a central hub through which they, as well as other students or the public, can access them.

Many of the available tools are integral in helping students improve their digital reading and writing abilities throughout their college career. Use of these tools, even if introduced in specific assignments or classes, should extend beyond a single assignment or course, so that students will be able to appreciate the multiple uses of a single tool, as well as begin to experiment with ways to connect several tools together to enhance their own work.

One example of a tool we have begun to use is the hypothesis annotation application (web.hypothes.is/), an online, free, and open-source annotation app that allows users to add annotation and highlighting to any website, including online PDFs. Access to annotations can be available to the public, restricted to a specific group, or kept private, depending on the needs of the annotator. Any student or faculty member who uses hypothesis can link their profile, which includes their public annotations, on their domain, and individual comments can be shared through social media or email.

This particular tool is especially helpful in overcoming a number of the problems of digital reading compared to print reading. It is essential to acknowledge that digital reading encompasses a different set of skills than print reading and that the skills required for one do not all readily transfer to the other (Ackerman and Goldsmith; Coiro, "Predicting Reading Comprehension"). In preparing students for literacy in the digital world, we must acknowledge these differences and enable students to think about reading digitally in ways that take advantage of technology rather than simply trying to adapt it to print literacy.

For example, it has often been noted that digital readers suffer from lack of sustained attention to the text due to various reasons such as the multitasking associated with working online, and note-taking is one way to assist continued attention on the part of the reader. While in some respects, taking notes online has been proven less effective in terms of long-term retention than taking notes by hand, due in part to the speed at which the notetaker can type compared to the slow pace of writing by hand (Mueller and Oppenheimer), digital note-taking also offers numerous advantages over taking notes by hand, and through continued use and reflection, the digital notetaker will be able to capitalize on these advantages.

First, annotations can take full advantage of the interactivity of the web and include links to images, videos, other websites, other annotations. Students can not only benefit from the interconnectedness that digital reading affords, but can take control of creating these connections for themselves by forming relations between different types of digital media and relating them to their own work. A student working through an online text can provide an annotation with a link to a blog they have created, to coursework they have done for another class, to the work of their professor or other students, and so on, creating an interconnected web of related academic work that situates their own learning within a larger academic community.

Hypothesis also allows all comments on a page to be searched, both by keyword and by tags added to the annotations. Tags are also listed on the user's profile page, allowing the ability to cross-reference annotations by subjects across all annotated digital texts. Being able to cross-reference annotations across multiple assignments allows a student to more fully realize the programmatic nature of their work, as well as providing an extensive resource for any future work they might do. It connects their work with their own learning goals and objectives rather so that they do not remain limited to individual course outcomes.

The annotations are also fully collaborative in nature, since they can be shared or viewed by others. For example, even if access to the annotations are limited to a group set up for a specific class, students and teachers are able to see and reply to each other's comments, allowing them to benefit from the insights, reading style, interests, and abilities of others as they perform their own reading, turning what is too often a lone activity to a collaborative group effort. This collaboration provides in effect a peer review of their writing even at its earliest and most informal stage, so that they can get feedback from a variety of others at the very beginning of the writing process, and allows them to reflect more productively on their writing and their audience.

Enhancing Digital Reading and Writing Using Assignments

Assignments in specific courses are the most common means for helping students improve their digital reading and writing skills. We would argue, however, that most programs or majors do not take full advantage of the power of the programmatic assignment to develop skills, especially for digital reading and writing. In this subsection, we will describe the potential of common assignments and assignment themes for programs and/or majors.

Before offering a specific example of an assignment adaptable for FYE, FYC, ME, or CE, we want to provide a general overview of a commitment to project design. We regularly initiate conversations across campus about learning and project design. We encourage more collaborative approaches (faculty with faculty and, especially, faculty with students) that privilege informal and situated learning and promote decision-making, student self-monitoring, and lifelong learning through every step of each project, each course, their entire academic experience at our university. We have said this before, but it's worth repeating: digital reading and writing require time, the time necessary for students to work, to play, to make mistakes, to share, to collaborate: to learn. We want our projects (like students' learning) to be developmental and recursive, with students moving back and forth among the stages of the project as they work toward submission of project deliverables.

We start with a basic template for all projects in our courses. Briefly, we provide a description, a framework for understanding the deliverables, a timeline for completing all of the work, and a brief set of readings and resources to get students started toward achieving the initial project aims. But we expect students to take control of the projects and develop them to fit their learning goals by contributing resources that they have used and reviewed relevant to the project and to share their insights with the rest of the class: a first step towards building competencies in digital reading and writing. More importantly, we want students to engage with the class, to share knowledge and ask questions, to be sensitive to their own learning needs while, at the same time, contributing to the larger ongoing classroom conversations. This open atmosphere helps students learn about and learn how to choose and use a wide range of strategies for digital reading and writing that will aid in their critical learning and reflective practices.

Each project includes a planning stage and a reflecting stage, a time when students can articulate what they want to learn and how they will do it. This means our projects need to be purposeful, have meaning to the students so they engage with the work (even if it's purely for their own reasons), so they feel like they are accomplishing things, DOING something. While we want students to look inward for their learning goals, we also expect outward participation, as well. At the early stages of any project, students are gathering resources for understanding concepts more fully and for completing the work. These early stages help students explore and establish a context for the project, so they understand it well enough to begin to discuss how their work should be evaluated.

A critical stage of any project is developing evaluation criteria as a class. This should include an explicit understanding that part of their reflection should address the ways that they met the criteria relative to their own learning goals for the project. Once the evaluation criteria is negotiated and agreed upon, drafts of the deliverables can be completed, for the first time. For every project, to develop digital writing skills, student work should go through multiple drafts, with time set aside for peer review and teacher review before they submit their work for evaluation. The goal here is to model recursivity, to encourage trust in multiple perspectives, to allow for the time necessary to submit quality materials, to continue to develop digital reading and writing skills.

We talk about performing higher-order revisions and lower-order edits before they submit a deliverable for evaluation. And the deliverables should be the only items evaluated. For us, the majority of the work should be participatory, a contribution to their own learning and to the learning of their classmates. The key to our project design, of course, is time. We have to be patient and provide the time for students to explore, the time to experiment, the time to fail, before they make the move to final completion. And we think the final outcomes are stellar.

By promoting an open and collaborative environment, one that encourages and rewards sharing, experimentation, personalization, we find our students are genuinely interested in helping one another. Less experienced students ask questions, more advanced students ask questions; when they set personal goals for learning, everyone looks for ways to enhance their skills and help others do the same. To conclude this subsection, we want to offer a specific example of an assignment adaptable for FYE, FYC, ME, or CE.

In essence, our project example is an analysis project. In this particular iteration, we focus on students analyzing privacy policy. The project could be individual, but we prefer a collaborative project at all levels. The goal of this project is for students to work with a team to select a privacy policy posted by a social media platform or other organization (including academic institutions) that posts a privacy policy statement; to identify background resources for analyzing the policy effectively; to develop criteria based on these resources to analyze the policy; then to create a report of findings to share with the class.

To get students started, we provide an initial set of resources. For example, we might post the following:

- From High School to Harvard, Students Urge for Clarity on Privacy Rights

  (Abamu)

- Have You Read the _____ Privacy (Data) Policy Lately?

  (Pasquini)

- iTunes Terms and Conditions: The Graphic Novel

  (Sikoryak)

The goal here is to not only provide students with a starting point, but also to show them that digital resources don't have to be limited to text.

A project like this should take a minimum of six weeks, depending on the level of complexity built in to the workload and the level of complexity expected for the deliverables. Our preference is for three deliverables:

1. Planning Document—This could take a variety of different formats, including a memo. The key is to highlight that the audience is the teacher and the purpose is to start a conversation about completing the project effectively. The planning document should identify the policy, summarize the organization who posted the policy, offer an initial set of criteria for analyzing the policy, describe the mode of delivery and why the team made that choice, and provide a project schedule and workload breakdown.
2. Resource List—Again, this could take a variety of different formats but should serve as a preview for the report. In first-year courses, it could just be an annotated bibliography. At the upper levels, we prefer a literature review. In either case, the document should, at the very least, include a brief introduction/overview of the resources and a brief annotation of each.
3. Final Report—Our preference for the final deliverable is a final report of the team's findings that provides, at a minimum, the following information:

   - Describe the platform/organization who posted the policy
   - Provide background information/materials for performing policy analysis
   - Articulate and justify the team's method and criteria used for analyzing the policy
   - State the findings from the team's analysis
   - Reflect on what the team learned and explicit takeaways for readers

The key to an assignment like this is its adaptability. Students can perform an analysis at different levels of sophistication, from first year to fourth year; more importantly, students can build on the work they have done in previous years to extend their thinking and to offer proof of their digital reading and writing development. This kind of transparency, where students are asked to openly acknowledge previous work and build on it, provides more explicit connections between courses, between the work they have done and the work they will do.

Conclusion

In conclusion, we see digital reading and writing as a complex rhetorical activity that allows students to think about their work in more innovative and creative ways so that they may move beyond consuming of information to the generation of knowledge. "The Internet presents an optimal context for practice with these knowledge-creating processes since learners are connected with infinite texts, global perspectives, and a multitude of digital tools that enable the construction and communication of creative ideas" (Coiro, "Purposeful, Critical, and Flexible" 54). DoOO as a platform for student work offers the space, freedom, and flexibility necessary for students to practice their reading and writing in a variety of situations and contexts, formal and informal, collaborative and reflective. By creating a space on the web that allows students to create their own online identity and to consider multiple audiences of their professors, their peers, and the public, DoOO enables students to realize more clearly the connections between their digital reading and writing, the technologies and tools they use, and their courses and assignments throughout their education and beyond.

Works Cited

Abamu, Jenny. "From High School to Harvard, Students Urge for Clarity on Privacy Rights." *Edsurge*, 13 June 2017, www.edsurge.com/news/2017-06-13-from-high-school-to-harvard-students-urge-for-clarity-on-privacy-rights.

Ackerman, Rakefet, and Morris Goldsmith. "Metacognitive Regulation of Text Learning: On Screen versus Paper." *Journal of Experimental Psychology: Applied*, vol. 17, no. 1, 2011, pp. 18–32.

Bromley, Karen. "Best Practices in Teaching Writing." *Best Practices in Literacy Instruction*, Guilford P, 2015, pp. 295–318.

Coiro, Julie. "Predicting Reading Comprehension on the Internet: Contributions of Offline Reading Skills, Online Reading Skills, and Prior Knowledge." *Journal of Literacy Research*, vol. 43, no. 4, 2011, pp. 352–92.

———. "Purposeful, Critical, and Flexible: Vital Dimensions of Online Reading and Learning." *Reading at a Crossroads? Disjunctures and Continuities in Current Conceptions and Practices*, Routledge, 2015, pp. 53–64.

"A Digital Humanities Manifesto." *The Digital Humanities Manifesto 2.0*, manifesto.humanities.ucla.edu/2009/05/29/the-digital-humanities-manifesto-20/.

Finer, Bryna Siegel, and Jamie White-Farnham. *Writing Program Architecture: Thirty Cases for Reference and Research*, University Press of Colorado, 2017.

Groom, Jim. "Preparing Students for a Connected Future." *Eventbrite*, 24 July 2016, www.eventbrite.com.au/e/preparing-students-for-a-connected-future-jim-groom-registration-35714991501.

Haas, Christina, and Linda Flower. "Rhetorical Reading Strategies and the Construction of Meaning." *College Composition and Communication*, vol. 39, no. 2, 1988, pp. 167–83.

Haswell, Richard. "Context and Rhetorical Reading Strategies: Haas and Flower (1988) Revisited." *Written Communication*, vol. 16, no. 1, 1999, pp. 3–27.

LeFurgy, Bill. "Introduction." *Perspectives on Personal Digital Archiving: National Digital Information Infrastructure and Preservation Program*, Library of Congress, 2013, pp. 3–4, www.digitalpreservation.gov/documents/ebookpdf_march18.pdf.

Long, Christopher. *Investing in Online Scholarly Presence*, 30 Aug. 2016, www.cal.msu.edu/news/webhostingservice.

Mueller, Pam A., and Daniel M. Oppenheimer. "The Pen Is Mightier Than the Keyboard: Advantages of Longhand over Laptop Note Taking." *Psychological Science*, vol. 25, no. 6, 2014, pp. 1159–68.

Pasquini, Laura. "Have You Read the ___ Privacy (Data) Policy Lately?" *techKNOWtools*, 21 June 2017, www.techknowtools.wordpress.com/2017/06/21/breakdrink-10/.

Sikoryak, R. *ITunes Terms and Conditions: The Graphic Novel*, 17 Sep. 2015, www.itunestandc.tumblr.com/tagged/comics/chrono.

UNLV Domains. www.mydomain.unlv.edu/. Accessed 17 July 2018.

UNLV General Education. www.unlv.edu/provost/gen-ed. Accessed 17 July 2018.

Warren, James E. "Rhetorical Reading and the Development of Disciplinary Literacy across the High School Curriculum." *Across the Disciplines*, vol. 10, 2013, www.wac.colostate.edu/atd/articles/warren2013.cfm.

13 Trending Information

Mapping Students' Information Literacies Against WPA Learning Outcomes in First-Year Writing

Jeanne Law Bohannon and Ella Greer

Composition instructors have long-observed experiences of first-year writers and their attitudes towards bibliographic research. Veterans of these courses are also exceedingly familiar with the compliments and complaints that these students offer in course feedback and informally in class about information literacy instruction. In recent years this type of research has moved increasingly to digital spaces, shifting the material reality of information literacy to what some see as Andrea Lunsford's vision of a "literacy revolution," and that others see as a "dynamic and often uncertain information ecosystem" in which teachers must provide a core set of values to frame "what counts" as validity in terms of evaluating sources (Framework for Information Literacy for Higher Education, Association of College and Research Libraries). Still other scholars, notably Jim Gee, take an overarching view of literacy as a student's ability to "control second uses of language" such as mediated, digital spaces (1989, 2007). In his 2007 book *What Video Games Have to Teach Us About Learning and Literacy*, Gee theorizes how his original concept of new literacies can now be applied to visuality of information found in online gaming platforms and students uses of information literacy to collaborate as they play video games. For our research described in this chapter, we consider all of these notions of information literacy, but we frame our own observations around the Association of College and Research Libraries (AARL) guidelines for higher education.

To start, what we know is that writing instruction is inextricably linked to the teaching of research competencies and information literacy. The case study research we present in this chapter offers a compromise that describes what first-year students report they do when performing internet searches for academic purposes as well as what they actually do when they perform those searches. Our case study at Kennesaw State University (KSU) is a networked component of the Learning Information Literacy Across the Curriculum (LILAC) project, a multi-institutional, empirical research study that has collected more than 450 data artifacts on how students conduct information searches online. Founded by Dr. Janice Walker and Dr. Kat Blackwell-Starnes at Georgia Southern University in 2013 and funded by a grant from the Conference on College Composition and Communication (CCCC), LILAC currently has five participating universities in the U.S., ranging from R-1 to comprehensive missions. KSU is a founding partner in the LILAC project.

From Campfire Stories to Case Studies

We have all heard colleagues talk about what happens in our first-year writing courses when the word "research" comes up. Across types and sizes of institutions, students often say: *"First I check out Wikipedia for an overview of the topic I want to research, but my teacher says it's not a credible source so I won't cite it."* During our research for the LILAC (Learning Information Literacy across the Curriculum) Project we heard this statement in many instances from student participants.

Maybe this situation also rings familiar, as remembered by Ella from a college class:

> English class was held in the library that afternoon and the librar-
> ian would attempt to walk us through the mysterious algorithm of
> JSTOR and Galileo. If you were anything like me, you half listened
> as you took the opportunity to catch up on other school work or pass
> notes to friends. We all left the resource room feeling like the hour
> was wasted, of course we knew how to use a search bar! We would
> then go home and work on our research paper by googling the thesis
> statement and skimming the first couple of sources that popped up.

To assess students' actual behaviors when they seek information in digital spaces, LILAC collects and analyzes screen-captured data containing a video record of screen activity and students' voice narrative while conducting bibliographic research on a topic. LILAC researchers collect this qualitative data in addition to survey data that aims to unpack students' experiences, attitudes, and evaluation of their information literacy. As of 2018, LILAC researchers have collected data from more than 450 participants, some of which is available in publications such as the Purdue Information Literacy Handbook, vols. 1–2, as well as publicly on YouTube.

Our case study uses LILAC Project protocols to examine first-year students' information-seeking behaviors for evidence of how theorized transformations towards multimodal information-seeking in first-year writing are—or are not—shaping student research and composition practices. In this case study, we have used LILAC Research-Aloud-Protocols (RAPs) and a coding scheme developed with the support of a 2013 CCCC research grant for LILAC to analyze what students actually do online when seeking information on a topic either from their original school-work or supplied by LILAC. We study how they save information they find, and what they say about their decisions.

What and Why

We implemented a mixed methods approach to study what students say they know about information literacy and how they actually integrate it into their online bibliographic research. In our methodology we draw from Ann Berthoff's theory of the hybridity of writing instruction, which emphasizes that, "reading and writing are in dialogue with one another . . . and whatever learned about reading is something learned about writing" (85–6). We have collected and analyzed qualitative data describing students' information-seeking behaviors in digital environments (bibliographic research) using video records of screen activity and students' voice narratives while source-searching for a topic. This data is in addition to survey data that describes students' demographics, psychographics, and their attitudes towards information literacies. As a networked component of the LILAC project, which has collected more than 400 data artifacts, this chapter examines the information-seeking behaviors of 50 first-year students at a 36,000-student, public state university (R-3) and discusses pedagogical implications directly mapped against WPA outcomes for students' writing in first-year composition courses. Readers will be able to apply our findings and recommendations across diverse first-year writing learning environments, creating a practical balance between theory and praxis while encouraging readers to look for information literacy trends in their own courses.

WPA Outcomes and Our Case Study

In 2014, the Council of Writing Program Administrators released its *Outcome Statement for First-year Composition (3.0)*. The *Statement* describes, "the writing knowledge, practices, and attitudes that undergraduate students develop in first-year composition" as outcomes that support students as they move beyond first-year college writing into diverse "disciplinary, professional, and civic lines." Our case study presented in this chapter focuses on two of these outcomes, "Critical Thinking, Reading, and Composing," and "Knowledge of Conventions" as they focus on information literacy.

Specifically, our case study maps our findings against particular WPA outcomes, as points of reference to examine perceived information-seeking behaviors and possible challenges students face. We also discuss pedagogical implications by addressing these questions, which come directly from the WPA outcomes previously noted:

From "*Critical Thinking, Reading, and Composing*":

1. How do first-year writers at comprehensive universities locate and evaluate various genres of sources specifically for credibility and currency (timeliness)?

From "*Knowledge of Conventions*":

2. How do these first-year writers use citation conventions effectively?

Preliminary Findings to Indicate:

3. How can our case study findings inform possible pedagogical approaches to improve information-seeking behaviors of first-year writers?

In answering the above questions, we offer findings that describe students' information-seeking behaviors and possible solutions based on our research and the findings of previous LILAC studies.

Review of Related Literature

The standards of writing and processing information have changed as the fields of composition have grown and field-specific theories have trended and fallen from favor, but the methods of teaching literacy have remained the same. The rumors of yesteryear about the dangers of Wikipedia and how .org and .gov websites are the only credible sources remain pervasive in the classrooms. We know that writing instruction is inextricably linked to the teaching of research competencies and information literacy at many institutions including comprehensive universities like KSU, Georgia Southern University, and others in both public and private spheres. Composition pedagogies need to address the conceptual and practical competencies required of today's researchers and writers. For example, the New Media Literacies group cites "transmedia navigation"—the "ability to follow the flow of stories and information across multiple media"—as a core competency "that young people need in our new media landscape" (Project New Media Literacies).

Our case study's methodology borrows from Berthoff's theory of the recursiveness of writing instruction, which emphasizes a rejection of linear models and encourages instructors to "invent courses which are consonant with the idea of the composing process as a continuum of forming" ("Recognition, Representation, and Revision," 32).

Literacy practices that students engage in based in the past combined with standards based on future expectations puts first-year writers in a difficult position. They are constantly reminded that they possess the most access to information by leaps and bounds, but they lack the skills to access this information properly. As a result, students' research becomes an exercise of creating a tapestry of several different yet like-minded articles wherein the final product shows block quotes weaved together with transitional sentences rather than being examples of critical thinking and the ability to integrate their own ideas with those of others.

Mina, Bohannon, and Li note the importance of overcoming that patch-writing practice in the forthcoming *Purdue Information Literacy Hand-book:* "both writing instructors and librarians have to better understand and to scaffold the development of information-seeking behaviors of these students, particularly in the first-year writing (FYW) classroom" (Mina et al.). These classrooms spaces are, for many students, the gateway to discipline-specific writing and research, and the first place where they are introduced to information literacy related to academic writing.

Expected WPA outcomes for First-Year Writing students include focus-ing on a purpose and an audience, evaluating sources and integrating their own ideas into the work, and learning how to document their work appropriately.

Understanding (the) students' (capacity of/level for) information lit-eracy skills, particularly as they seek information in online spaces, will help future curriculum to integrate teaching strategies to increase learning these skills. This has the potential to also improve student writing in own disciplines by helping them better assess credible sources from which they create a foundation of research that demonstrates an increased ability to quote, paraphrase, and summarize research without patchwriting from their online sources.

Andrew Asher, a principal investigator for the Ethnographic Research in Illinois Academic Libraries (ERIAL) Project reminds us that "students do not have adequate information literacy skills when they come to college . . . [a]nd they're not getting adequate training as they're going through the cur-riculum" (Kolowich). Here is where we find a primary locus of bibliographic research instruction in higher education—the first-year writing classroom and the ubiquitous research paper as well as students' need for IL instruction in this curricular space.

In 2008, Els Kuiper and Monique Volman concluded that students in secondary school environments are not adept at searching online for academic sources. In their study, the researchers concluded that students do not possess the competency to locate reliable information online (Kui-per 241–68). While their study focused on high school students, we can draw parallels from their work because the overwhelming majority of first-year writers studied by the LILAC project are less than two years out of high school.

Educational scholars remind us that, although many "digital natives" (Prensky, 2001) possess proficiency in digital information literacies like social media and texting, "this does not necessarily mean that they are skilled in the effective use of online information, perhaps the most impor-tant aspect of the Internet" (Leu et al. 344). Their study also touches on the need to provide students with best practices for writing and research that embrace the digital.

Asher concluded that "Student overuse of simple search leads to prob-lems of having too much information or not enough information . . .

both stemming from a lack of sufficient conceptual understanding of how information is organized," he said. Those libraries that have tried to teach good search principles have failed, he continued, because they have spent "too much time trying to teach tools and not enough time trying to teach concepts" (Kolowich). Gaps in how students internalize information literacy instruction can show us when and where possible instructional changes need to occur. A consideration of current data is important, but a combined approach to observing how students actually perform information literacy is a vital key to developing pedagogical strategies that will increase those literacy skills.

Methodology

For our case study at Kennesaw State University, we recruited students from across more than fifteen sections of first-year writing courses, both English 1101 and 1102. The difference in the courses was considered, but since we recruited in summer semester, the diverse groups of students enrolled in the courses negated possible "difference" effects. We do acknowledge, however, that individual students might be outliers in our data given the number of times they have been enrolled in a course.

Demographic Data

Participants in this case study were enrolled in an R-3, comprehensive public university, with 36,000+ students (third largest in Georgia), located in North Metro Atlanta. For the 2016–2017 academic year, this university enrolled 5,498 new freshmen and 2,471 transfer students.

Participants in the LILAC "Trending Information" study were all classified as first-year writers, based on their enrollment in face-to-face English 1101 courses. We did not consider how many times they had taken a course. The overall average age of participants was twenty-eight, and the gender make-up was roughly equal. Based on answers to the LILAC survey and observations, we classified forty-two participants as native English speakers and eight participants as multilingual students, who speak English in addition to a home language. More than 47% of participants reported that they are strong writers; 66% indicated that they believed "writing will be important in my career."

LILAC Overview and Framing

We collected and analyzed qualitative data describing students' information-seeking behaviors in digital environments (bibliographic research) using video records of screen activity and students' voice narratives while source-searching for a topic. This data is in addition to survey data that describes students' demographics, psychographics, and their attitudes towards information literacies. For inter-rater reliability, both of us coded all fifty videos separately, using the current version of the LILAC coding template (Appendix 13B). We then entered our data into an Excel spreadsheet to compare how often we agreed on categories of analysis. With 91% agreement, we believe that our combined analysis is both valid and reliable, making it applicable for other institutions and researchers.

As part of the larger LILAC initiative, our study is a mixed methods design, which is a new approach in describing and evaluating students' digital information-seeking behaviors. LILAC is the first empirical project of its kind to utilize both a survey of perceived information-seeking behaviors and research aloud protocols (RAPs) to collect actual behavioral data from students.

Mixed Methods—Surveys and RAPs

To begin each research session, participants first complete a 5 minute survey about their prior instruction and perceptions of information literacy skills. The survey also captures demographics and psychographics from participants. We tabulate this information to gain an overview; we then compare surveys with associated videos of RAPs, which participants complete in the last 15-minutes of the session.

We observed students' onscreen information-seeking processes, using Camtasia Studio software to capture their screen activity and voice narratives (RAPs) while they conduct digital bibliographic research on a given topic. The protocol's purpose is to observe actual information-seeking behaviors and strategies to determine how students are performing mapped against WPA outcomes and offer recommendations as to where pedagogical intervention might be needed. Such a protocol allows for determining the independent and dependent nature of information behaviors and strategies.

From the data collected and analyzed through a qualitative coding template of participant behaviors and quantitative survey data, we provide results that show how students perform secondary research, how they feel about doing it, and what we, as instructors, can do to increase their growth in this area as they move through academic programs at their universities and ultimately in their post-graduation lives.

Discussion

Self-Reported Survey Data

More than 84% of participants reported that they complete most of their research online, while only 32% usually employ library databases. Of all participants, 33% indicated that they "sometimes forget where they obtain their information altogether" (LILAC Survey, Appendix 13A). When asked if they understand what denotes scholarly, peer-reviewed sources, 57% reported they did. In terms of searching for sources online, participants gave credibility to domains in the following order: .EDU (53%); GOV (47%); .ORG (40%); .COM (13%). Only 9% of participants gave credence to news APPs. Approximately 72% of participants reported that they possessed adequate online research skills.

Digging deeper into the survey data of what they said they do, we found that, when evaluating sources, 39% of first-year writers in this case study use information to support their own opinions; while more than 6% don't think they need to do research if they already know what they want to say. However, 54% know how to evaluate library source information, and 82% know how to evaluate web source information. When asked about multimodal sources, 24% reported that they do not know how to cite them. More than half of students surveyed reported using digital citation generators. Another 32% confess to waiting until the last minute to write up their essays. Interestingly, 40% of students indicated that they knew how to ask for a librarian's help when they were stuck, with 44% reporting that their library research skills were adequate to write up their research. In terms of the type of information literacy instruction provided, 58% received hands-on or workshop learning experiences and 2% received this instruction as an online tutorial. The reported data indicated to use that first-years writers had issues with citing certain genres of sources, problems with using library databases, and including opposing opinions in their research. Conversely, the data also showed that these writers thought they knew how to cite digital information. Our qualitative method proved otherwise.

Observed RAP Session Behaviors

The second part of our case study focused on collecting qualitative data that would help determine independent and dependent nature of information behaviors and strategies. Asking students to talk about what they are doing and why they are making the choices they make while they are in the process of conductive research is an effective tool for these purposes. During the RAP sessions, participants provided observable data that allowed us to identify various information-seeking behaviors in videos (e.g., use of Google, use of library sources, etc.), using a protocol analysis template to compare what students say they have been taught and what they think they know with what students actually do.

As we observed student's information-seeking behaviors through the recorded RAP sessions, we discovered trends that indicated that we argue can map against WPA outcomes, specifically:

1. How do first-year writers at comprehensive universities locate and evaluate various genres of sources specifically for credibility and currency (timeliness)?
    —From "*Critical Thinking, Reading, and Composing:*"

2. How do these first-year writers use citation conventions effectively?
—From *"Knowledge of Conventions:"*

To answer these questions, we begin first with the search engine students choose from the initial home screen. All fifty participants in our case study navigated to Google prior to searching for either topic information or other websites. In their first search, 17% of students went to our University's homepage, 15% landed on Wikipedia, 5% on Google Scholar, and the remainder searched for their topic via the Google search engine. Regarding types of search, we observed that 46% of participants used key words, 25% used natural language inquiry, 13% used Boolean operators, and the remaining participants in single digits using an author or title search.

We also found that most students would type in an entire phrase for their topic search such as "childhood obesity," rather than a specific thought or opinion. This rhetorical choice caused us to make note that perhaps they were planning on writing their papers by cramming in as much information about childhood obesity they could rather than writing a paper with a clear thesis and stance/opinion on an aspect of the issue. We noted here also that of the suggested topic list on the instructions page (Appendix 13C), students chose the topic "childhood obesity" over any other topic listed, besides their own off-lit topic.

Question five of the coding sheet tracked how first-year writers evaluated search results on their initial topic search. Figure 13.1 shows the division of categories as well as frequency of choice, which were multifaceted and not as clear as other findings. However, we noted that 24% of participants chose a source based on its popularity in the search results list (the higher up the list, the more popular); 13% chose sources based on the title of the website or article; and 10% based on credibility. We measured credibility as utterances during RAP sessions. For example, some participants verbally articulated that they chose websites such as CNN based on its news reputation. Similar results occurred with government websites. We did note that they avoided multimodal sites that contained videos and podcasts in place or in addition to alphanumeric text.

The remaining percentages were in single digits and included publication type as well as relevance to topic, with currency ranked at just 1%. We measured currency based on verbal articulations of timeliness and chronological dates as reasons for search results evaluation. These results indicate two actualities. First, they tell us that students value .gov websites but avoid multimodal platforms such as YouTube, TedTalks, and podcasts. This finding is important as we seek to develop teaching strategies for information literacy that address a diversity of reliable search results.

Second, these results tell us that students need instruction on how to evaluate search results in online bibliographic research practices because they seem to choose sources to evaluate based on popularity and title. This

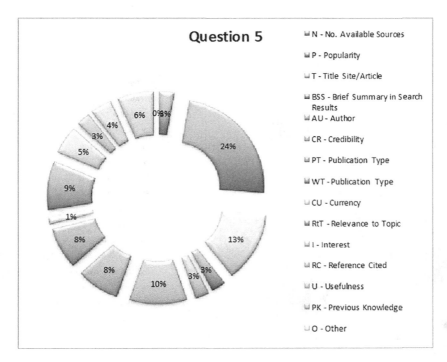

Figure 13.1 LILAC coding template question 5

practice creates a specious process of research that is then followed by an evaluation of sources on those websites.

Figure 13.1 is the result also of an overarching phenomenon we observed in most participants' behavior. We found that the overwhelming majority of students did not look further than the first page of search results for their sources. What this key piece of evidence tells us is that there is a limited critical evaluation of search results that occurs as first-year writers search for information online, because we can see that they simply do not navigate to the second page of search results.

Question six of the LILAC coding template specified how student writers evaluated sources that they found after navigating to a search result in their initial information search. Subsequently, we tracked source evaluation through this question. Figure 13.2 shows a similar multilateral distribution to that of Figure 13.1, with key indicators still existing in double digits, but possessing a spread that is even more dispersed.

What we can glean from Figure 13.2 is interesting because the data seem to delineate an opposing finding that differs from participants' observed avoidance of multimodal sources. In fact, we found that 14%

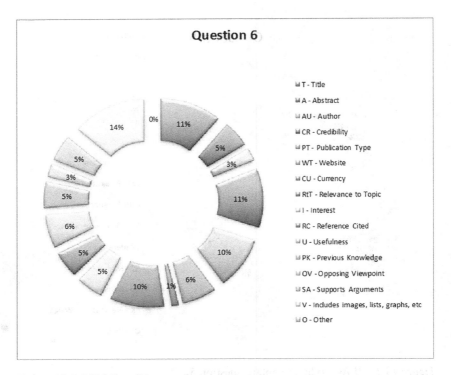

Figure 13.2 LILAC coding template question 6

of participants (the largest percentage) evaluated sources based on their visual content, including infographics, lists, and images. Participants stated the importance of these sources as timely and reliable. In equal numbers, students also chose to use sources because of title or credibility (11%). Here, they articulated credibility as a source that appeared to them to be "scholarly" even when said sources were not located on a .edu or a .gov site. Students also articulated credibility based on any source that did not come from Wikipedia. For example, several students mentioned that they scanned Wikipedia during the search for ideas, but they would not use it as a source because of a rule from their professor. Of further interest is our finding that 10% of participants evaluated sources based on their relevance to topics. We observed that a majority of students reinforced what they reported in the survey: they chose sources that supported their perspectives on their chosen topics. This result suggests the need for instructors to work with students on information literacy to develop more inclusive approaches in their bibliographic research practices. We will discuss this result more in-depth further in this chapter in the section on Pedagogical Possibilities.

Assessing the second WPA outcome, which details how students use citation conventions effectively, we found that our RAP session data provided a rich snapshot of how students perform this practice in online spaces. For example, many students opened tabs across the top of their web browser and kept those tabs open to keep track of sources they evaluated. Less than half, however, articulated that they would use these tabs to later create citations of their sources. We did not confirm what students reported in the survey regarding use of online citation generators, because we did not observe any participant using these tools. Further, we observed no tracking of sources other than tabbing. The only indication of citation conventions came from two students, who noted verbally that the citations for their sources were located on the "right-hand side of the library site." What we took from these comments was that at least 4% of students in our case study knew where to locate citations on the university library source pages. What remains elusive, however, is a clear signal of how students are employing these citations suggestions in their online information-seeking for academic purposes.

Pedagogical Possibilities

At the beginning of our chapter, a third research question (how can our case study findings inform possible pedagogical approaches to improve information-seeking behaviors of first-year writers?) asked how our case study findings might inform pedagogical approaches to improve information-seeking behaviors of first-year writers. While we admit wholeheartedly that a study of fifty first-year writers might not be applicable across all FYW contexts, we did glean data that might provide pedagogical possibilities for writing teachers and librarians doing information literacy instruction.

Most importantly, we encourage partnerships between instructors and librarians, providing interactive learning opportunities where students actually practice searching and evaluating sources in real time, alongside peers and experts, on the same topic. We found more consistency among students who used the same topic to search for sources; we assert that these similarities could lead students receiving information literacy instruction in a workshopping environment towards a deeper comprehension of how to determine credibility and currency of sources. Our experiences with participants further suggest the need for multiple instructional sessions, not the "one-offs" that are typical in our university and possibly others. We propose that first-year students are exposed to information literacy instruction in both library and classroom lab settings, where they can either use university technology or bring their own devices to practice source-searching and evaluation in large and small groups.

A pedagogical strategy that has worked for Jeanne in the past is also integrating democratic teaching methods into this instruction. For example, in a large group setting, students decide on an idea to search, then narrow that idea down to a topic. Usually a student leads the session while Jeanne and a librarian facilitate from the sidelines. Students then divide up into groups or teams that take on specific genres to search. One group searches for multimodal content, while others may search for academic, background, or popular sources. Once the groups reconvene, student representatives discuss their processes and how they determined validity of sources. In essence, the students learn from one another and by "doing" the work of online information-seeking.

Learning appropriate use of library web page citation suggestions works much the same, with librarians often taking the lead, introducing students to online citation resources such as Purdue OWL and university-specific digital guides, and *then* teaching students how to use these resources when they practice citing their own sources in academic and professional writing. Finally, we strongly recommend working with students on relevant and rhetorical use of Wikipedia as a resource. We know that students use this site as a departure point for bibliographic research, so we must embrace strategies for teaching its use as a tool for students. Several recent empirical studies, including a 2014 *PLoS ONE* article, suggest a high reliability for Wikipedia. The authors of this particular study analyzed the reliability of pharmacological information on Wikipedia versus a textbook. They found that Wikipedia was just as reliable up to 99% for accuracy and 91% for completeness (Kraenbring et al.). We advocate for instructors to use Wikipedia and its use as both a resource and opportunity to teach rhetorical choices that lead to effective source evaluation and citation practices. We encourage readers who have practiced with Wikipedia to continue to do this vital work and to present and publish their teaching methods so that our field can benefit from their innovations.

Concluding Thoughts

Teacher-scholars in higher education need to know why students receiving instruction on information literacy skills, including instruction in locating, evaluating, using, and citing information-sources, do not transfer this knowledge with them beyond the confines of a specific assignment or classroom. The LILAC Project provides snapshots of student populations from diverse institutions and academic contexts, identifying where the disconnects lie between what students have been taught and what they are actually doing and then providing instructors with possible solutions at the point of need rather than divorced from the research and writing process itself.

Our mixed methods research seeks to help composition instructors better understand how students are performing bibliographic research online, what they learn from specific information literacy instruction, and what pedagogical interventions can we design to enhance information literacy skills in college and professional careers.

The discussion and recommendations reported in this chapter indicate a clear purpose for empirical information literacy research across academic fields as well as a need to continue this type of work in tandem with classroom and library instructional applications. LILAC researchers continue to conduct studies at diverse institutions with participants of varying matriculations, ranging from first-year writers to graduate students. Given the collaborative, multi-institutional nature of the LILAC project, we invite instructors and librarians to network with our group. Check out LILAC projects, presentations, publications, and collaboration opportunities on our website http://lilac-group.blogspot.com/, or by following us on Twitter: @LILACProject.

Works Cited

Berthoff, Ann. *Forming, Thinking, Writing: The Composing Imagination*, Upper Montclair, NJ, Boynton Cook, 2013.

———. "Recognition, Representation, and Revision." *The Journal of Basic Writing*, vol. 2, no. 3, 1981, pp. 19–32.

———."Framework for Information Literacy for Higher Education." *American Library Association*, 9 Feb. 2015, www.ala.org/acrl/standards/ilframework.

Gee, James P. "What Is Literacy?" *Journal of Education*, vol. 171, no. 1, 1989.

———. *What Video Games Have to Teach Us about Learning and Literacy*, New York, St. Martins Press, 2007.

Kolowich, Steve. "Searching for Better Research Habits." *Inside Higher Ed.*, 29 Sep. 2010, www.insidehighered.com/news/2010/09/29/search.

Kraenbring, Jona, et al. "Accuracy and Completeness of Drug Information in Wikipedia: A Comparison with Standard Textbooks of Pharmacology." *PLoS One*, https://journals.plos.org/plosone/article?id=10.1371/journal.pone. 0106930.

Kuiper, Els, and Monique Volman. "The Web as a Source of Information for Students in K-12 Education." *Handbook of Research on New Literacies*, New York, Routledge, 2008.

Leu, Don, Lisa Zawilinski, Ellen Fozani, and Nicole Timbrell. "Best Practices in Teaching the New Literacies of Online Research and Comprehension." *Best Practices in Literacy Instruction*, edited by Linda B. Gambrell and Lesley Mandel Morrow, Guilford Press, 2015, pp. 343-364.

Mina, Lilian, Jeanne Bohannon, and Jinrong Li. "Google, Baidu, the Library, and ARCL Framework: Assessing Information-Seeking Behaviors of First-Year Multilingual Writers through Research-Aloud Protocols." *Purdue Information Literacy Handbook*, Purdue University Press, 2018.

Prensky, Marc. "Digital Natives, Digital Immigrants." *On the Horizon*, vol. 9, 2001, pp. 1–6.

"Transmedia Education: The 7 Principles Revisited." *Project New Media Literacies*, 24 June 2010, www.newmedialiteracies.org/2010/06/transmedia_blog_1/.

"WPA Outcomes Statement for First-Year Composition (3.0)." *Council of Writing ProgramAdministrators*, 17 July 2014, www.wpacouncil.org/positions/outcomes.html.

14 New Assessments for *New* Reading

An Evidence-Based Approach

G. Travis Adams

Over the last decade, composition's surge in attention to reading has been traced and retraced thoroughly in monographs and edited collections by Salvatori and Donahue, Carillo, Horning, Sullivan, Tinberg, Blau, Keller, and through recently published articles in *College English, Pedagogy, Teaching English in the Two-Year College, Reader,* and *Writing Lab Newsletter,* to name a few. This renewed attention emphasizes the value in exploring college reading's complexity and its importance to teaching writing. One overdue outcome of this attention has been the development of reading pedagogies that push students to read across a wide range of texts both digital and "print" and for a growing range of purposes. Such a development is fitting, particularly at a time when, as Keller argues in *Chasing Literacy,* "what counts as effective reading and writing becomes a moving target—over time and from context to context" (8). In fact, I find myself greatly encouraged by Keller's work; by Sullivan, Tinberg and Blau's *Deep Reading;* by Carillo's *Securing a Place for Reading;* by Horning's *What Is College Reading?;* by Hewett's *Reading to Learn and Writing to Teach;* and by this volume because collectively we are articulating a solidly theorized reading pedagogy that arrives at a time when the nature of reading and texts is undergoing significant changes that impact composition instructors and students.

"New" Reading Pedagogy

Compositionists must now understand articulations of reading pedagogy labeled as "deep reading" by Sullivan, as "college-level" reading by Horning, and as "mindful" reading by Carillo. Understanding, embracing, and employing this "New"[1] reading pedagogy begins by recognizing that deep, mindful, and college level are relatively synonymous terms offered to frame an evolving set of core beliefs about reading's place in composition classrooms and in the lives of our students. With "'Deep Reading' as a Threshold Concept in Composition Studies," Patrick Sullivan describes deep reading as a pedagogy "most essentially designed to provide opportunities for students to engage in metacognitive thinking about the process of learning, and to help students assess and reassess their own mental models for understanding the world" (147). Carillo's mindful reading focuses on "promoting the development of metacognitive practices that help students develop knowledge about reading, knowledge that will prove useful as they move among many contexts and classes" (*Securing* 117). In the introduction to *What Is College Reading?*, Alice Horning summarizes Carillo, Bunn, Berthoff, and others who, via "New" reading "ask students to first respond to the text, then comment on the moves they made as readers, and finally, assess the particular meaning of the text their recursive reading produced" (5). Continuing an articulation of college-level reading, and thus "New" reading, Horning defines it "as a complex, recursive process in which readers actively and critically understand and create meaning through connections to texts" (5). Horning then traces five key terms that frame what students and faculty must in turn do:

> Because college reading is complex, it needs to be taught in every discipline and every course. Because it is a recursive activity, students need to be reminded that they need to work on reading as they work on subject learning and mastery. Because it is an active process, reading assignments need to be set up so that students must do the reading and engage with the material in some overt way. Because reading should always be critical, students must learn the elements of critical evaluation of everything they read (authority, accuracy, currency, relevancy, appropriateness, bias) and be able to apply them online and on paper. And finally, because of the need for connection, faculty must help students read in context, not only within their courses, but also within their disciplines, to make connections to materials and ideas beyond the classroom.
>
> (7)

Named any which way, "New" reading represents an explicit shift toward active attention to reading processes and strategies from teachers and students. Of course, such frameworks for reading will not simply manifest themselves in composition classrooms now that we've articulated core values.

For teachers, integrating "New" reading into the classroom involves reconsidering many traditional instructional frameworks around reading that tended, as Sullivan argues, to focus on knowledge mastery and promote approaches to reading that allow students to see reading as an exercise of the short-term memory and as a process consisting mostly or only of moving one's eyes across text on a page (148). Like Sullivan, Carillo clarifies that a pedagogy more attuned to reading "offers students opportunities to reflect on their ways of reading, to imagine and make connections across contexts, to adapt reading strategies to various contexts, and to experience firsthand the amount of time it takes to read mindfully" ("Preparing"

203). Carillo, Sullivan, and Horning make clear that significant steps must be taken to reframe reading in the composition classroom so that students are invited into and supported throughout this reading work.

One step we must take is to clarify our expectations. This involves careful introspection for instructors, similar to what Karen Manarin describes in "Reading Value: Student Choice in Reading Strategies." Manarin shares that upon surveying students about reading, she "had to consider what I meant by reading and what, as an English professor, I was or wasn't doing to help these students read" (282). Adler-Kassner and Estrem have expressed the "critical need for composition instructors to carefully define how we want students to be as readers, and *why* [. . .] participating in these ways is important for [students] as readers and writers" (39). Thus, we must communicate clearly to students what we are asking them to do—which is to change the way they read—and why that change is necessary. We want students to read in ways that allow them to engage in written and oral discussions of texts, and we want them to be readers that are constantly learning about how writing works from the texts they consume. Thankfully, we can now turn to texts like Carillo's *A Writer's Guide to Mindful Reading* for a model of making expectations clear to students.[2] Via the mindful reading framework, Carillo articulates four reasons why students need to develop as readers:

1. You will be faced with more reading.
2. The types of reading you will be assigned will vary drastically depending on the discipline and the course.
3. You will be expected to read more complex texts.
4. You will be asked to complete more complex tasks associated with your reading.

(vi)

Carillo then includes suggestions for annotating texts digitally, thus presenting expectations and offering a connected strategy. In so doing, Carillo also models how, once embraced by individual instructors or programs, "New" reading must be consistently framed across syllabi, assignments, activities, and in-class discussions (online or in person).

Our expectations will need to be clearer than ever, particularly as "New" reading pushes against students whose relationships with reading may immediately put them at odds with such pedagogies. Keller helps us understand that we are teaching students overwhelmed by the sheer number of texts they encounter and for whom:

> Acceleration is one response to accumulation, to the overabundance of texts and media options: when faced with so many texts, readers tend to read faster, skimming, scanning, and sorting.

(153)

Instructors will need to communicate what *is* expected of students when teachers no longer see reading as "some compartmentalizable skill that is independent of context or of the reader herself" (Carillo, "Preparing" 203). And as Sullivan clarifies, embracing "New" reading underscores the need to "frame the deep structures of our teaching practice in accessible and powerful ways" (155). As instructors, we must help students develop strategies for processing such a wide range of texts across contexts. This work will be challenging, in part because students also need help finding "a means for making decisions about which contexts demand with approaches" (Carillo, *Securing* 128). No longer can we focus just on how we want students to read print essays assigned for FYC, as students may choose to read digital versions of textbooks, and instructors may assign a far wider range of texts (blogs, websites, news articles, journal articles, memos, business plans, advertisements) written for diverse audiences and purposes and accessed via a far greater range of mediums and tools (textbooks, e-books, digital files, e-readers, etc.). Given this reality, instructors have to recognize that teaching students to read as writers "is actually more challenging than teaching a single reading approach since it involves helping students develop ways of reading that are characterized by rhetorical adaptability" (Carillo, *Securing* 129). This will be true for traditional face-to-face classrooms and especially for online courses like those Hewett explores in *Reading to Learn and Writing to Teach*.

Noting that "getting students to engage actively in learning can be challenging online" (103), Hewett suggests a range of reading exercises designed to "easily fit within most writing assignments" (104). Designing reading-based assignments is a second key step toward embracing "New" reading. Assignments, after all, are fundamental for communicating expectations to students. Thus, if our goal is to "help develop new mental models for students, we must design learning activities that require them to think deeply, creatively, and reflectively about complex problems" (Sullivan 157). Yet, designing assignments that position reading to fit well with writing assignments and processes also requires us to explore a tension between adding (or significantly modifying) reading assignments and assessing reading. For example, when Hewett suggests that reading elements can be added to most writing assignments "without requiring significantly more work than already has been built into the assignment" (258), she introduces a tension between whether we value the reading work enough to ask students to do it and as instructors to read, respond, and grade such work. Hewett offers that the range of reading lessons/activities she describes "do not need to be graded by the teacher" (105), thus suggesting that quick responses will be enough for students because "such personal contact about any literacy lesson assures students that the lesson is not merely busywork; they can see that the teacher reads and cares about what they are experiencing" (105). Hewett recognizes—and I agree—that not every instance of reading needs to be graded and that quick responses validate student work. However, this also highlights the tension between what instructors value and what we can reasonably expect students to take seriously when and if such reading is not evaluated. To this tension, Horning offers:

> students generally don't read much extended nonfiction prose of the kind used in college courses [. . .] and they won't unless teachers assign reading in a specific and intentional way and make what students do count in their grades.
>
> (7)

Note particularly that Horning's push is for what students do to count in their grades, not necessarily for every single instance to be graded. So, making clear how ungraded reading activities count toward a grade addresses some of this tension. At the same time, tension remains around exactly when or how to grade "New" reading.

As a reflection of "New" reading's pedagogical generativity, we can now with relative ease point to a broad spectrum of "New" reading assignments including:

- Anson's Writing to Read Assignments
- Bunn's guiding questions for Reading Like a Writer
- Carillo's Passage-Based Paper and Reading Journal
- Morris's genre-based reading
- Edwards' Recirculation and Envelope Exercise
- Miller's slow reading
- Hewett's reading focused lessons and tasks
- Horning's Inquiry Project (this volume),
- Licastro's annotations/commentary via social annotation tools (this volume),
- McIntosh's embracing of digital annotations, clipping, and journaling (this volume)
- Morris's collaborative annotations (this volume)

These assignments ask students to—via digital or print texts—explore "making the private act of reading public" (Miller 159). After all, when we create assignments that focus our and our students' attention on reading, we are exposing strategies and processes that are typically invisible. By asking students to make visible the previously invisible, each of the assignments listed above is certainly evidence of "New" reading that we can, and should, require of our students. After all, each such assignment, not only reflects a collective conception of reading pedagogy for composition classrooms, but they also reflect disciplinary values articulated in documents including the WPA Outcomes, asking in various ways for students to demonstrate rhetorical knowledge, critical thinking, reading, and composing processes, and knowledge of conventions (Council of Writing Program Administrators).

Unfortunately, even as we have reached a historical moment in which we can—and should—tap into a wealth of thoughtfully theorized and designed "New" reading assignments for FYC, we are left largely without articulations of how to grade reading assignments and how, if at all, we are to count the informal and often more invisible reading work students do as they engage writing assignments and process the full range of texts encountered in and for our courses. For example, in *A Writer's Guide to Mindful Reading* Carillo devotes an entire chapter to "Developing a Repertoire of Reading Strategies," walking students through previewing, skimming, says/does approach, rhetorical reading, read aloud to paraphrase, mapping, believing/doubting, reading like a writer, and reading/evaluating online sources (9–24), each presented in detail, well contextualized, and with prompts for practicing each strategy. Carillo also provides students with additional assignments and activities through which they can make their reading visible; these include a reading journal, reading difficulty inventory, the passage-based paper, and the source synthesis (25–34). Given this framing, students should understand a range of strategies available to them, but nothing makes clear how any of this reading work factors into the students' grade or how instructors should approach evaluating this work.

Not discussing the grading of "New" reading assignments reflects a broad tradition of separating our grading practices from much of our published scholarship. We operate under the assumption that teachers will fold new pedagogical elements into their grading schemes on their own. And, pragmatically, not addressing the assessment of reading keeps work focused. The consequence, however, is that we leave students guessing as to how their reading work will be graded and we leave instructors without models which would help them improve as teachers—and graders—of reading. As Tinberg has noted, teachers must "engage in conversations with colleagues about the challenges of reading (for themselves and their students or employees) and strategies for assisting others to improve as readers" (262–3). Within and beyond FYC, assessing student reading is a challenge that we need to discuss more frequently not just on individual campuses, but in our scholarly work as well.

In the remainder of this chapter, I highlight the gap between progressive calls for collaborative writing assessment (e.g., Gallagher & Turley) and the range of "New" reading assignments and expectations. I then offer an evidence-based reading assessment framework that allows students to demonstrate reading in writing courses across time, genres, purposes, technologies, and texts. Such a framework promotes a realignment of the ways we assess student reading with the ways in which compositionists have crafted writing assessments that recognize the complexity, process, and individuality of writing.

Aligning "New" Reading and Writing Assessment

"New" expectations for student reading and the growing reliance on digital texts and tools complicate reading in our classrooms for teachers and students. In terms of assessment, reading presents a range of challenges because of the range of strategies, assignments, and processes involved as well as the individual nature of many aspects of the reading process. Reading is also a challenge because we have long relied on limited means for assessing it. As Morris notes in "From Twilight to the Satanic Verses: Unexpected Discoveries about Reading and Writing in the High School Classroom," at the secondary level, there has been an overreliance on graphic organizers, posters, and other traditional means of assessing student reading (25). Morris shares that despite having assessments provided by the College Board, colleagues "often chose different assessments that usually took the form of multiple-choice tests (graded by Scantron), essays to further prepare for the state writing test (graded for form rather than content), or art projects" (25). Like Morris, I believe it is time for teachers to hold ourselves to a "higher and more rigorous standard" for teaching reading (31). Part of this higher standard comes via the recognition that we "have to commit to teaching reading as a unique process that can involve multiple approaches, which will lead to eventual and *real* mastery" (Morris 31). And, at the same time, teachers must understand that reading assessment can be "loud and chaotic or completely silent" (Morris 31–2). Of course, writing teachers should be familiar with loud, chaotic, and silent.

After all, reading is not unlike writing; both are highly complex, often invisible, and personal processes. Over the last fifteen years, writing assessment scholarship has shifted to fully embrace writing as a process of rhetorical, genre, and reader/writer-based decision-making and revision. We have a solid body of research and practice embracing portfolios, contract grading systems, and reflective writing for assessment (at course and program levels) of student writing. In *Our Better Judgement: Teacher Leadership for Writing Assessment*, Chris Gallagher and Eric Turley trace writing assessment's history, highlighting the shift toward an inquiry framework for assessment that involves students in the process and results in much richer and useful assessment of student writing and learning. Gallagher and Turley remind us that assessment is "the process of gathering, analyzing, and using information about student writing for the purpose of supporting students as writers, informing writing instruction/curriculum/professional development, and/or making decisions about students as writers" (17). Substituting "reading" and "readers" for writing and writers in Gallagher and Turley's definition of assessment should help us see the need for reading assessment that goes beyond testing whether or not students have read assigned texts. Our goal must be to "design assessments in ways that reveal information about what we want to know" (Gallagher and Turley 18). If we want to know how our students are reading, we need assessments that allow us to see our students as readers and writers, and we need to analyze the evidence provided via assessment to help our students learn and to continuously re-shape courses and programs.

Shifting from traditional reading assessment (i.e., quizzes, comprehension questions, and reading responses) to assessments of student reading that value individual reading styles/strategies and the reading process will align reading and writing assessment. Again, we can look to Gallagher and Turley for key advice. First, they offer that "writing assessment need not result in a grade, a score, or in fact any final evaluative judgment" (18). So, like Hewett, Gallagher and Turley help us understand that as we align writing with reading assessment not every instance of reading or our assessment of it must result in points earned. Second, they stress that assessment of writing can come via formative as well summative assessments, with emphasis on developing context-specific formative assessments because those assessments best get at actually improving teaching and learning (Gallagher and Turley 18). Gallaher and Turley's advice echoes what Scott Filkins has written about reading assessment. Filkins advocates a shift away from reading assessments that happen at the end of a course or unit (summative) to one in which teachers participate in assessment "*with* [students], all along the way" ("Rethinking" 51). Such a shift allows instructors to experience reading assessment as an "attempt to understand my students better as readers" ("Rethinking" 51), thus shifting the focus toward supporting our students as readers.

By rethinking reading assessment to work in support of students rather than to test them, Filkins points out that teachers will "want to look for ways to get your students to offer up such information about their processes, habits, and attitudes" ("Rethinking" 51). Filkins lands on two tools for gathering information about student reading. One is student annotations of texts, the other is one-on-one reading conferences (Filkins, "Rethinking" 51). Conferences promote "embedded, individualized instruction. As students are reading [. . .] you can talk with students about how they're preparing to read and how it's going as they are working through a text" (Filkins, "Rethinking" 52). Again, looking at student annotations and having conversations about reading throughout a course shifts assessment away from testing if students have read, so that evidence of reading "helps [instructors] know what to model for students and to guide them to (and through)" (Filkins, "Rethinking" 52).

As I have shifted my own classroom approach to reading assessment, thinking in terms of evidence has been a game changer. Like Filkins, I have long worried that students enter and leave my classroom "believing that the purpose of reading was to answer someone else's questions about texts they didn't care about" (*Beyond* 15). If I'm choosing the texts, if I'm identifying the questions, and if I'm articulating the strategies students are to use for reading a text, then even a well-crafted reading assignment privileges what I'm asking for rather than showing me how students read, what is important to them, and what choices and connections they draw. Shifting to an evidence-based assessment of student reading—in which "New" reading assignments play a role—repositions reading "as a constructive act in which students make meaning by combining their lived experiences with the content on the page" (Filkins, *Beyond* 16). In an evidence-based assessment system, teachers still create writing-to-read assignments, but students choose what combination of assignments, annotations, notes, etc., to draw on as evidence of their reading. Students articulate, via written reflection or conversation, what processes and strategies were at work in that evidence as well as what they learned through the process.

Early in my FYC we read Bunn's "How to Read Like a Writer" and talk about the expectations for reading. This initial conversation surfaces reading habits and histories, often revealing how students have previously been expected to read, what they've actually done to get by, and that being held more accountable for their reading in college is unexpected and potentially nerve-racking. To alleviate some of this nervousness, I have worked with students to articulate how to make an evidence-based case that they have read at an A, B, or C level for the course; they can assemble and present their evidence in individual conferencing moments (10–30 minute conversations focused on reading evidence) and/or in an end of term portfolio, thus aligning reading with the common FYC practice of required writing portfolios.[3] Just as I use rubrics to guide conversations about writing projects in process and for assessment at the end of the term, I now use a Reading As a Writer (RAW) rubric to facilitate conversations about reading throughout the course and for final assessment of reading evidence.

The RAW rubric, drafted and revised with significant initial and ongoing student input, began with language pulled from Bunn's "How to Read Like a Writer" and the Association of American Colleges and Universities' "Reading Value Rubric." As you can see in Figure 14.1, the rubric employs five categories, each articulating a scale of expectations for strategies, processes, and thinking work students must show evidence of by the end of a semester.

In use, the rubric helps students understand that not all reading is equal and that they must show what they are doing not only to comprehend texts but also to use texts as writers (see, specifically Reading for Choices and Reading for Application). FYC, after all, is a writing course in which everything we read is intended for our growth as writers. The rubric also sets an expectation that students demonstrate a process for reading before, during, and after the actual act of moving eyeballs across paper or pixels (Reading Process) and that students can show the ways their reading strategies are shaped by the variety of texts they read, whether

	A	B	C
Reading Comprehension	Consistently explores how specific textual features and genre conventions contribute to the effectiveness of the author's message; questions, notes, annotations draw connections between features and how/why texts were produced or make meaning.	Consistently identifies specific textual features (e.g, sentence structure, word choices, transitions) that contribute to the author's message; questions, annotations, notes engage how/why texts were produced or make meaning.	Demonstrates ability to accurately paraphrase or summarize the information communicated in texts.
Reading Process	Demonstrates planning/strategizing/question posing before/during/after reading, including consistent written planning/reflection. Connects individual texts to others currently or previously assigned/read, including revisiting texts to apply new concepts, frameworks, or strategies; treats texts as part of an ongoing conversation.	Demonstrates planning/strategizing/question posing before/during/after reading, including some level of written planning/reflection. Draws connections between/across texts over time.	Demonstrates basic planning/strategizing/ question posing but does so inconsistently before/during/after reading. Texts are treated as individual artifacts/experiences.
Purposeful Reading	Provides evidence of reading via a range of strategies driven by features of specific assignment, texts, or genres; notes or makes clear how reading is shaped by particular discourse communities, disciplines, or groups of readers/audiences.	Demonstrates reading purposefully, choosing among reading strategies based on features of specific assignments, texts, or genres.	Relies on external authority for reading purpose; relies heavily on one reading strategy applied across reading tasks and genres.
Reading for Choices	Consistently identifies and analyses choices/moves made by the author(s) of assigned texts, research sources, and/or texts from other courses/contexts. Considers how those choices effect readers including and beyond themselves. Consistently explores different choices authors may have made and the effect of alternative choices.	Consistently identifies and analyses choices/ moves made by the author(s) of assigned texts. Shows consideration of how those choices effect readers including and beyond themselves. On occasion, explores different choices authors may have made and the effect of such choices.	Demonstrates ability to identify choices/moves made by the author(s) of assigned texts. Shows basic consideration of how those choices impact own reading. Comments/analysis of choices/ moves is primarily evaluative (good/bad/like/ dislike)
Reading for Application	Consistently identifies features, choices, moves, etc. in written texts that could be tried in his/her own writing and does so beyond prompts from assignments/activities. Shows multiple instances of application in one or more written projects.	Consistently identifies features, choices, moves, etc. in written texts that could be tried in his/her own writing and does so beyond prompts from assignments/activities. Shows evidence of application in at least one writing project.	Demonstrates an ability to identify features, choices, moves, etc. in written texts that could be tried in his/her own writing but does so only on rare occasions or when directly prompted by assignments/activities. Little or no evidence of application in own writing.

This rubric is not meant as a way to grade your reading of individual texts, but rather as a tool for evaluating your reading as a whole. Evidence for RAW should be whatever best captures YOUR reading as a writer and may include any combination of the following, plus whatever else best represents your reading: annotations, dual entry journals, reading log, reading responses, notes, reflective/analysis portions of writing projects, screen captures, discussion question responses, completed class activities, rhetorical moves/style analysis sheets, etc.

Note: Rubric adapted from the Association of American Colleges and Universities' "Reading Value Rubric" and is deeply informed by Mike Bunn's "How to Read Like a Writer." I am indebted to the students in English 1160, 2400, and 2420 who have contributed to this rubric. – G. Travis Adams, University of Nebraska Omaha. Revised 12/19/2017

Figure 14.1 RAW Rubric sets expectations for student reading

that variety is due to genre, purpose, or other features of the text (including if the text is read digitally) (Purposeful Reading). Rather than asking students to prove they are reading solely via specific moments I've crafted, students use the RAW rubric to gather whatever makes clear what they are doing (and why) before, during, and after reading. This includes:

- Annotating
- Journaling
- Writing responses
- Dialogue or dual-entry journals
- Cloze sentences or sentence stems
- Direct responses to in-class discussion questions
- Move/style analysis tables
- Writing project reflections
- Reading & class notes
- Drawings/comics
- Sculpture, finger paints, poetry . . .

Yes, the preceding list moves from what might be familiar and logical to what might very well stretch beyond what students might ever produce in our courses but reaching out to the extremes of something like finger painting illustrates to students and colleagues that as teacher I do not care what constitutes evidence of student reading. I care deeply and only that such evidence represents students' actual reading process and practices and that students can describe what they did and why. So, if and when a student arrives in my office, points to a finger painting as evidence of reading or includes such evidence in a portfolio, I'll eagerly listen to or read the ways in which the finger painting illustrates the reading process or the connections being made between texts consumed and produced.

To this end, I would offer that with evidence-based assessment of reading, we must work to help students balance evidence that comes from teacher created reading moments ("New" reading assignments) and evidence that captures real snapshots of student reading in as unaltered forms as possible. In his work, Keller uses the term "foraging" to describe students' "purposeful wandering across texts, evaluating and possibly gathering and using materials along the way" (166). FYC teachers should model and teach strategies to help students forage efficiently. Concurrently, evidence-based assessment does not simply dismiss foraging. Students can be rewarded for foraging, if they can articulate what they are doing and why foraging aligns with their purposes for reading and writing.

Through reading conferences and feedback on RAW, I guide students away from re-typing or reorganizing annotations, notes, journals, or other evidence just to make it easier for me to manage. I am not interested in students doing all kinds of additional work to re-package their reading evidence. In many cases, they are already doing additional work to explain their RAW evidence orally or in writing, and evaluating RAW evidence adds to my workload as well. So, as much as possible, my effort has been to have students present RAW evidence in its original form, with as minimal explanatory additions or organization as possible. And, as I look at evidence early on in a semester, I make clear what is obvious to me and what I need help understanding.

By the end of a semester, students should know what counts for RAW evidence and how to explain what instructors should see in that evidence. Of course, the evidence itself will be highly individualized, as readers employ different strategies and tools to the same text. For instructors, this means being open to a wide range of evidence including pen and paper notes (yes, even students reading digital versions of texts may choose to take physical notes), annotations, evidence shared via Google Docs, PDF files crammed with colored comment bubbles, OneNote documents, digital (and physical) sticky notes, LMS discussion thread snips, and scanned pages or digital photos of textbooks/articles (increasingly simple thanks to free smartphone scanner apps). We must recognize evidence of reading in all such forms, as this is simply the reality of how our students read.

Conclusion

Of course, I am not suggesting that anyone simply take the RAW rubric, add reading conferences to their syllabus, and march into the next semester. Rather, I hope that the RAW rubric and evidence-based assessment will help individual instructors as well as writing programs consider local contexts (course objectives, pedagogical values, and students) and develop reading assessments that recognize and reward the full range of reading processes, strategies, and products. Employed as part of a system built around "New" reading and reflecting active conversations about reading in FYC, the RAW rubric facilitates a process of assessing reading that aligns well with the WPA Outcomes Statement for First-Year Composition and with other calls for new assessments of reading. Evidence-based assessment of reading speaks back to scholars like Salvatori and Donahue, who argue that we must increase our focus on the "'reader within' the readings they produce, for such readings emerge from repertoires that, while possibly shared, can also be highly discrete" (332). Evidence-based reading assessment allows teachers to see these discrete reading moments and to reward students whose creative strategies for engaging with texts may go unrecognized by both traditional reading assessments and a given teacher's selection of "New" reading assignments. Moving to evidence-based assessment also allows us to embrace the reality that students will enter and leave the FYC course with a range of reading skills and competencies, just as they do with writing.

As Manarin reminds us, while we can and likely will see student progress in reading over the course of a semester, much like writing, developing into a critical reader "is a long, and not necessarily linear, process" (292). Manarin, like others, calls for recognizing that students need "explicit instruction and practice with reading strategies" and that as teachers we should "talk about reading as a series of choices students can control" and "provide feedback on reading" (294). Embracing "New" reading and evidence-based assessment, gets at the core of reading's importance to FYC, since paying attention to how our students read is not just about making sure they are able to read for a single writing course. When we put a rich, nuanced articulation and assessment of "New" reading at the center of FYC, we also communicate—to students, to administrators, and to the community—that reading is, as Manarin puts it, about "the ability of people to learn, the ability of people to sift through various forms of rhetoric, the ability of people to participate in a democracy" (295). As we navigate the digital age and help our students write, think, and read their way through it as well, our shift to "New" reading and to evidence-based assessment of reading will prepare students to be better writers and readers and citizens, make us better teachers of writing and reading, and improve writing programs overall.

Notes

1. My use of "New" is intentionally tongue in cheek. Like Anson and others, I recognize that FYC instructors, textbooks, and scholars have valued, taught, and scaffolded these ways of reading for decades. I use "New" to refer to articulations that arise at this particular moment in time and because it provides one umbrella term to include others now in use—deep, mindful, reading like writers, etc.
2. Carillo's *A Writer's Guide to Mindful Reading*, follows a tradition of FYC textbooks that variously emphasize reading's connection to writing, including Bartholomae and Petrosky's *Ways of Reading*; Ballenger and Payne's *The Curious Reader*; Marshall's *Composing Inquiry*; and Bean, Chappell, and Gillam's *Reading Rhetorically*, to name a few.
3. At least as far back as the mid-1990s, scholars made compelling cases for adopting portfolio-based assessment of reading. Casazza describes a shift toward portfolio-based assessment of reading in part because the primary curricular goals "are to promote critical thinking, comprehension, monitoring, and the integration of reading with writing" (289).

Works Cited

Adler-Kassner, Linda, and Heidi Estrem. "Reading Practices in the Writing Classroom." *WPA: Writing Program Administration*, vol. 31, no. 1–2, 2007, pp. 35–47.

Anson, Chris. "Writing to Read, Revisited." Horning, Gollnitz, and Haller, pp. 21–39.

Bunn, Mike. "How to Read Like a Writer." *Writing Spaces: Readings on Writing*. vol. 2, Parlor P, 2011, pp. 71–86.

Carillo, Ellen. "Preparing College-Level Readers to Define Reading as More Than Mastery." Sullivan, Tinberg, and Blau, pp. 188–209.

———. *Securing a Place for Reading in Composition*, Utah State University Press, 2015.

———. *A Writer's Guide to Mindful Reading*, University Press of Colorado, 2017.

Casazza, Martha E. "Enriching the Developmental Teaching and Learning Environment with Portfolio Assessment." *Forum for Reading*, vol. 26, 1995–1996. In Paulson, E. "College Reading Research and Practice: Articles from the Journal of College Literacy and Learning." *International Reading Association*, 2003, pp. 1–24.

Council of Writing Program Administrators. "WPA Outcomes Statement for First-Year Composition (v3.0)." 1 Nov. 2017, http://wpacouncil.org/positions/outcomes.html.

Edwards, Mike. "Unpacking the Universal Library: Digital Reading and the Recirculation of Economic Value." *Pedagogy: Critical Approaches to Teaching Literature, Language, Composition, and Culture*, vol. 16, no. 1, 2016, pp. 125–36.

Filkins, Scott. *Beyond Standardized Truth: Improving Teaching and Learning through Inquiry-Based Reading Assessment*, NCTE, 2012.

———. "Rethinking Adolescent Reading Assessment: From Accountability to Care." *English Journal*, vol. 103, no. 1, 2013, pp. 48–53.

Gallagher, Chris, and Eric Turley. *Our Better Judgement: Teacher Leadership for Writing Assessment*, NCTE, 2012.

Hewett, Beth. *Reading to Learn and Writing to Teach: Literacy Strategies for Online Writing Instruction*, Bedford, Macmillan, 2015.

Horning, Alice S. "Introduction." Horning, Gollnitz, and Haller, pp. 3–18.

Horning, Alice S., Deborah-Lee Gollnitz, and Cynthia R. Haller, editors. *What Is College Reading?*, University Press of Colorado, 2017.

Keller, Dan. *Chasing Literacy: Reading and Writing in an Age of Acceleration*, Utah State University Press, 2014.

Manarin, Karen. "Reading Value: Student Choice in Reading Strategies." *Pedagogy*, vol. 12, no. 2, 2012, pp. 281–97.

Miller, Richard. "On Digital Reading." *Pedagogy: Critical Approaches to Teaching Literature, Language, Composition, and Culture*, vol. 16, no. 1, 2016, pp. 153–64.

Morris, Sam. "From Twilight to the Satanic Verses: Unexpected Discoveries about Reading and Writing in the High School Classroom." Sullivan, Tinberg, and Blau, pp. 23–32.

Sullivan, Patrick, Howard Tinberg, and Sheridan Blau, editors. *Deep Reading: Teaching Reading in the Writing Classroom*, NCTE, 2017.

Tinberg, Howard. "When Writers Encounter Reading in a Community College First-Year Composition Course." Sullivan, Tinberg, and Blau, pp. 244–64.

Afterword
"A Rapprochement of Reading and Writing"

Lynée Lewis Gaillet

Contributors to *Digital Reading and Writing in Composition Studies* fully explore contemporary integrations of reading and writing, along with the theoretical and pedagogical alignment of these two acts brokered by digital reading and composing. *Digital Reading and Writing in Composition Studies* joins impressive recent works such as Katie Comer, Michael Harker, and Ben McCorkle's *The Archive as Classroom: Pedagogical Approaches to Digital Archive of Literacy Narratives*, a collection of essays exploring ways to mine digital works for pedagogical projects that are in-line with current composition scholarship. Both collections focus on the collaborative nature of research, reading, and writing; ground discussions within a broad definition of literacy studies; and provide teacher-tested classroom heuristics and assignments for integrating acts of digital/rhetorical reading and composing in innovative approaches.

Composition scholar-teachers are currently seeking ways to establish a vertical writing curriculum, help students develop an authoritative voice while examining their own positionality on self-selected topics, and join public conversations in the process of becoming rhetorical activists. *Digital Reading and Writing in Composition Studies* also addresses these issues, offering teachers pedagogical advice that builds upon students' existing familiarity with digital research and (often extensive) experience composing in digital spaces. Contributors suggest new lines of inquiry and encourage the creation of born-digital work.

While connections between the acts of reading and writing are now acknowledged, explored, and celebrated in the pages of rhetoric and composition scholarship and in our pedagogical texts, that has not always been the case. Ironically, many of the earlier divides between reading and writing that characterized our field were disciplinary rather than solely theoretical or pedagogical. Winifred Bryan Horner, holder of the Radford Chair in Rhetoric and Composition at Texas Christian University, addressed these disciplinary differences between reading and writing scholar-teachers, setting the stage for enduring, widespread academic discussions on the topic. In an unpublished piece written shortly before her death in 2014, Professor Horner explains:

> In my book, *Composition and Literature: Bridging the Gap* (University of Chicago Press, 1983), I saw the gap between composition and literature as largely professional: the salary and status differences that existed between the professors who taught literature courses and the graduate students and adjuncts who taught composition. The gap was not theoretical; it was real in terms of teaching loads, salaries, tenure, and professional standing. My strategy for addressing this gap was simple. I organized a conference panel for the MLA Teaching of Writing division and enlisted participation from well-respected literature scholars who chose to teach composition courses and thus saw that endeavor as not only closely connected with their teaching and research in literature but as important and rewarding. The first scholar whose help I enlisted was Wayne Booth, whose reputation was without par in the English discipline. The session drew a large audience of not only composition teachers but also literature professors who had been forced to teach composition and were searching for new ideas. I had long been distressed at the low status given the teaching of composition by English departments of the time. Senior professors regarded the composition course as a "service course" and blamed bad writing on the high schools who blamed it on the elementary schools who blamed it on the parents.
>
> (unpublished manuscript submitted to author)

This divide raged on. Ten years after the publication of *Composition and Literature*, Erika Lindemann and Gary Tate's discussion of "Two Views on the Use of Literature in Composition" appeared in the March 1993 issue of *College English*. These opinion pieces touched an academic nerve and ignited a new debate over the role reading should play in writing instruction. The fallout from these two polar articles and the resulting/responding scholarship in some ways further divided the field between those scholars and teachers who viewed writing instruction as a "service" course vs. those who saw writing instruction as a "humanist" course, focusing on the intrinsic value of writing as an expression of ideas. In arguing against including literature in a writing course, Lindemann claims that these classes should provide "guided practice in reading and writing the discourses of the academy and the professions" (312).

These disciplinary debates had very real consequences (notably many writing and rhetoric concentrations separated from English departments to form stand-alone programs). As a field, we have thankfully moved away from the vehement twentieth-century debates about composition vs. literature in First-Year Writing (FYW) courses for the most part (arguments which were more about turf wars than literacy skills) given the growth and recognition of rhetoric and composition programs, shifts in the very nature of what constitutes a university education, connections between college and career readiness, the rise of social media, and, of course, digital publishing and composing. However, those of us housed in traditional English departments are still at war of another kind. The battle now wages over attracting students in an educational climate characterized by shrinking numbers of majors in humanities departments. The conflict has become external rather than internal as English departments fight for tenure-track hires to support majors and expanding graduate education, develop certificates and MA programs focused on career preparation, and overhaul curriculum to attract new undergraduate majors. Yet, the external battle is still characterized by reading vs. writing in many ways, as indicated in a recent article "The Evolving English Major," published in *Inside Higher Ed*. This article highlights "A Changing Major: The Report of the 2016–17 ADE Ad Hoc Committee on the English Major," released July 18, 2018, and claims that "[b]achelor's degrees conferred to English majors are down 20 percent since 2012." The article's tagline encapsulates the current iteration of the reading/writing divide: "Of the specializations within major [sic], writing is doing relatively well, and literature not so much." Following the publication of the *Inside Higher Ed* article, leading rhetoric and writing scholars responded in a multitude of ways in posts to the Council of Writing Program Administrators listserv. Members suggested that English departments fight for survival by focusing on the production of texts, writ large (Doug Hesse); encouraging the Modern Language Association to be more inclusive of writing and rhetoric programs (Laurie McMilan); and changing traditional department names to something other than "English" (Andrea Lunsford). Indeed, perhaps a name change is the next logical step in the fight for English department survival, but it is up to forward-looking departments to create monikers that reflect departments housing literary studies, writing and rhetoric programs, and creative writing instruction. That won't be an easy task apart from adopting the simple tag of "English Studies," which may not be a radical enough departure, in the same way that merely adding new courses to traditional curriculum will likely only broaden appeal to existing declared majors.

The ADE Report attests, "responsive departments that know how to market their worth to students are finding ways to thrive." As the first Department Chair trained in rhetoric/composition of my traditional English department, I am actively seeking ways to respond to recent challenges and to blend traditional reading/writing tasks in innovative ways— all while maintaining our collegial working relationships. My department houses literary studies (with the most departmental faculty members working in that concentration by far), rhetoric and composition (with far fewer faculty members), and creative writing (with even fewer faculty hires). Yet our numbers of undergraduate students line up inversely: creative writing student numbers are increasing, rhetoric and composition holding steady, and literary studies shrinking year after year. To address what is often characterized as a reading/writing divide, our concentrations have worked together to revise curriculum in each of the three areas to better address student need, appeal more broadly to students from across the curriculum, and prepare students for graduate school and alt-ac careers. At the graduate level, the English and History departments have partnered to first garner a 25K National Endowment for the Humanities (NEH) Next Generation grant, and then create programming to address the dearth of jobs for graduate students in both departments, broaden graduate students' understanding of and training in diverse research methodologies, address Graduate Teaching Assistant preparation to teach core undergraduate classes, and expand career training. The newly formed institutional Humanities Center serves as a corollary to the NEH initiatives, to address needs of faculty who also face dwindling internal/external research support and publishing challenges blurred by digital publishing practices across humanities disciplines—that in many ways echo issues foregrounded in *Digital Reading and Writing in Composition Studies*.

Thirty years ago, in *The Rise of Fall of English*, Robert Scholes looked to the past in making radical assertions about a future of English that takes risks, muddles through, and ultimately may "risk annoying both traditionalists and avant-gardists by adopting a militant middle position on many of the questions that currently vex English studies" (ix). Now, the very survival of English departments may depend upon creating what Scholes labels a "middle position" stance. Pedagogical means for adopting this position and attracting majors, while helping to ensure English department's longevity are inherently suggested by the contributors to *Digital Reading and Writing in Composition Studies*, who examine a rapprochement of reading and composing resulting from shifts in technology, digital collaborative reading and writing strategies, incoming students' skill sets, and the increasing need for information literacy.

Works Cited

Comer, Katie, Michael Harker, and Ben McCorkle, editors. *The Archive as Classroom: Pedagogical Approaches to Digital Archive of Literacy Narratives*, Logan, UT, Utah State University Press, 2019.

Council of Wring Program Administrators. *Listserv. wpa-l Digest—19 July 2018 to 20 July 2018 (#2018–289)*. Wpa.org. Accessed 20 July 2018.

Flaherty, Colleen. "The Evolving English Major." *Inside Higher Ed.*, 18 July 2018, www.insidehighered.com/news/2018/07/18/new-analysis-english-departments-says-numbers-majors-are-way-down-2012-its-not-death?utm_source=Inside+Higher+Ed&utm_campaign=70c138edeb-DNU_COPY_01&utm_medium=email&utm_term=0_1fcbc04421–70c138edeb-233914333&mc_cid=70c138edeb&mc_eid=a313f4c9f9. Accessed 18 July 2018.

Horner, Winifred Bryan. *Composition and Literature: Bridging the Gap*, Chicago, University of Chicago P, 1983.

———. Unpublished manuscript, 2012.

Lindemann, Erika, and Gary Tate. "Two Views on the Use of Literature in Composition." *College English*, vol. 55, Mar. 1993, pp. 311–21.

Scholes, Robert. *The Rise and Fall of English: Reconstructing English as a Discipline*, Yale University Press, 1999.

Index